IMAGES
of America

POCAHONTAS AND RANDOLPH COUNTY

On the Cover: Ray and Joe Sallee opened Sallee Brothers Handle Mill on the banks of the Black River in Pocahontas in 1909. The mill was well suited to take advantage of the large hardwood forests that occupied the vast acres of farmland in Randolph County today. Logs were cut and either floated down the river or transported by barge to the mill. Once at the mill, the logs were cut into blanks for handles and baseball bats. The finished products were shipped to St. Louis and New Orleans. Sallee Brothers ceased operation in 1984. (Courtesy of Randolph County Heritage Museum.)

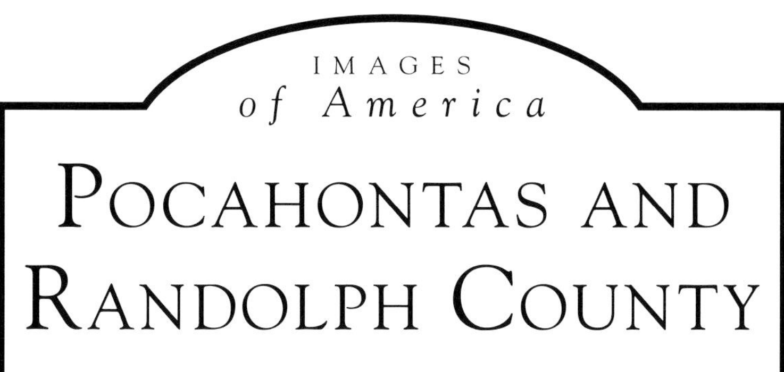

Rodney Harris, PhD

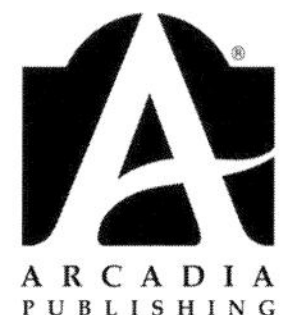

ISBN 978-1-4671-0899-7

Published by Arcadia Publishing
Charleston, South Carolina

Printed in the United States of America

Library of Congress Control Number: 2022939462

For all general information, please contact Arcadia Publishing:
Telephone 843-853-2070
Fax 843-853-0044
E-mail sales@arcadiapublishing.com
For customer service and orders:
Toll-Free 1-888-313-2665

Visit us on the Internet at www.arcadiapublishing.com

This book is dedicated to the men and women who established the Randolph County Heritage Museum, the volunteers who have donated countless hours to keep the museum open, and the donors who have generously given to keep the museum financially viable.

Contents

Acknowledgments

The generous support of Five Rivers Historic Preservation Inc. and the Randolph County Heritage Museum (RCHM) allowed me to organize and write this book. I am indebted to the museum directors who proceeded me—Karen Parish, Cindy Robinett, and John Allen French—for their dedicated work preserving such an archive of historic photographs and documenting the history of Randolph County. The idea for this project was first developed in 2018 as a way to document the photographic history of Pocahontas and Randolph County while providing funds to the museum. This book would not be possible without the help of a dedicated group of volunteers who keep the RCHM open on a daily basis. These volunteers are the real heroes when it comes to preserving the history and heritage of our communities and county. In fact, the RCHM has no paid staff and operates solely on the work of volunteers. I am especially indebted to Mary Clark, the archivist for the museum, for all of her assistance, and to Jan Frier, one of our dedicated workers. Both Mary and Jan spent countless hours searching for images and scanning them to make this book a reality. Special thanks are also due to our whole team—Pat Lambert, Kerri King, Erma Hill, Rita Rowe, and Sandy Gipson—for their dedication to the museum. All the images in this book are part of the Randolph County Heritage Museum collection.

INTRODUCTION

Randolph County is where the Ozark foothills meet the Mississippi delta. In 1803, William Hix established a ferry on the Current River in northeast Randolph County. This ferry became a gateway for migrants entering Arkansas. Later, the Benge Route of the Trail of Tears would transverse the county beginning at this point, and a notable Civil War battle took place at the town of Pittman, which grew up at the ferry crossing. Pittman was notable for being the home of multiple grist mills, cotton gins, and other businesses.

Arkansas attracted diverse immigrants. In 1813, Lewis de Mun, a French immigrant born in Haiti, established a mill near modern-day Pocahontas. Implicated in Aaron Burr's plot to develop a new nation in the Louisiana Purchase, de Mun fled to family-owned lands in what is now Randolph County. In 1813, he built a water-powered mill on what would become known as Mill Creek near modern-day Pocahontas. The mill ground grain into flour. In 1815, Missouri Territory governor William Clark appointed de Mun to lead a commission to select a county seat for the newly established Lawrence County, and de Mun was later appointed chief administrator of the newly formed county. The county seat, Davidsonville, was on property partially owned by de Mun.

In 1815, James Boyd founded the first platted town in Arkansas in Randolph County. Davidsonville became the first post office in Arkansas in June 1817. In the 1820s, the federal government located the state's first land office in Davidsonville. However, the town declined due to illness, flooding, and competition from newer settlements such as Pocahontas and Batesville.

Around 1815, the settlement of Fourche de Thomas on the banks of the Fourche River in modern-day Randolph County emerged. Later, the settlement was referred to as Columbia. In 1818, Baptists founded the first Baptist church in Arkansas at Columbia. Both Columbia and Davidsonville sought to be the seat of political power in the region, leading to conflict. Ransom S. Bettis immigrated from Greenville, Missouri, and settled on the Black River around 1815. The settlement known as Bettis Bluff served as a trading post and prospered. In 1835, the town became Pocahontas. Thomas S. Drew immigrated to the area in 1825 and married Bettis's daughter Cinderella. From 1832 to 1835, he served as the chief administrative officer of Lawrence County. He was elected governor in 1844 and won re-election in 1846, but resigned shortly after taking office.

The Columbia settlement and Bettis Bluff both sought to become the seat of the newly created Randolph County. An election was called to determine the location. Bettis and Drew hosted a free barbecue with free whiskey on election day, which swayed most voters in favor of Bettis Bluff. A short time later, the settlement's name was changed from Bettis Bluff to Pocahontas, though the reason is unknown. One legend has it that residents and supporters of Columbia claimed Bettis Bluff had "poked-it-to-us," which became Pocahontas. The actual reason remains lost to history. Incorporated in 1857, Pocahontas celebrated its centennial in 1956–1957.

Pocahontas has been home to three county courthouses. The first was built around 1837 by Thomas O. Marr. This was a frame structure that served the county until 1870. By then, the wooden courthouse was in poor condition and in danger of collapsing. In 1875, the county moved into a new Italianate courthouse on the court square in Pocahontas on land donated by Thomas S. Drew. Today, this structure, referred to as the "old courthouse," remains. By 1940, it could no longer accommodate the growing county government, and county leaders constructed a new courthouse just south of the old one. This structure remains in use today.

Following the Civil War, it took time for the region's economy to rebound. The Union had burned a portion of Pocahontas in 1863, exacerbating the community's economic stagnation. What followed was an economic boom. At the high point, Pocahontas boasted seven hotels, and the port of Pocahontas bustled with activity as steamboat navigation led to the town becoming a commercial center. However, by the end of the 19th century, the steamboat era was waning. In 1896, the Hoxie, Pocahontas & Northern Railroad opened, bringing railroad traffic from Hoxie. In 1902, a rail line from Poplar Bluff, Missouri, to Pocahontas was under construction. These infrastructure improvements continued in 1911 when the St. Louis–San Francisco Railway built a rail bridge over the Black River at Pocahontas.

As the local economy expanded, Pocahontas boasted several industries. The town was home to button factories, which relied on shells harvested from the Black River. In addition, Pocahontas was home to a brick factory and a facility that produced parts for wagon wheels, the Sallee Brothers Handle Mill, and numerous others.

As the 20th century began, Pocahontas continued to experience limited economic growth. However, the Great Depression interrupted this. During the Depression, Pocahontas benefited from New Deal spending, such as constructing the Community House and golf course. Randolph County was also the home of a Civilian Conservation Corp camp at Five Mile Springs near Pocahontas. As the country entered the 1940s, the economy expanded. Pocahontas added new industries, such as an egg dehydration plant that supplied eggs for the army. In the mid-1940s, the Brown Shoe Company built a factory that became the area's largest employer. Over the next few decades, Pocahontas continued to attract new industrial plants and experienced prolonged economic expansion.

In 1956, Pocahontas celebrated its centennial. The celebration featured a parade, a beard contest, and a massive play about the city's founding, among other events. Speaker of the US House of Representatives Sam Rayburn attended at the invitation of Congressman Wilber D. Mills.

Arkansas approved a school consolidation plan in 1948, reducing the number of schools in Randolph County. This consolidation effort led to significant growth for local school districts. Despite the Brown vs. Board of Education ruling in 1954, Pocahontas maintained segregation until 1966. Today, the Pocahontas Colored School serves as the Eddie Mae Herrin Center, an African American cultural center. Pocahontas is also home to St. Paul Catholic School.

Pocahontas and Randolph County continued to experience economic growth during the late 20th century. In 1973, the state's ninth vo-tech school, Black River Vocational-Technical School, opened in Pocahontas. The county's largest employer, Brown Shoe Company, announced its closure, signaling an economic decline. Other industrial closures followed. In the early 2000s, the county saw an economic rebound with numerous chicken houses. Peco, a family-owned chicken processing facility, opened, becoming the area's largest employer.

One

The Beginning, Civil War, and the Aftermath

The first known human activity in today's Pocahontas and Randolph County was hunting expeditions from southern Missouri by the Osage. French hunters and trappers established temporary trading posts in the region but left no permanent settlements. The Osage agreed to give up their claims to the area in 1808, opening the door for settlement. Ransom S. Bettis arrived at the present site of Pocahontas in 1815 and built a small trading post. Soon, the settlement was known as Bettis Bluff and attracted other settlers. In 1826, Thomas S. Drew migrated to Bettis Bluff from Clark County in southwest Arkansas. Drew served as a peddler, teacher, lawyer, and railroad speculator. On February 2, 1827, he married Cinderella, the daughter of Bettis. Bettis gave the couple a large plantation as a wedding gift. Drew served as the chief administrator or judge of Lawrence County from 1832 to 1835. By the time the state legislature created Randolph County out of Lawrence County in 1835, Drew possessed considerable wealth and status. Bettis and Drew wanted their settlement to be the seat of the new county and hosted a barbecue with free alcohol on the day of the county-wide vote. The ploy worked. Bettis Bluff defeated the settlement of Columbia, becoming the county seat. Drew then donated the land for the first county courthouse because both Bettis and Drew hoped becoming the county seat would lead to more wealth through land speculation. In 1835, Bettis Bluff became Pocahontas. As speculators, Bettis and Drew controlled much of the land around Pocahontas and sold tracts to settlers such as Thomas O. Marr, William Looney, and George Mansker.

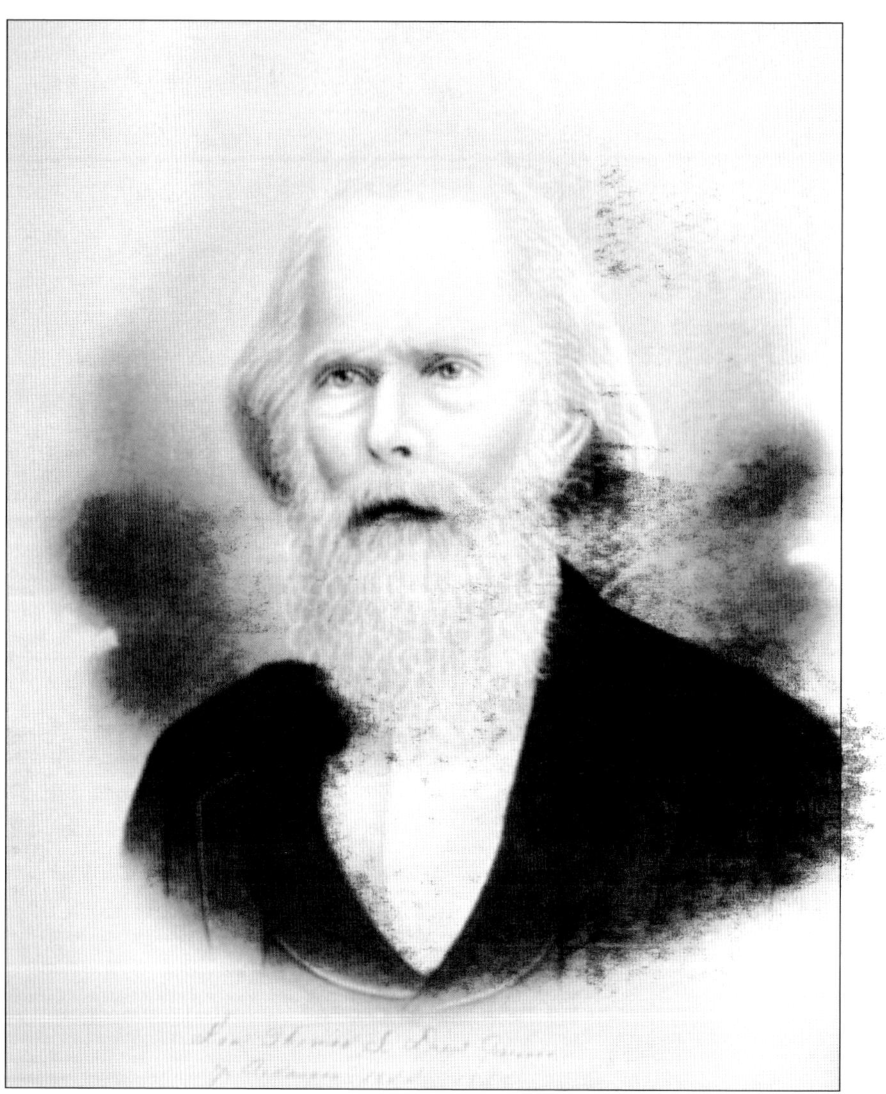

By 1836, the young man who came to northeast Arkansas as a peddler had passed the bar, married well, and achieved wealth through plantation and land speculation. When Congress agreed to grant Arkansas statehood in 1836, Thomas S. Drew stood out as an elite. He won a seat in the convention tasked with writing Arkansas's first state constitution. Due to his wealth, which allowed him to participate in politics as a southern gentleman, Drew made notable connections within the state. He became active in the state's Democratic Party and aligned with the dynasty or family that controlled the party. In 1843, the Democratic Party split over selecting a nominee for governor. After multiple attempts to choose a nominee, Drew emerged as a compromise candidate. Reelected for a second term, he resigned early for personal financial reasons and left Arkansas. As governor, Drew worked to improve the state's ports, clear rivers, and improve roads. He also proposed educational reforms and the creation of a state university. Unfortunately, Arkansas's poor financial situation hampered many of Drew's efforts following the panic of 1837. His legislative proposals met resistance in the general assembly, and few proposals became law. He resigned from office on January 10, 1849. Following his resignation, he traveled to California and spent much of his time trying to rebuild his finances, which had been harmed by serving as governor. The Civil War left Drew financially ruined, and he moved to Texas to live with one of his daughters.

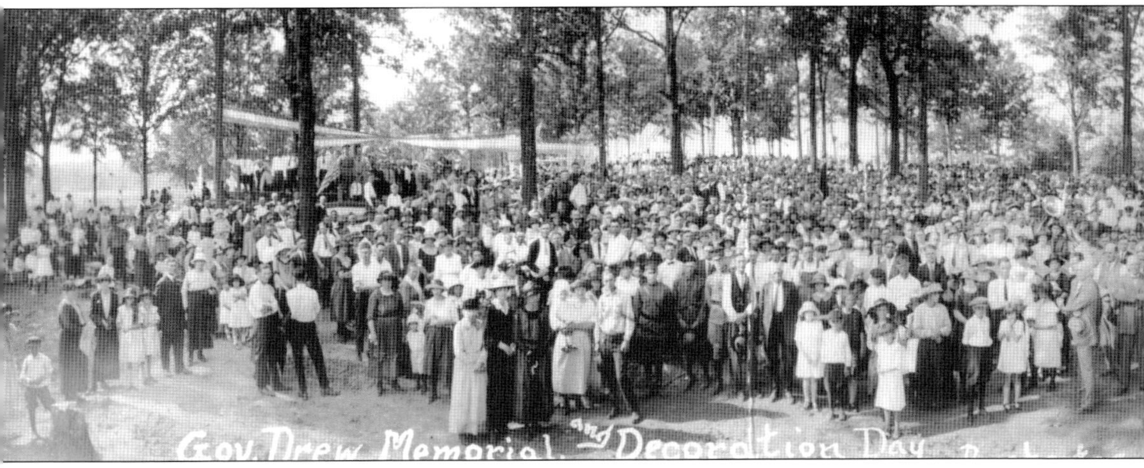

Following his resignation from the governor's office, Drew worked to restore his finances. He eventually moved to Texas to live near his daughter. He died in poverty there and was buried in the Old Baptist Cemetery in Lipan, Texas. However, the citizens of Pocahontas wished to have their governor buried in Pocahontas near his father-in-law Ransom Bettis. In 1923, the Arkansas General Assembly passed an act that created a committee to go to Texas and bring Drew home. The committee went to Lipan and had Governor Drew's body exhumed and returned to Pocahontas, where he was reburied with much fanfare.

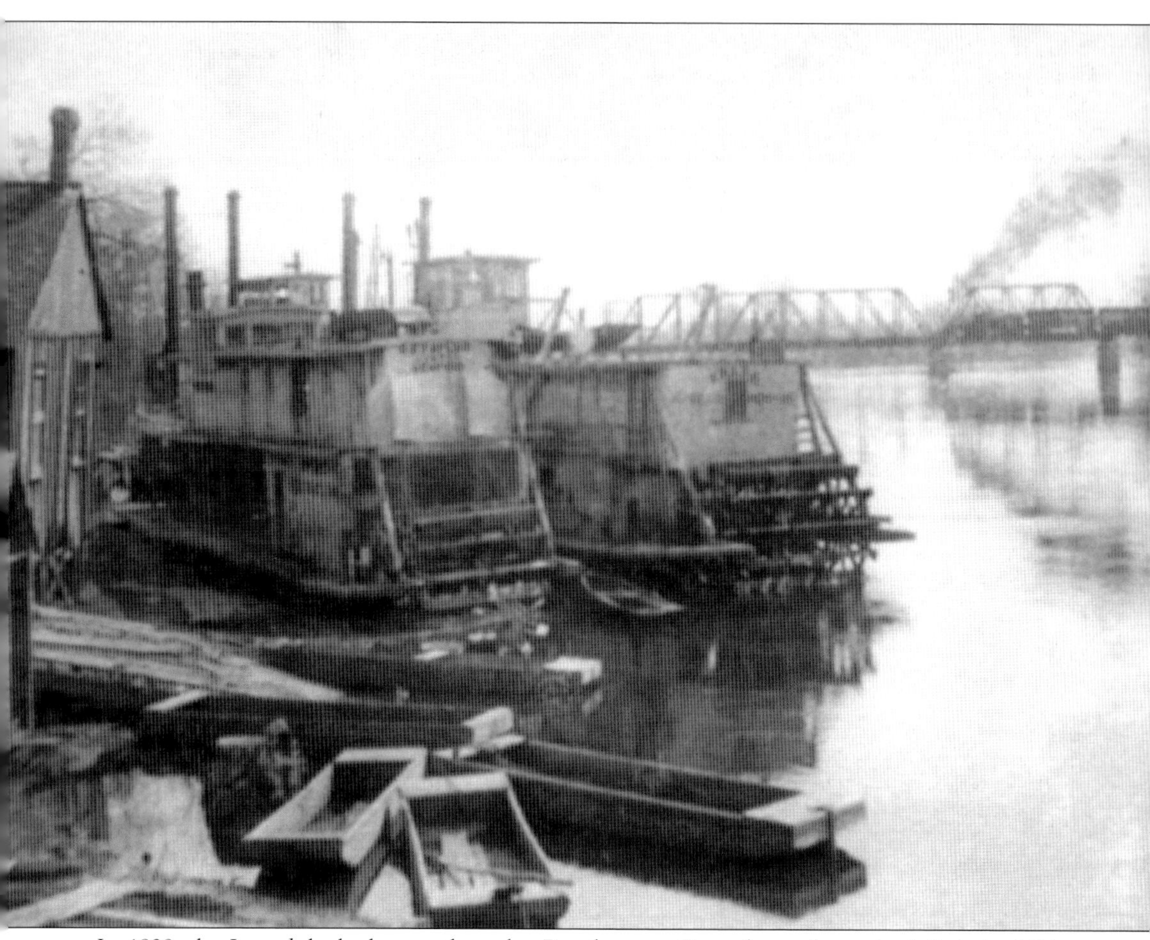

In 1829, the *Laurel* docked at modern-day Pocahontas. Steamboats from the Mississippi River traveled as far as Pocahontas, and some went on up the Current River as far as modern-day Biggers. These boats brought goods to the merchants of Randolph County and transported cargoes of cotton and other goods to the Port of New Orleans. Pocahontas became a noted port with a thriving waterfront that saw *The Fairy Queen*, *Clara Inman*, *Hope*, and *Black Dimond* all docked. However, the steamboat era was not without danger. In 1853, the *Julia Dean* sank 15 miles below Pocahontas. Boats had to watch for snags, sandbars, and rocks as they plied the local rivers.

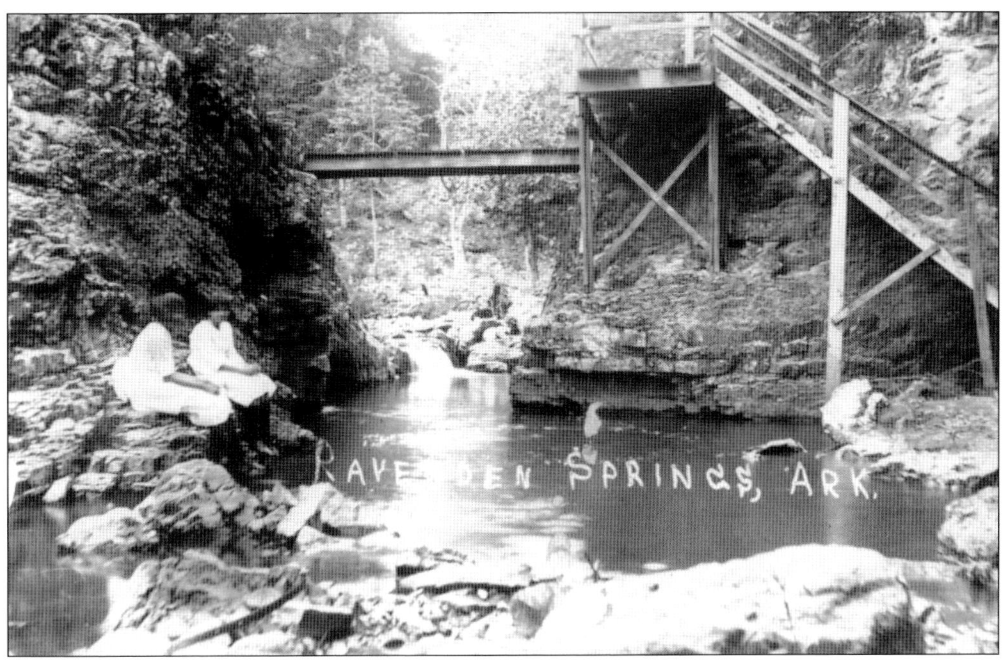

John Janes migrated to the creek that bears his name in 1809. A few years later, Caleb Lindsey, who lived at Fourche de Thomas, reportedly established the first school in Arkansas near modern-day Ravenden Springs. The legend holds that Lindsey taught the state's first school in a cave in Hall's Canyon.

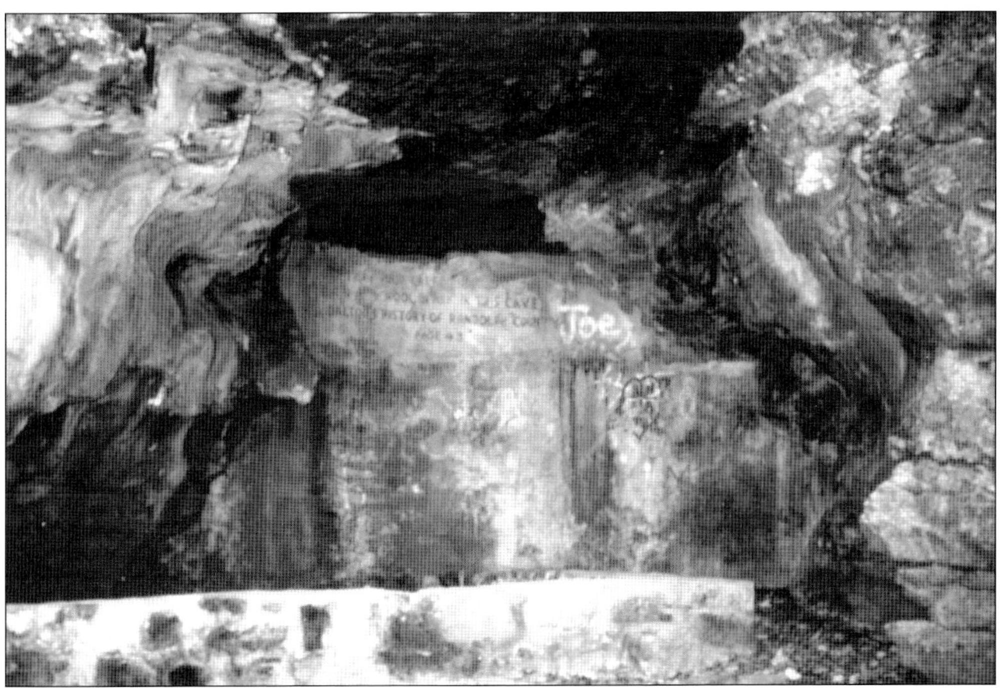

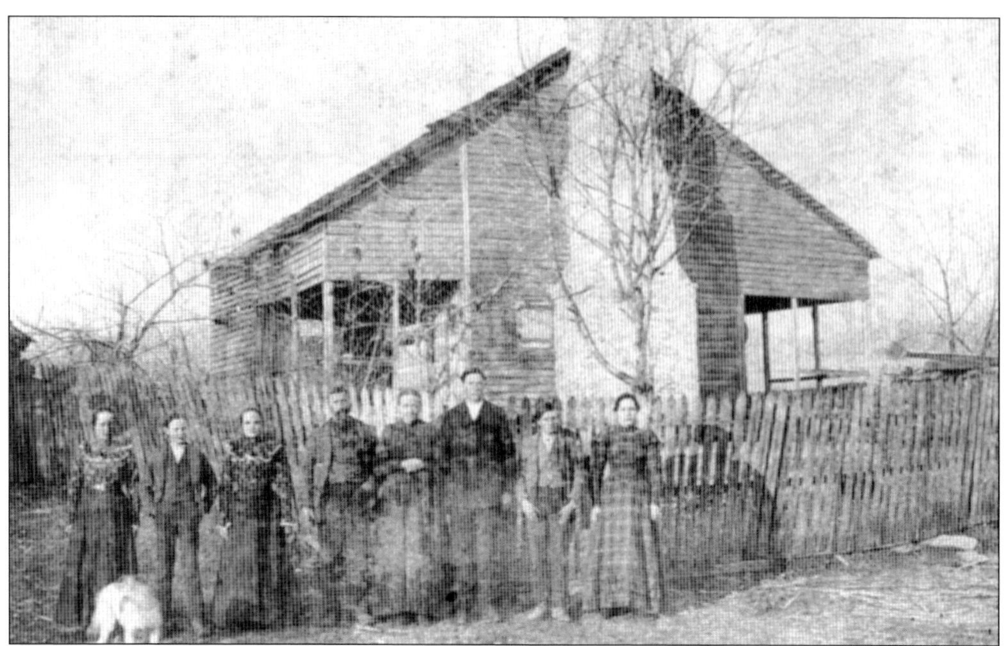

Reuben Rice constructed the Rice-Upshaw house in 1828 to serve as a trading post along the Eleven Point River. He migrated to the area in 1812 as part of a wagon train of white settlers and enslaved people. The home is one of the oldest surviving structures in the state and the only surviving trading center. The family produced fine cloth on a loom, which they sold. Rice was illiterate but became wealthy due to land speculation and trading. In 1835, he was chosen as one of three commissioners to oversee the construction of the first courthouse in Pocahontas.

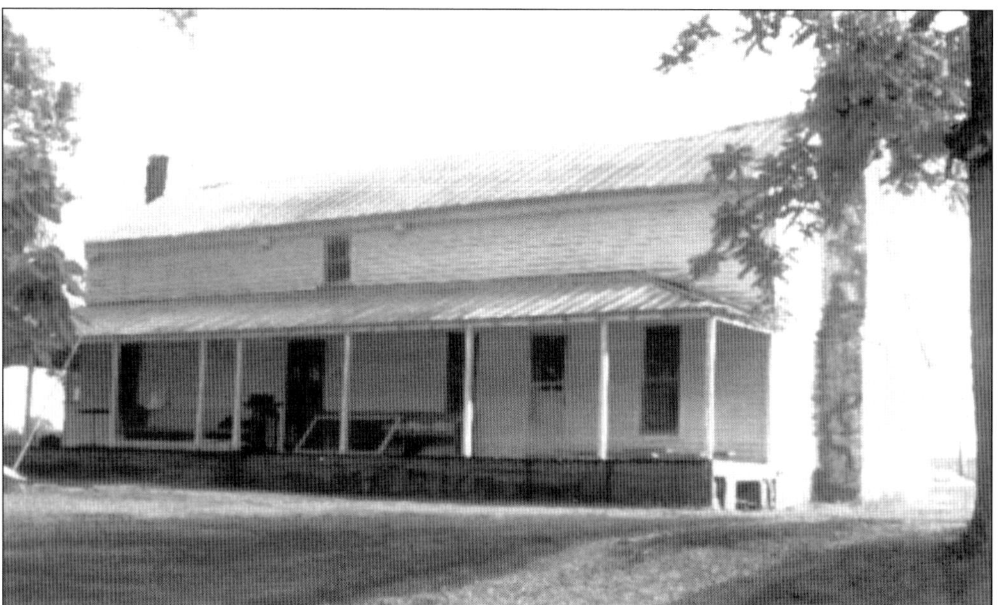

The William Looney Tavern on the west bank of the Eleven Point River near Dalton was constructed in 1833 and served as a tavern and distillery. Looney died in 1846 as one of the wealthiest men in the county. In 2006, the structure was listed in the National Register of Historic Places and has since been restored.

Brig. Gen. M. Jeff Thompson, often called the "Swamp Fox" of the Confederacy, commanded cavalry in the Trans-Mississippi Theater of the Civil War. Union troops captured Thompson at the St. Charles Hotel on the square in Pocahontas on August 22, 1863. Released on July 29, 1864, as part of an exchange for a Union general, Thompson was one of the last Confederate commanders to surrender at Jacksonport, Arkansas, on June 5, 1865.

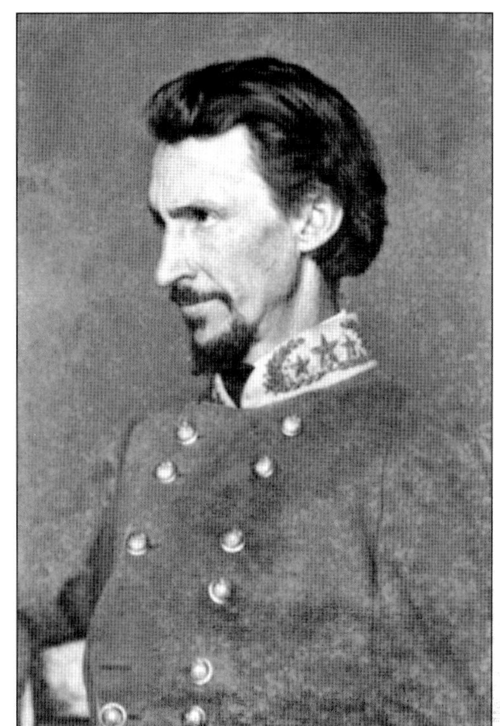

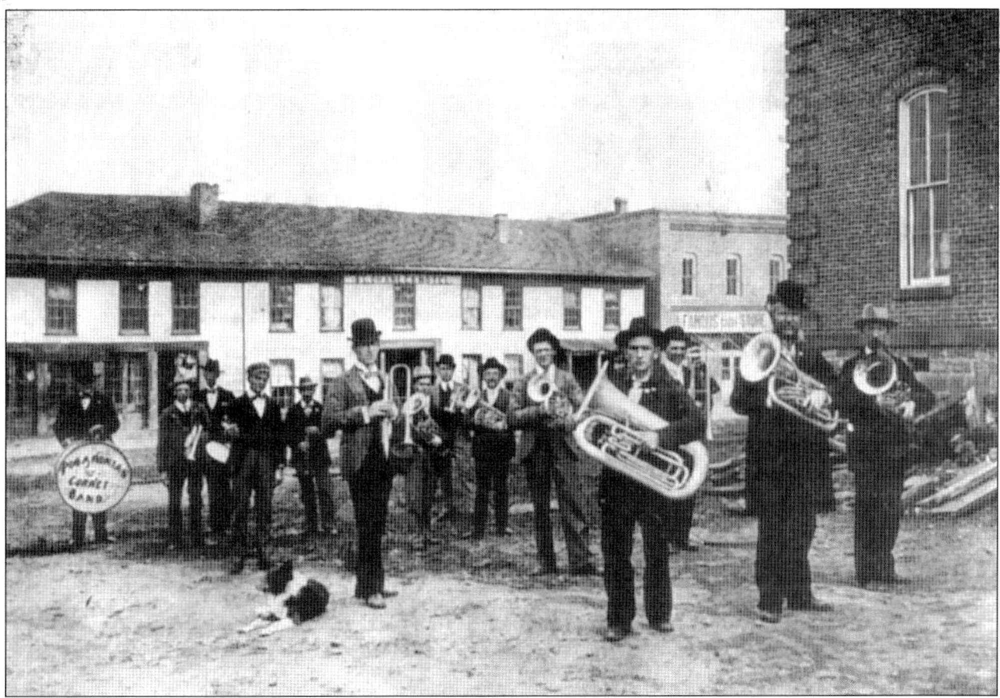

In 1853, William Allaire built the St. Charles Hotel on the east side of the Pocahontas Court Square. The hotel can be seen behind the brass band. Following Allaire's death, his widow, Nancy Jones, took over management. The two-story hotel housed small shops on the first floor and offered 20 rooms. In August 1863, Gen. Jeff Thompson was captured by Union soldiers here.

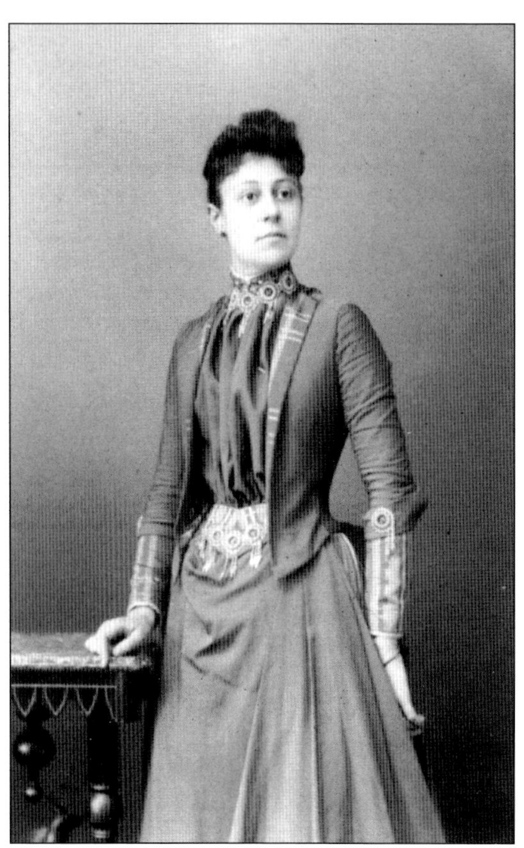

Thomas S. Drew was married to Cinderella Bettis, the daughter of Ransom Bettis. The Drews had two daughters. This photograph is of their granddaughter Emma Bennett when she was 22 years old. Drew suffered a financial setback after leaving Arkansas after the Civil War. Emma appears well-dressed, leading to speculation that the family had recovered some financial stability by this time.

This photograph of the south side of the Pocahontas Court Square around 1880 is the oldest known image of the square. The offices of the *Randolph Herald*, Will H. Skinner Druggist, Lee Brothers Saloon, and the Isaac Hirst Grocery can be seen. The *Herald* is the oldest known business in the county.

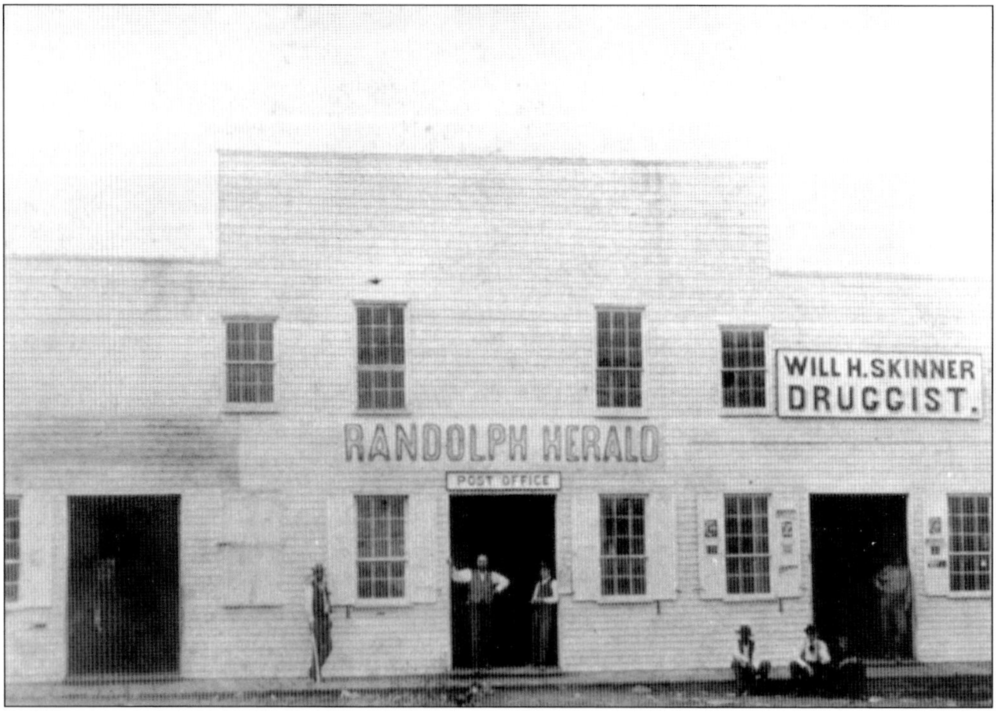

Two

Pocahontas and Her People

Pocahontas prospered in the late 19th century. During this time, the town saw businesses thrive. It could boast seven hotels, numerous steamboats docked at the port, and a level of economic growth. This success led to the construction of ornate business buildings and homes. In 1896, the Hoxie, Pocahontas & Northern Railroad was built from Hoxie in Lawrence County, and the construction of tracks to Poplar Bluff, Missouri, was completed. In 1911, the St. Louis–San Francisco Railway (Frisco) built a new railroad bridge over the Black River that remained until the late 1980s, when it was removed. Pocahontas was the location of button factories, a brick factory, cotton gins, and other industries such as the Sallee Brothers Handle Mill. The town became known for its vibrant business community and thriving economy. The county's other communities also partook in this prosperous economy. Cities such as Maynard, Biggers, Reyno, Ravenden Springs, Dalton, and others grew.

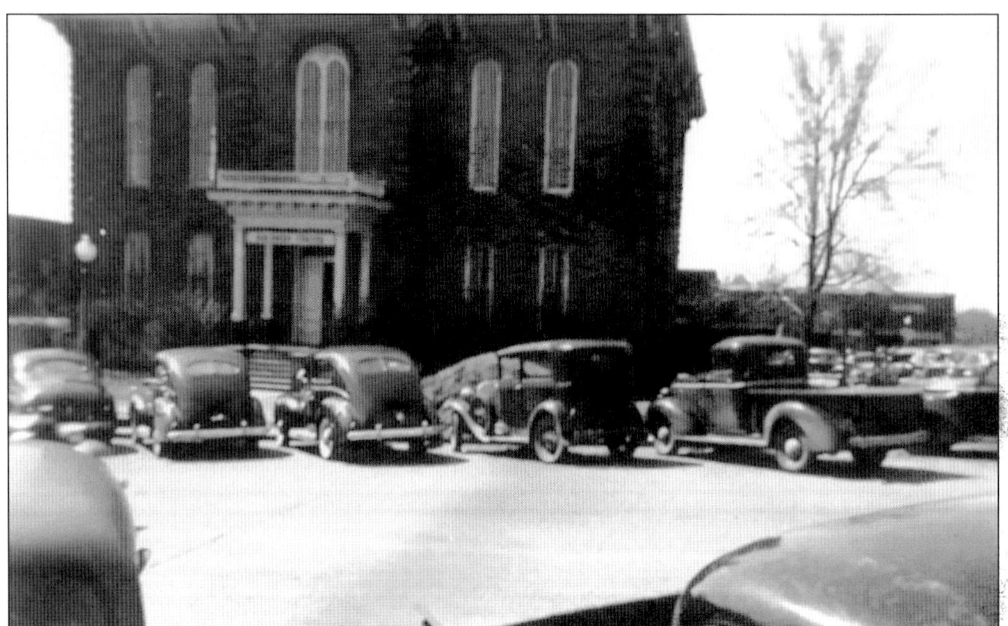

The old courthouse (pictured) is the central feature of the Pocahontas Court Square. Completed in 1875, the courthouse served the county until the construction of the "new courthouse" in 1940. The building replaced an earlier frame structure that previously served as the Randolph County Courthouse. (No photograph of this building exists.) The courthouse was built on land donated to the county in July 1837 by Thomas S. Drew and his wife, Cinderella, the daughter of the town's founder, Ransom Bettis. For many years, the building contained a vault added to the east side of the structure. This vault was removed in the 1930s. The old courthouse contained a large courtroom on the second floor with two smaller office rooms. The building has a central hall that runs the length of the building and contains a staircase. The first floor was used as office space for county offices.

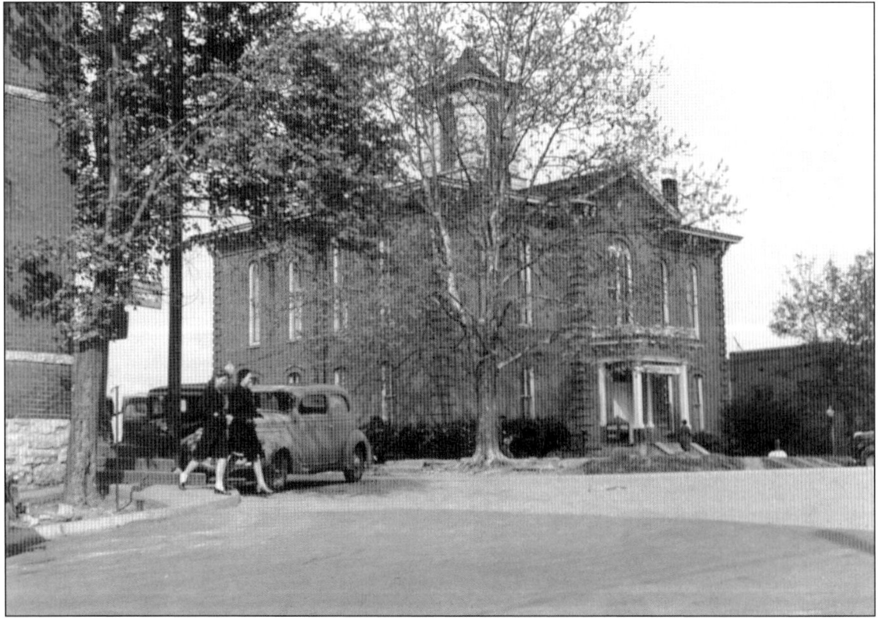

After the county offices moved to the new courthouse in 1940, the old courthouse was used for various purposes. During World War II, it was a USO club, providing entertainment for the men stationed at Walnut Ridge Army Airbase in nearby Walnut Ridge.

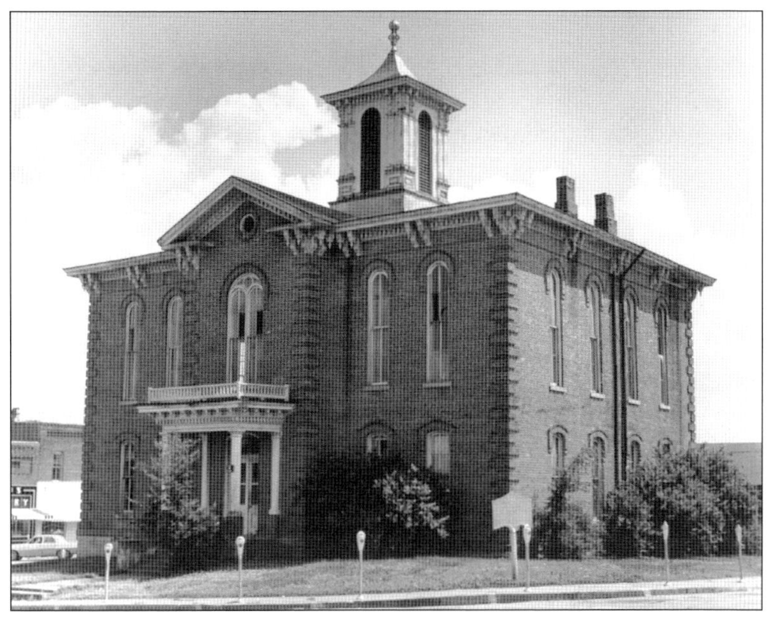

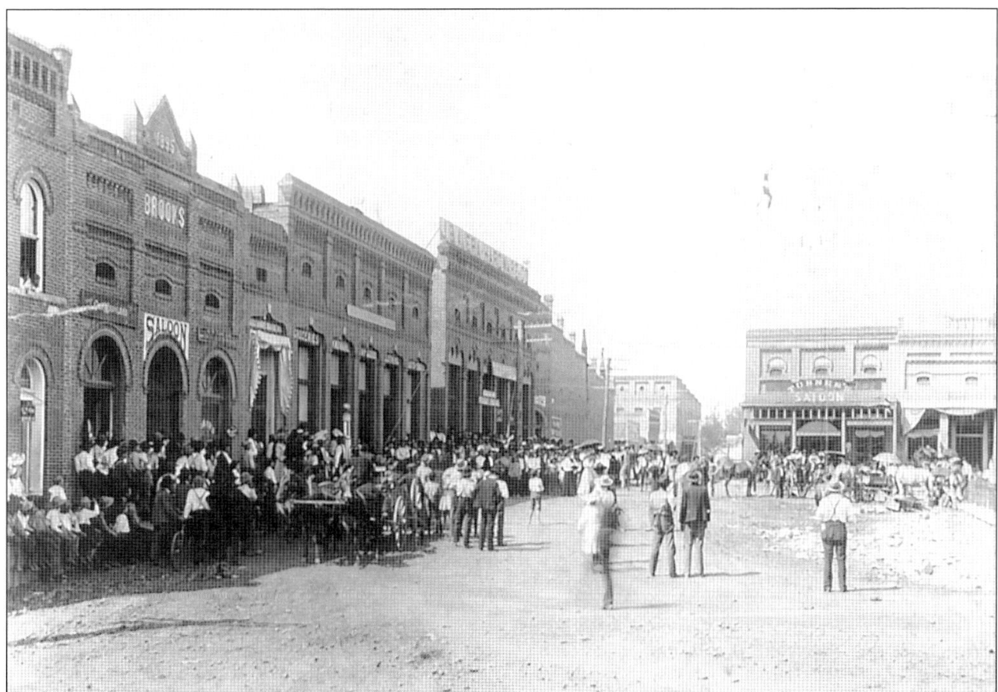

A large crowd has gathered for Merchants' Day in Pocahontas around 1900. A man is walking a high wire across Marr Street on the west side of the square. The wire stretched from the old courthouse to a building on the west side of the square. At least two saloons are visible.

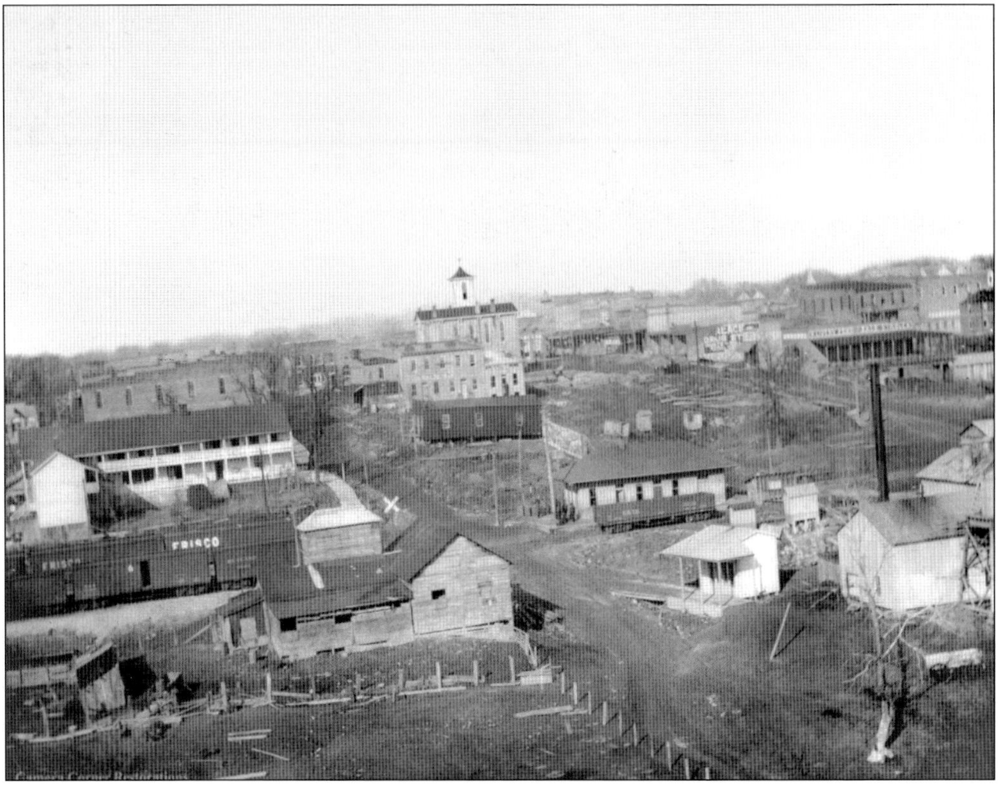

Downtown Pocahontas around 1900 is pictured here, with several landmarks visible, including the Biggers Hotel, the old depot (not the present building), the old courthouse, and other businesses along the court square. In the days before US Highway 67, Broadway Street and others ran to the river, and many businesses were located along the river. Note the dirt streets.

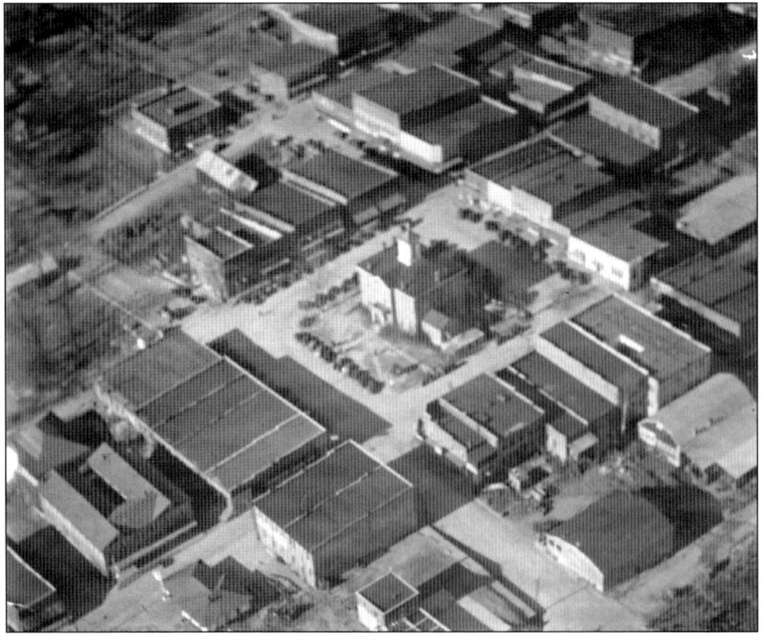

This aerial view of the Pocahontas Court Square was taken sometime before 1930, since the old courthouse still has the vault on the east side. The Highway 67 bypass was not built at this time. However, the new US Post Office was built and can be seen on Van Bibber Street.

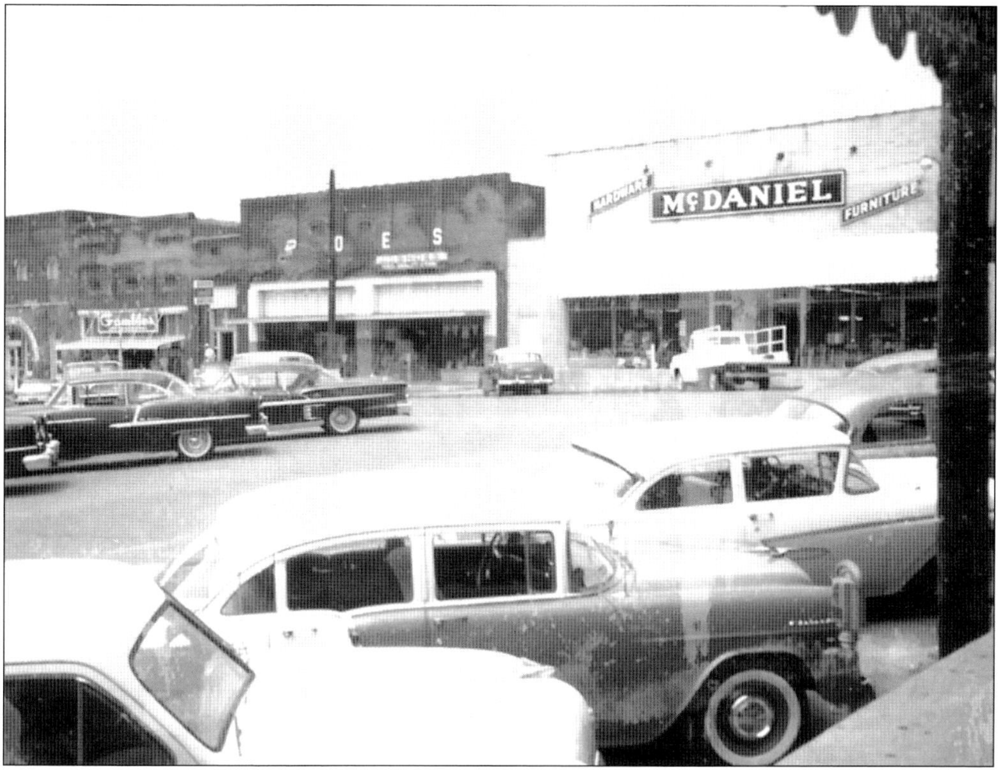

In the above image from the 1950s, the west side of the Pocahontas Court Square can be seen. Poe's department store is visible, as is McDaniel hardware and appliance store. The image below is of the same side of the square from an earlier date. The court square is deserted, and the building at the corner of Marr and Everett Streets that houses McDaniel's above had not yet been updated.

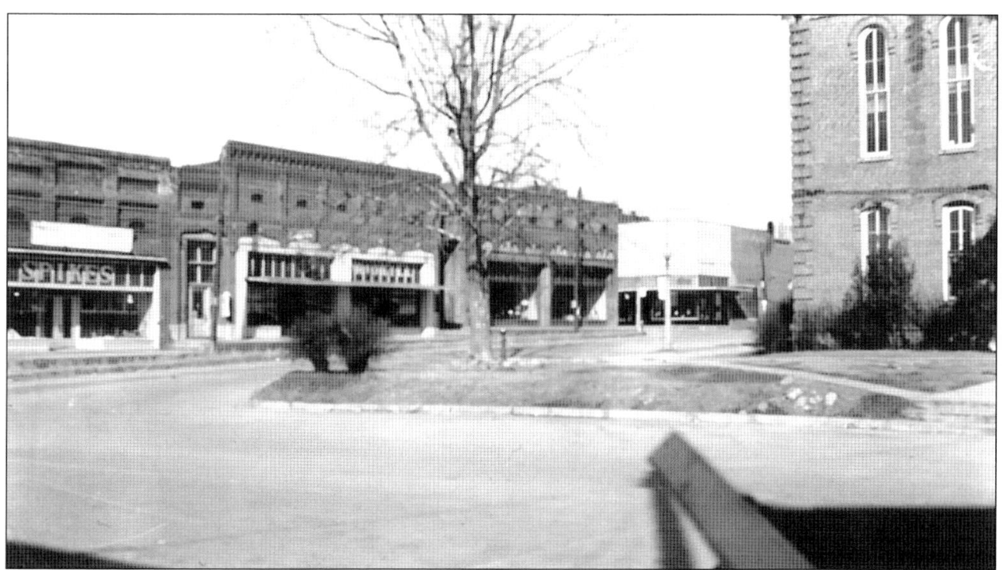

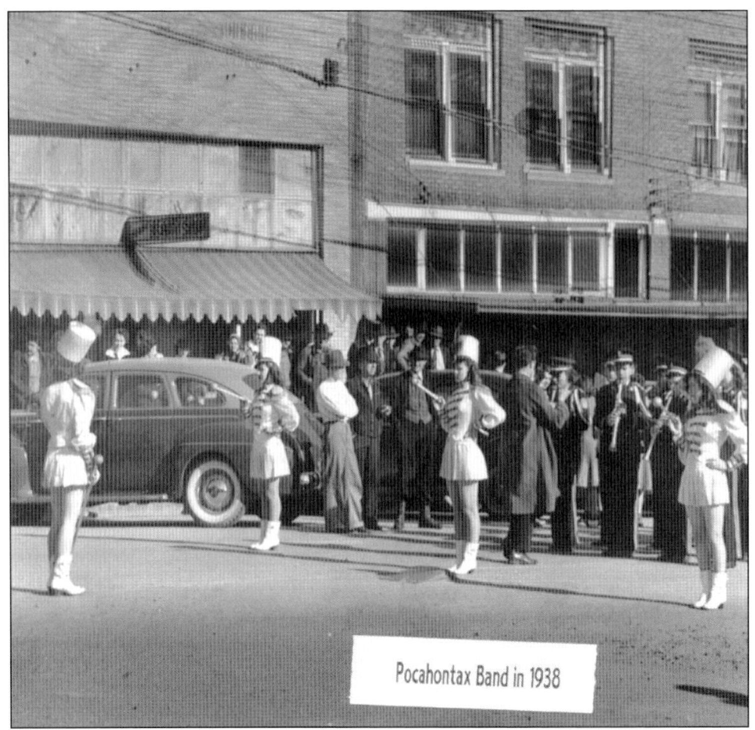

The Pocahontas school band marches in a parade on the court square in 1938. The buildings in the background now house Studio B Salon and the Randolph County Heritage Museum. The film appears to have been double exposed, making the right side of the photograph blurry.

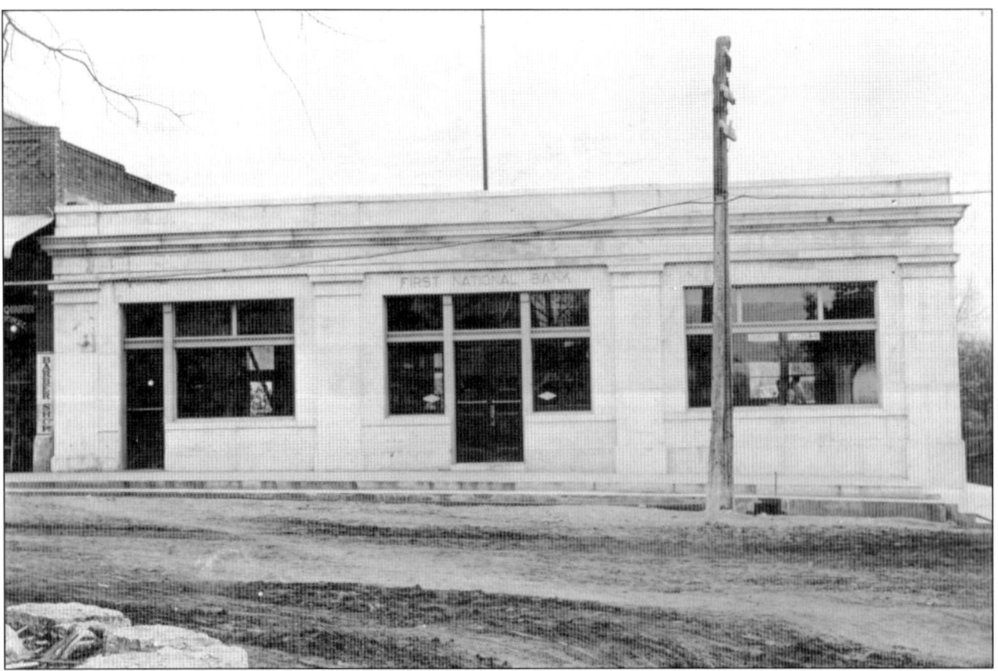

The First National Bank building has housed multiple financial institutions, including the Pocahontas Federal Savings and Loan, the Bank of Pocahontas, and Farmers and Merchants Bank. The building is on the square's north side, at the corner of Everett and Bettis Streets. It also housed the offices of a local attorney for many years.

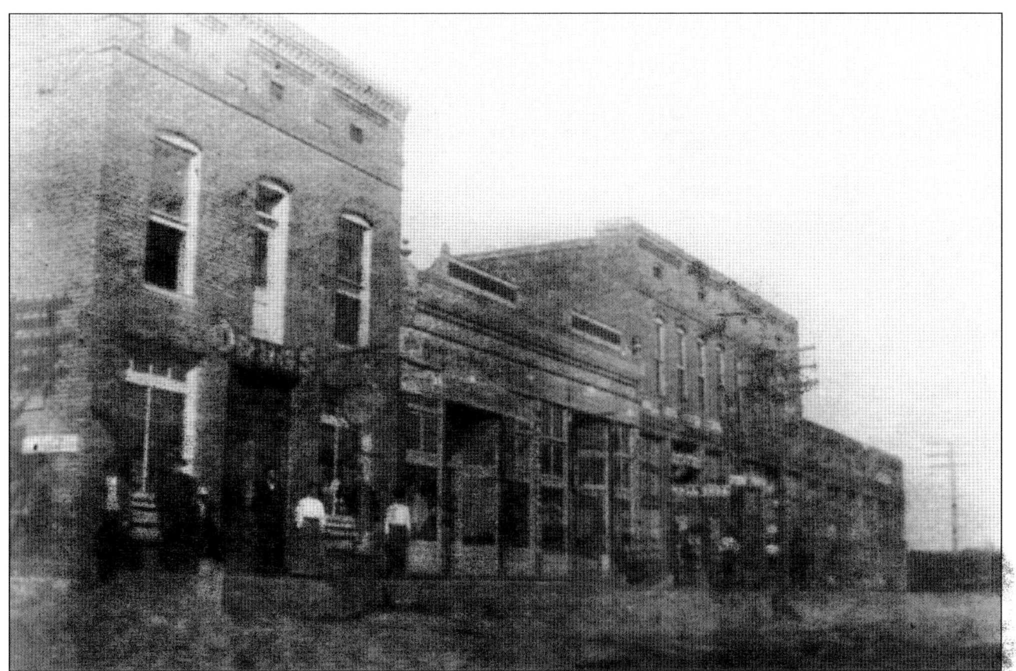

In this 1909 photograph, the two-story building on the south side of the Pocahontas Court Square is Pringle Drug Store. A drugstore has been at this location since before the Civil War. The DeClerk Saloon, Wall Shoe Store, and the Shannon General Store were also located here. The Shannon General Store building housed a hotel on the second floor. The DeClerk Saloon was one of several saloons on the court square.

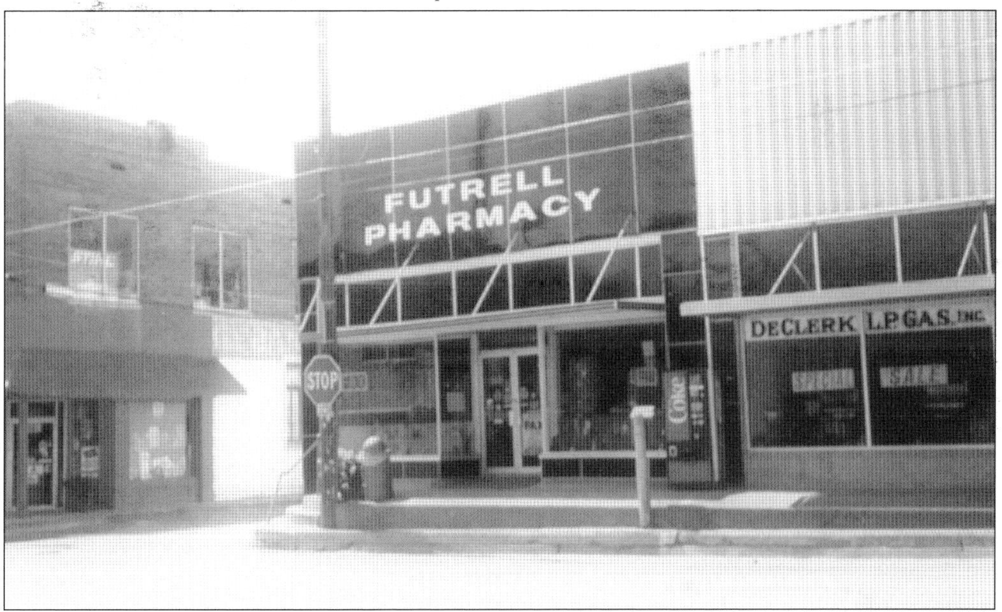

In 1909, Pringle Drug Store was in the two-story building seen in the previous image, but sometime after this, the south side of the square was damaged by a fire. The business became Johnston Drug Store and then was purchased by Phil Futrell. The Futrell family owned the pharmacy at the corner of Broadway and Bettis Streets from at least the 1930s until 2022.

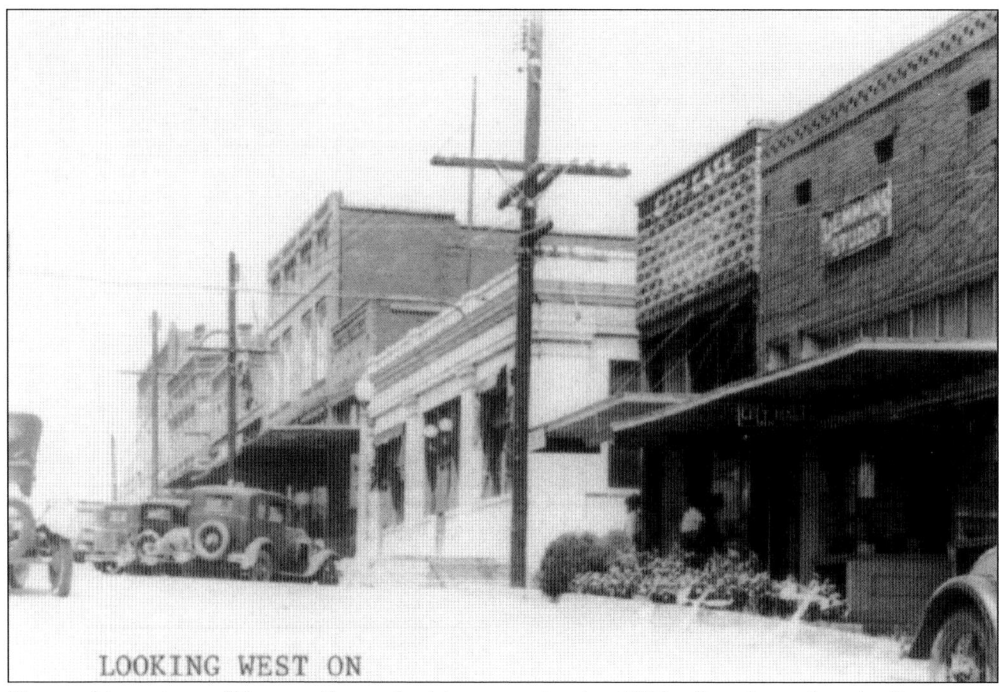

Pictured is a view of Everett Street looking west in the 1930s. On the right, the Lemmons photography studio can be seen, along with Pocahontas City Hall, which was in the building at the corner of Bettis and Everett Streets. The bank building that is the current home of the Randolph County Heritage Museum can also be seen.

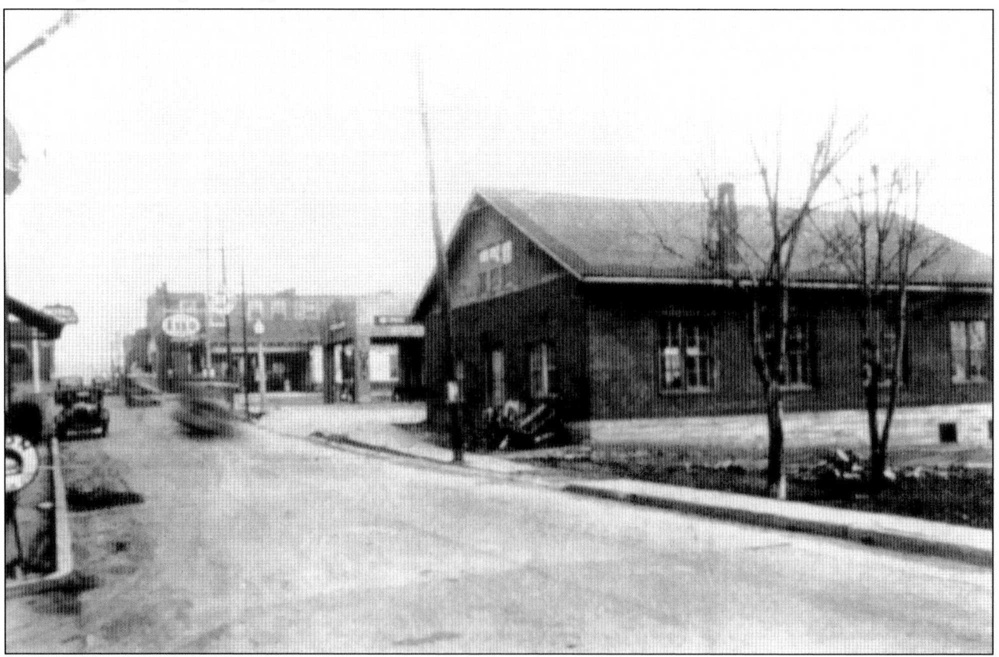

Bettis Street is pictured looking north around 1930, with the Hotel Randolph sign visible on the left. The building also housed the offices of Dr. M.A. Baltz. Decker's Sinclair station can be seen on the left. Farther north, the rear of Johnston's Drug Store can be seen.

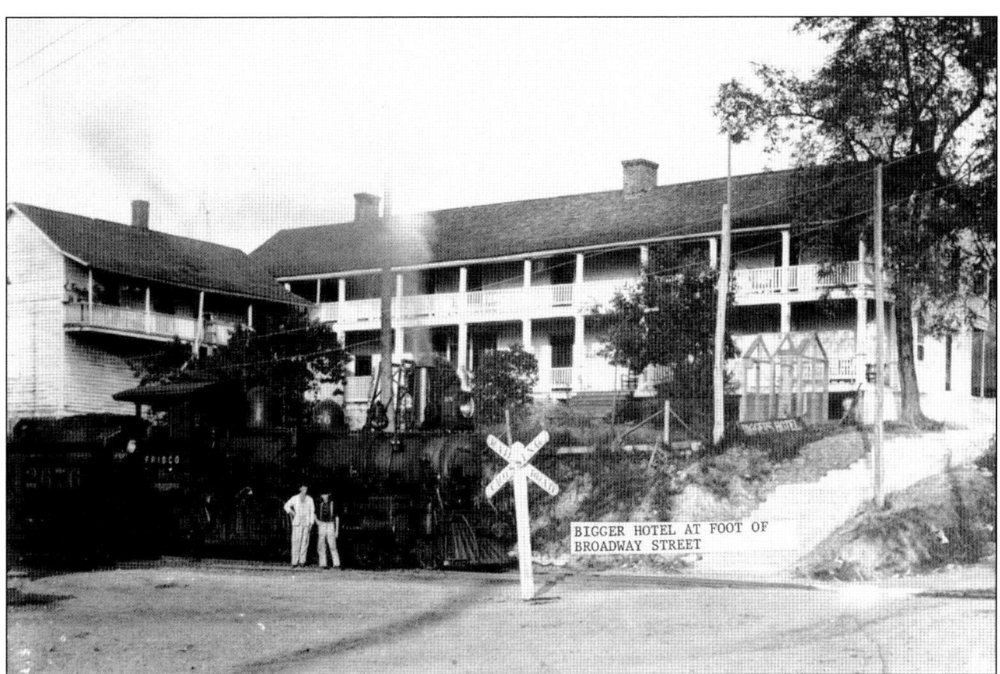

In 1881, B.F. Bigger and his wife, Ida, acquired the Heavener Hotel in Pocahontas, renaming it the Biggers Hotel. The hotel overlooked the Black River and the railroad tracks. A path and steps led to the Frisco depot. This porch was a popular spot for townspeople to spend Sunday afternoons. The hotel was known for its food and was a favorite location for parties and events.

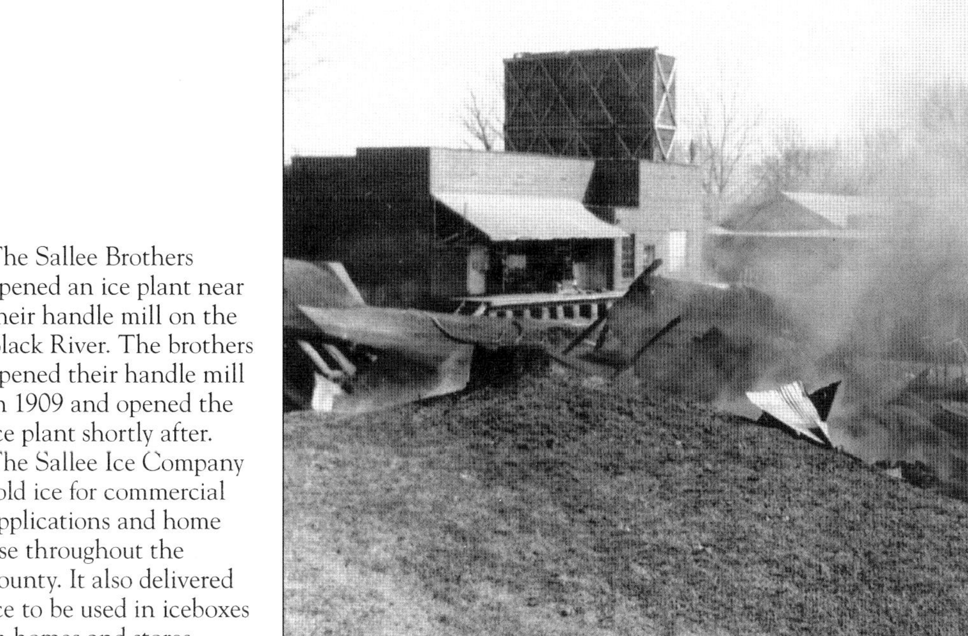

The Sallee Brothers opened an ice plant near their handle mill on the Black River. The brothers opened their handle mill in 1909 and opened the ice plant shortly after. The Sallee Ice Company sold ice for commercial applications and home use throughout the county. It also delivered ice to be used in iceboxes in homes and stores.

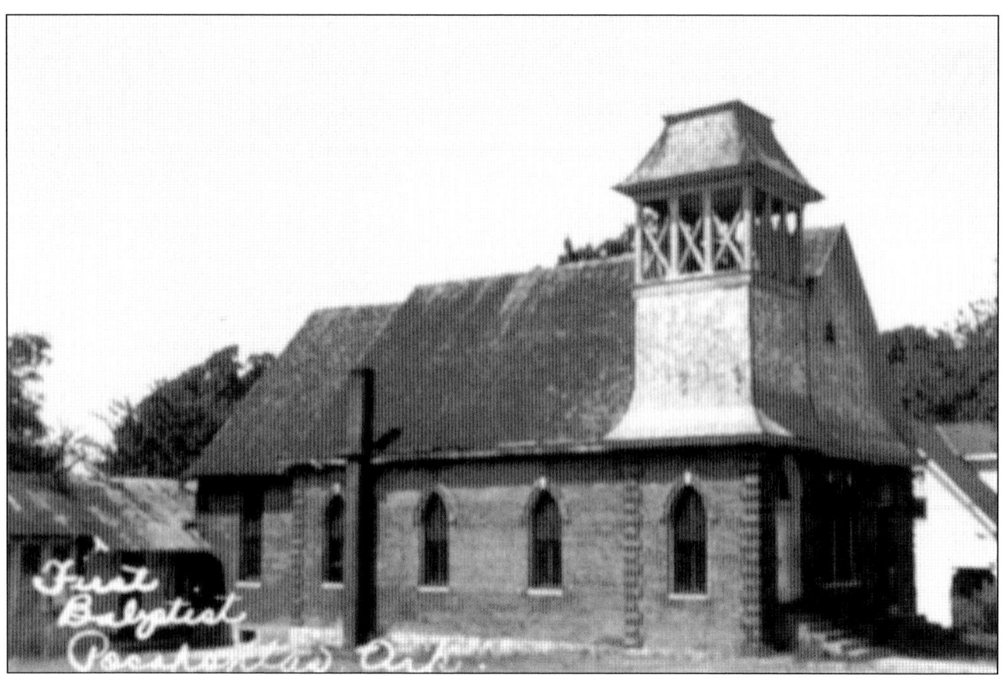

Rev. M.D. Bowers founded what is today First Baptist Church in 1899. The congregation first met in the Methodist church before being officially organized in 1900 by Rev. R.C. Medaris. The congregation then built a church building in 1901, which burned in 1948. At the time, a new sanctuary was already under construction and was completed in 1949. First Baptist has added classroom space and a significant addition with a fellowship hall in the years since the new building opened. Below is a large gathering outside the original building, which faced Church Street.

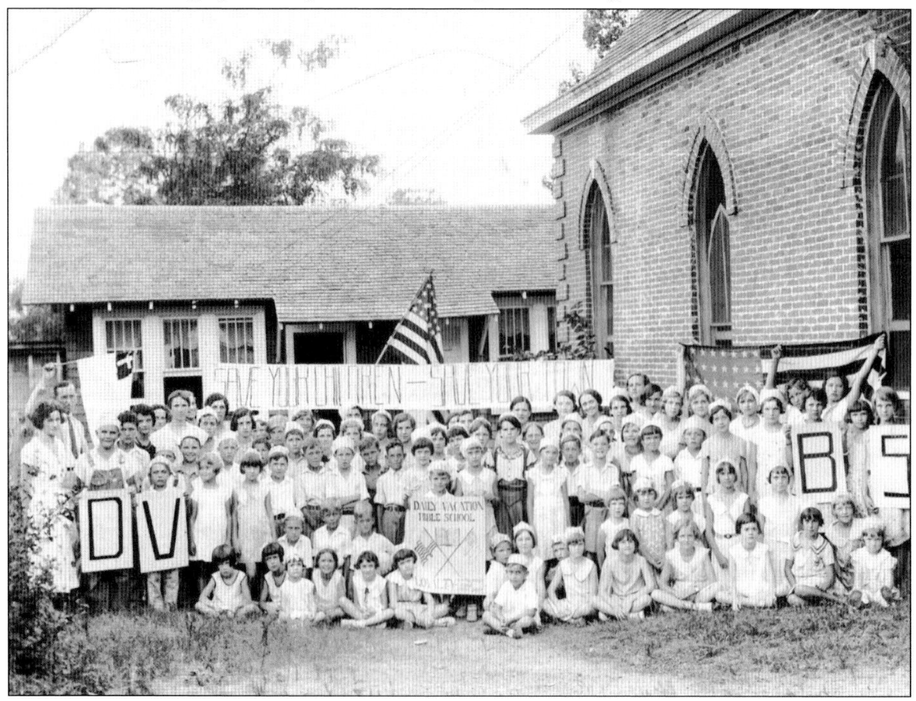

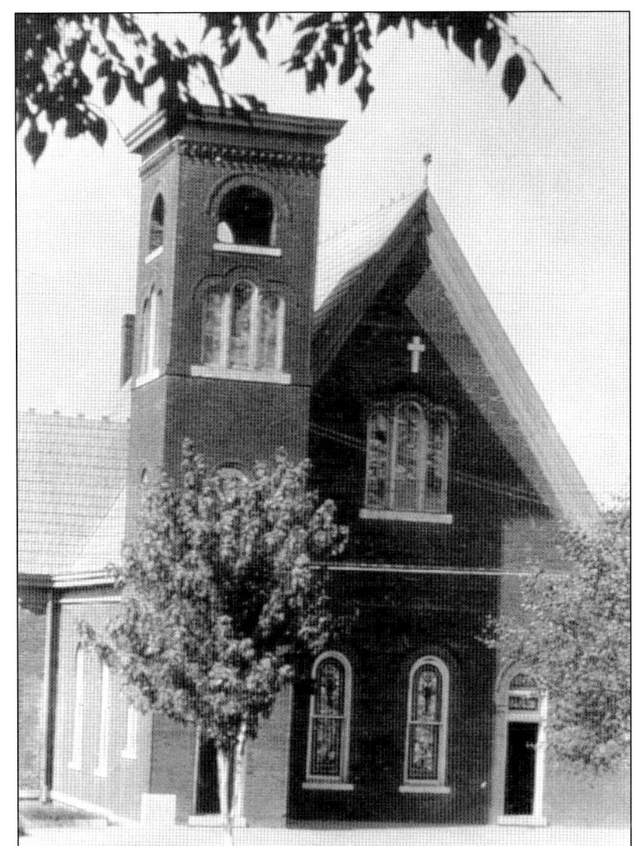

Pyburn Street Church of Christ was established in 1885 as the Pocahontas Church of Christ. The congregation first met in the Methodist church building. For the next 29 years, they met in the jury room of the old Randolph County Courthouse. In 1914, the congregation bought land and built a redbrick building with stained glass windows and a bell tower at Pyburn and Bryant Streets. In the 1950s, the congregation erected their new building.

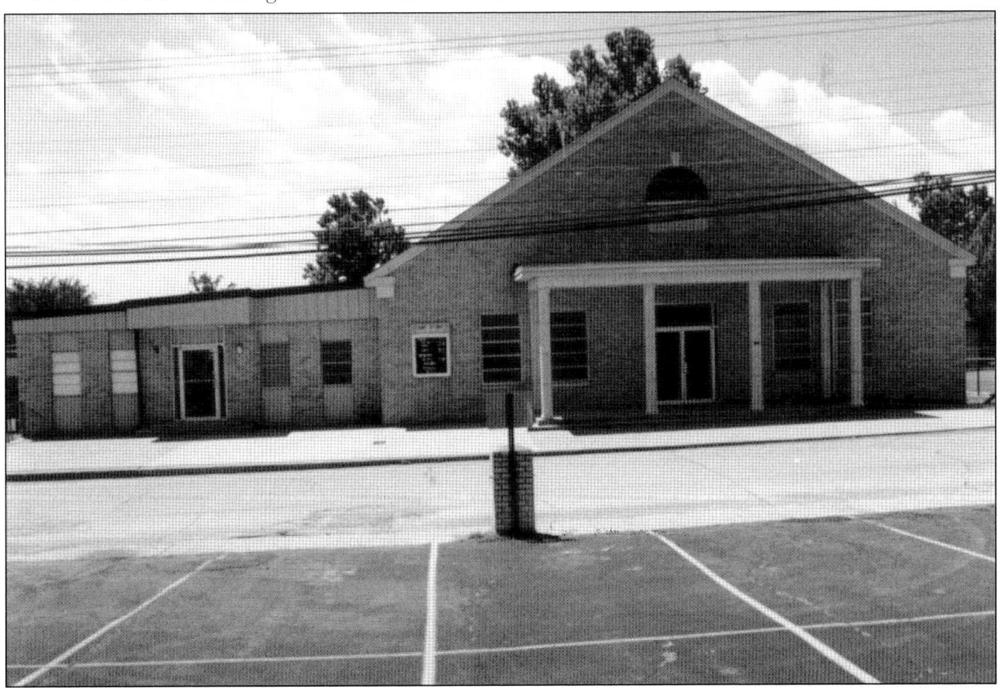

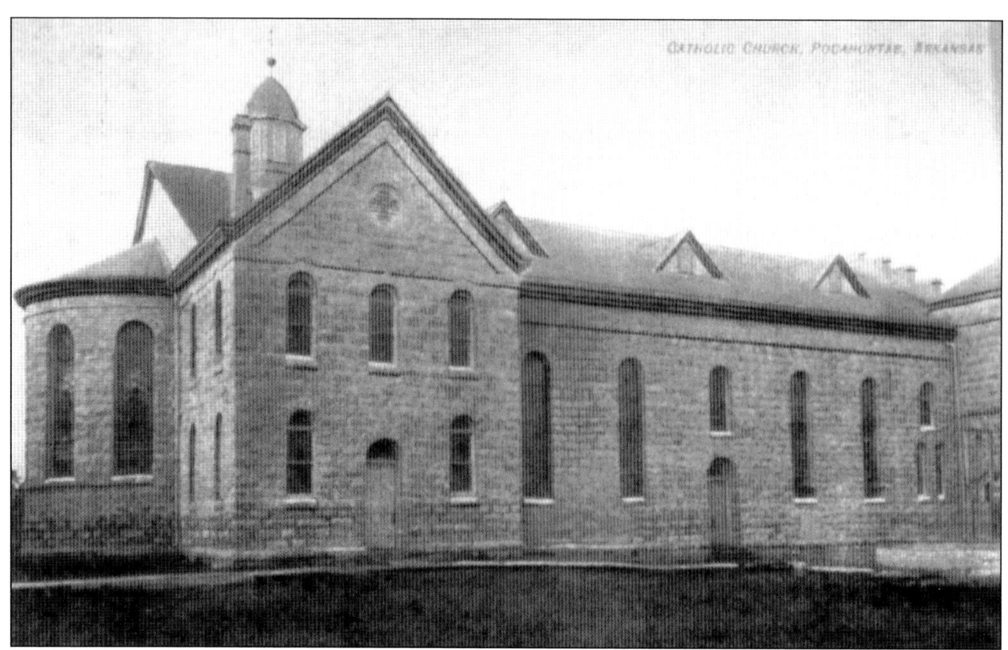

Saint Paul the Apostle Catholic Church was established in Pocahontas in 1868. Dr. James Esselman and Dr. Putman invited an Irish missionary priest, Rev. James P. O'Kean, to Pocahontas. Eventually, Bishop Edward Fitzgerald assigned O'Kean to Pocahontas. Area residents and many Protestants donated land and money to start the area's first Catholic church. In 1879, Rev. John Weibel came to Pocahontas. Weibel built the first school, started the first choir, and bought the first organ.

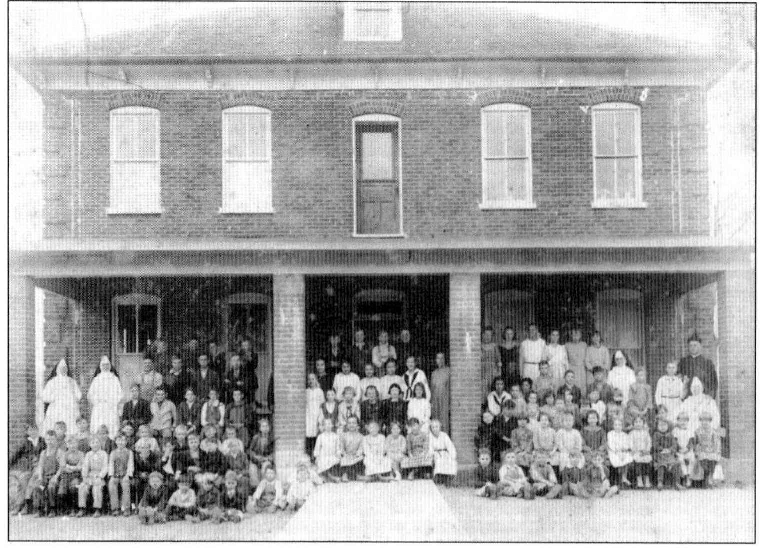

The Saint Paul's school eventually built a schoolhouse, and in 1939, the high school was started. The present school building was constructed in 1948. The school continued until 1990, when the high school closed. The elementary school remains open, and students transition to public school after completing elementary grades.

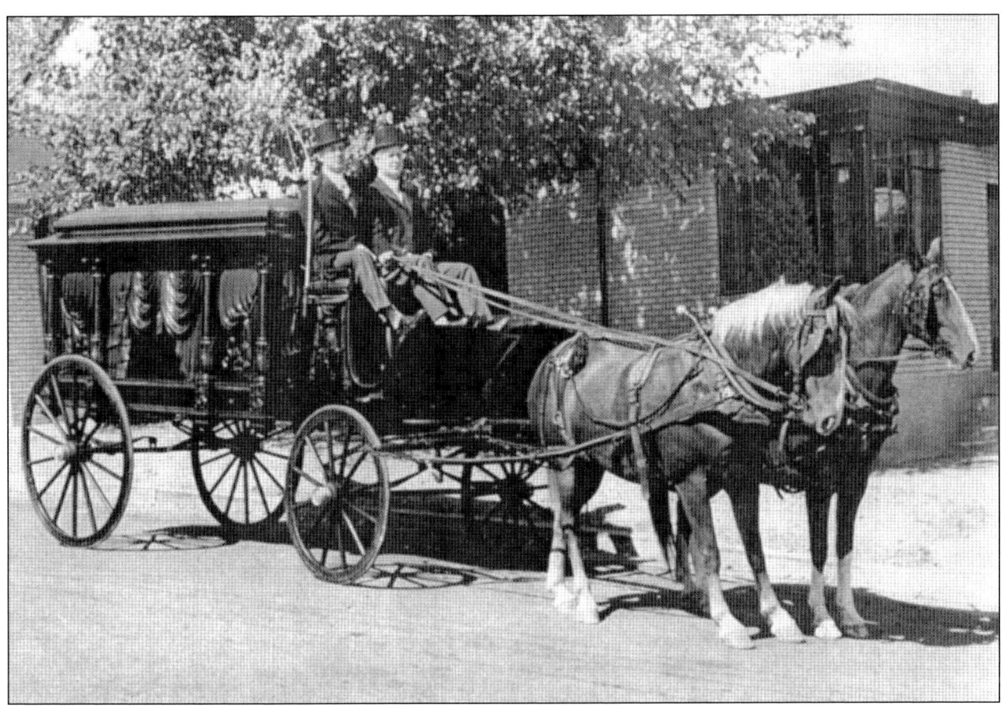

Clifford and Gardner McNabb, the owners of McNabb Funeral Home in Pocahontas, drive an antique hearse in the Pocahontas Centennial Parade in 1956. McNabb Funeral Home is still in business today.

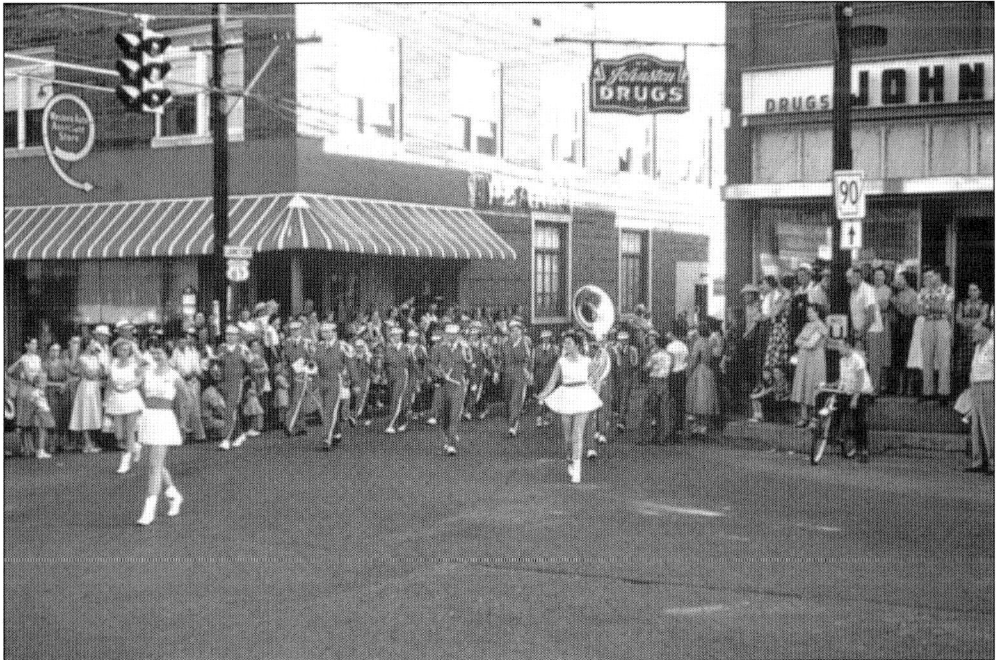

The Pocahontas High School band marches in a parade in downtown Pocahontas in the early 1950s. The band is passing through the intersection of Bettis and Broadway Streets. Johnston's Drug Store and Futrell's Western Auto can both be seen.

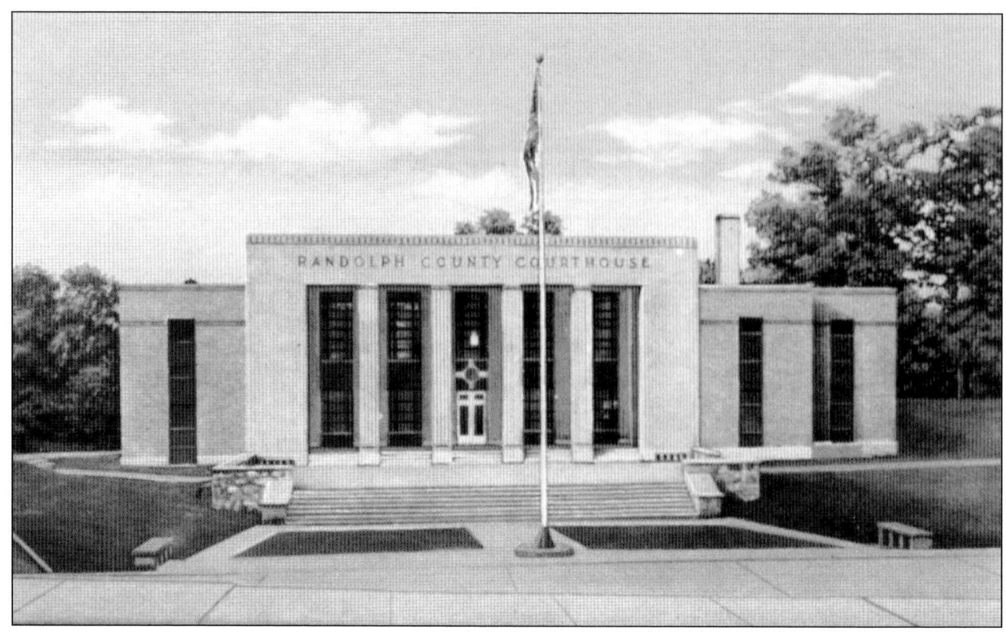

The New Randolph County Courthouse was built in 1940 with Works Progress Administration (WPA) funds. It was built in an Art Deco style of buff-colored brick and faced in gray concrete. This building replaced the 1870s courthouse. The new courthouse is still in use today.

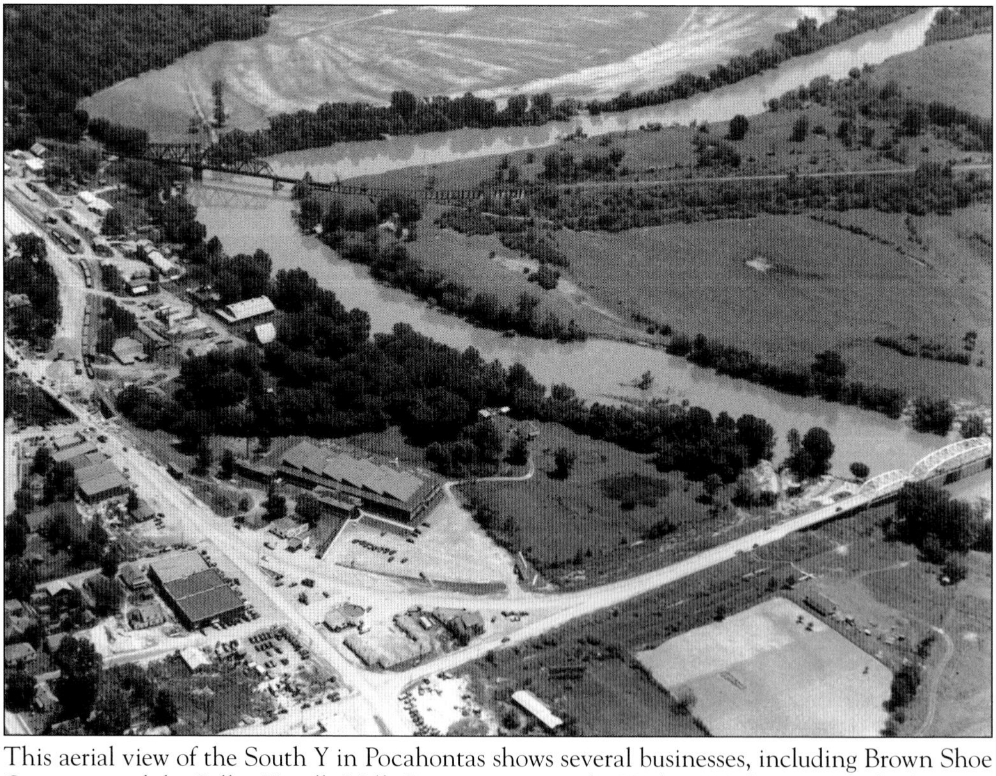

This aerial view of the South Y in Pocahontas shows several businesses, including Brown Shoe Company and the Sallee Handle Mill. Construction on the Highway 67 bypass can also be seen. The highway followed Bettis Street through court square before turning on Everett and Marr Streets.

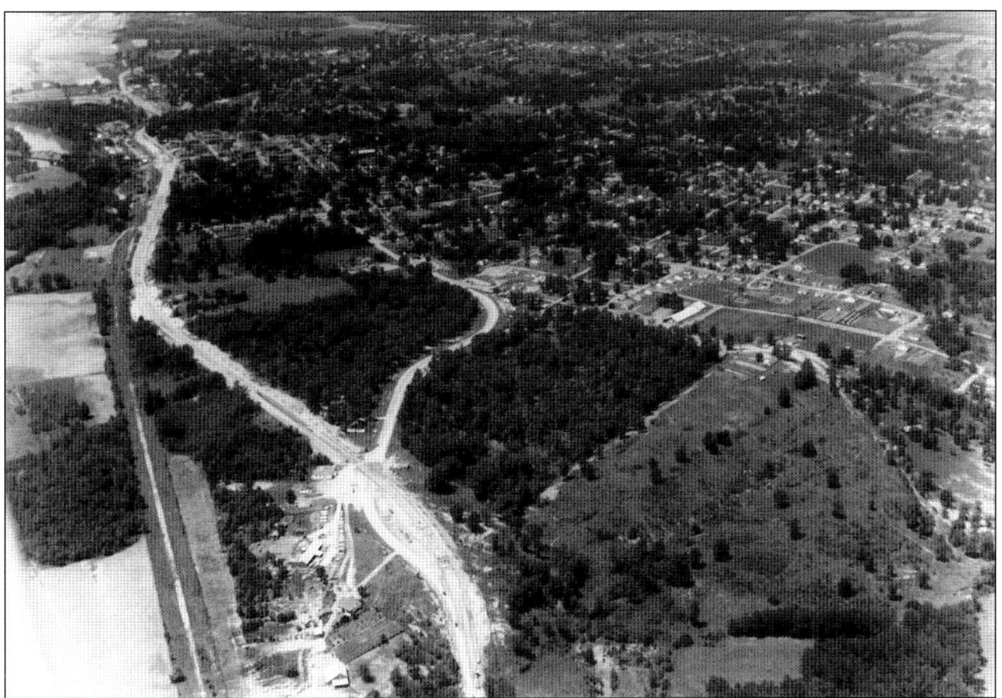

In this aerial view of the North Y looking south toward downtown, construction on the Highway 67 bypass can be seen. Note the large amount of undeveloped land that eventually became the Lakeview development and Baltz Lake.

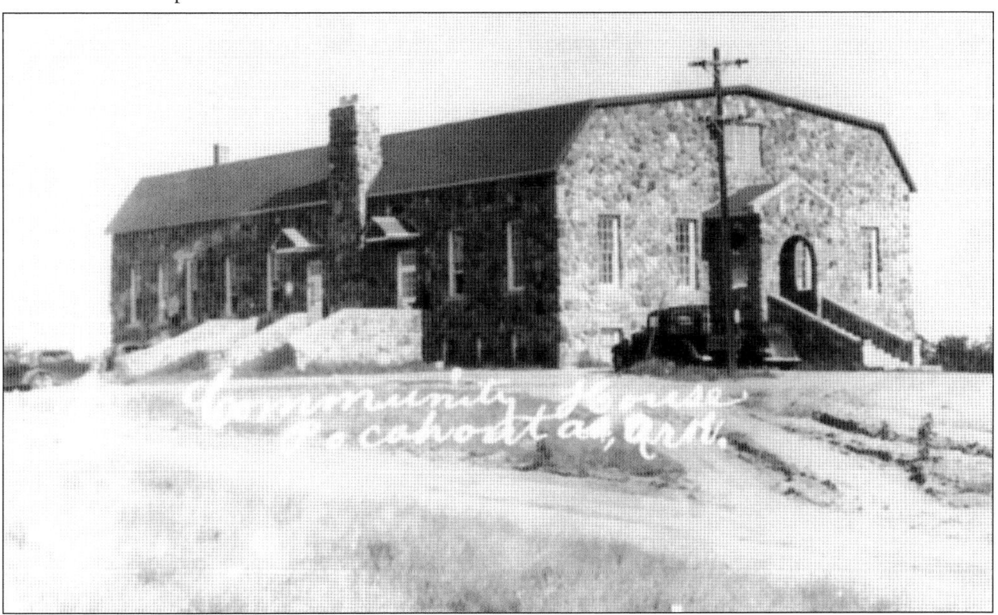

The WPA and the National Youth Administration constructed the Pocahontas Community House in 1939 as part of the New Deal. In 1941, Southern Baptist College, now Williams Baptist University, began in the building before moving to Walnut Ridge and the US Army Flying School. The "Old Rock Building" then became part of the new campus of Pocahontas Public Schools. The building currently serves as the cafeteria for the high school.

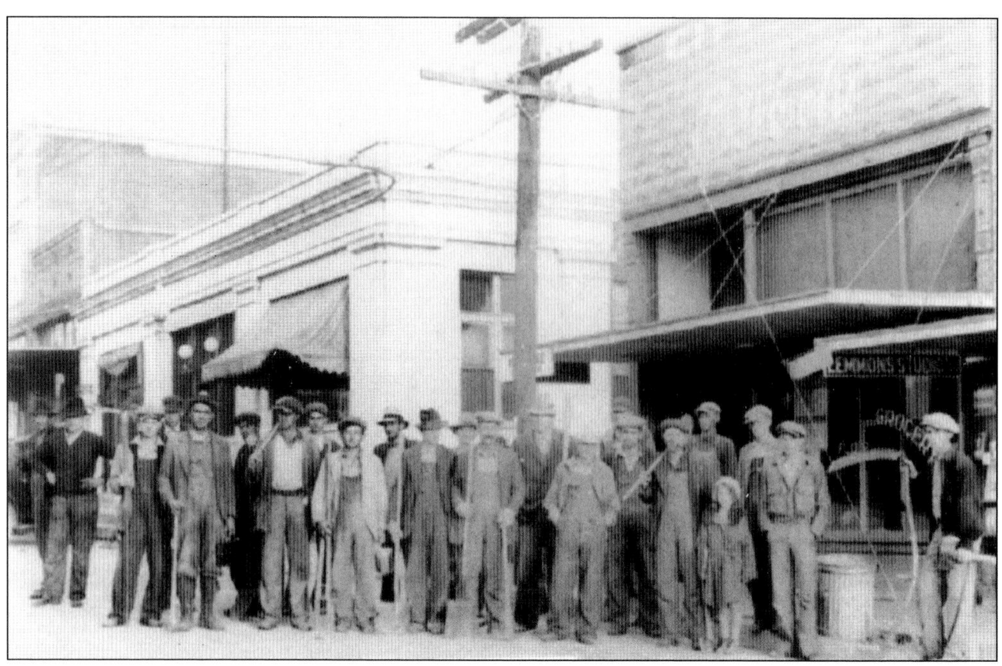

In 1932, WPA workers pose in front of Lemmons Studio on Everett Street. They appear to have been working downtown since they all have tools. The bank building can be seen behind them, with the awning. This building housed a succession of banks and later the Grider Law Firm for many years.

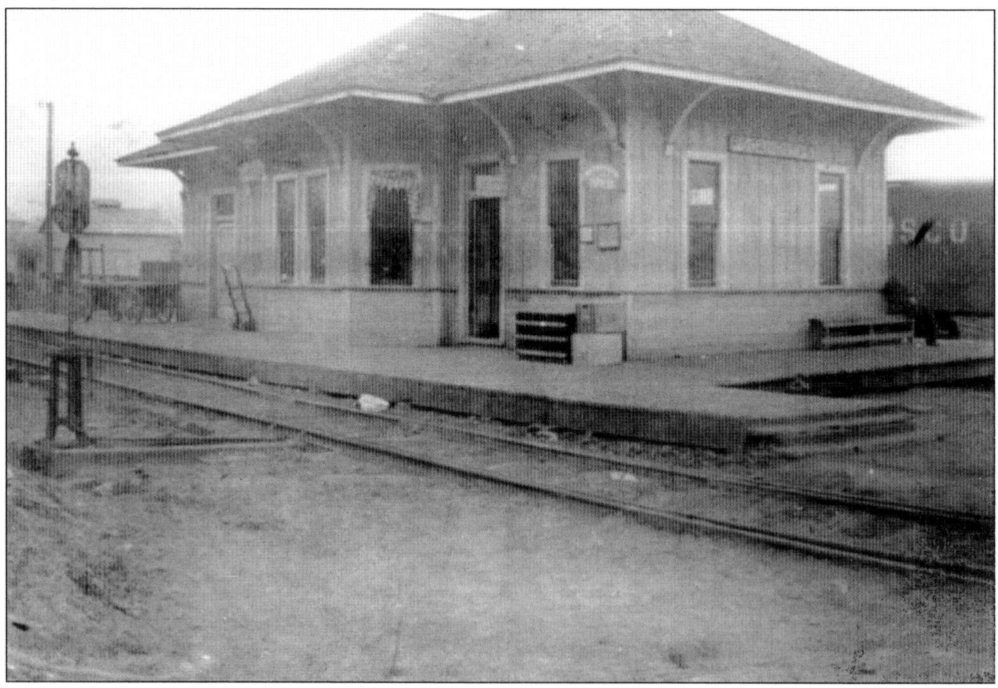

The older Frisco depot, which should not be confused with the present depot, was south of the current depot. This building was closer to the Biggers Hotel, where Broadway Street intersects with Highway 67.

In 1948, a massive explosion rocked downtown Pocahontas. It destroyed most of a city block and leveled the McNabb Funeral Home. The pastor at the local African Methodist Episcopal church, Rev. Henry Taylor, was killed in the explosion. Taylor worked for McNabb, and it is believed he struck a match in the basement while working on a heater.

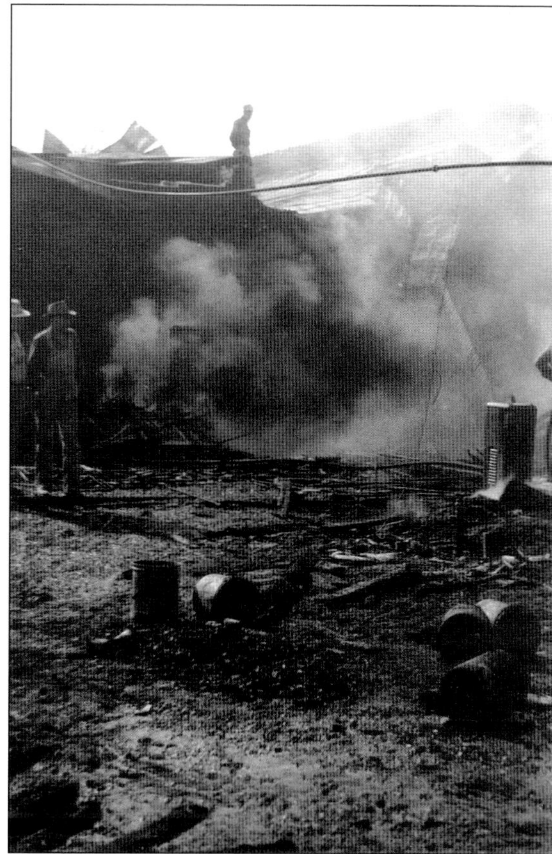

The Joe S. Decker service station was on Bettis Street behind the former Futrell Western Auto building. Bettis Street contained several service stations, a hotel, Dr. Baltz's office, and a few stately homes, such as the Sallee home at Rice and Bettis Streets.

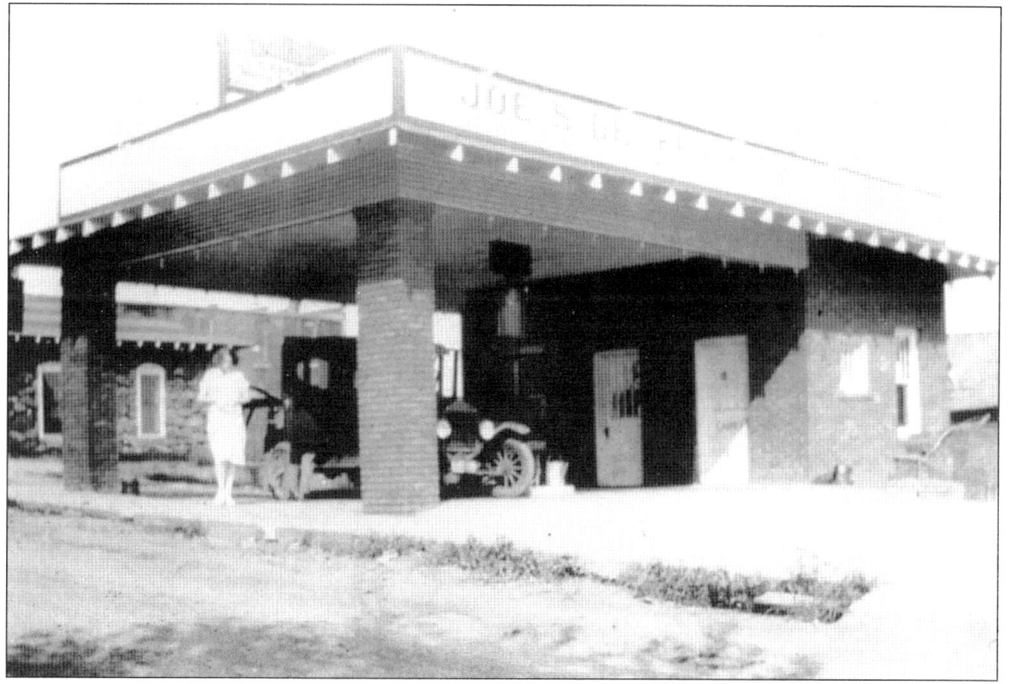

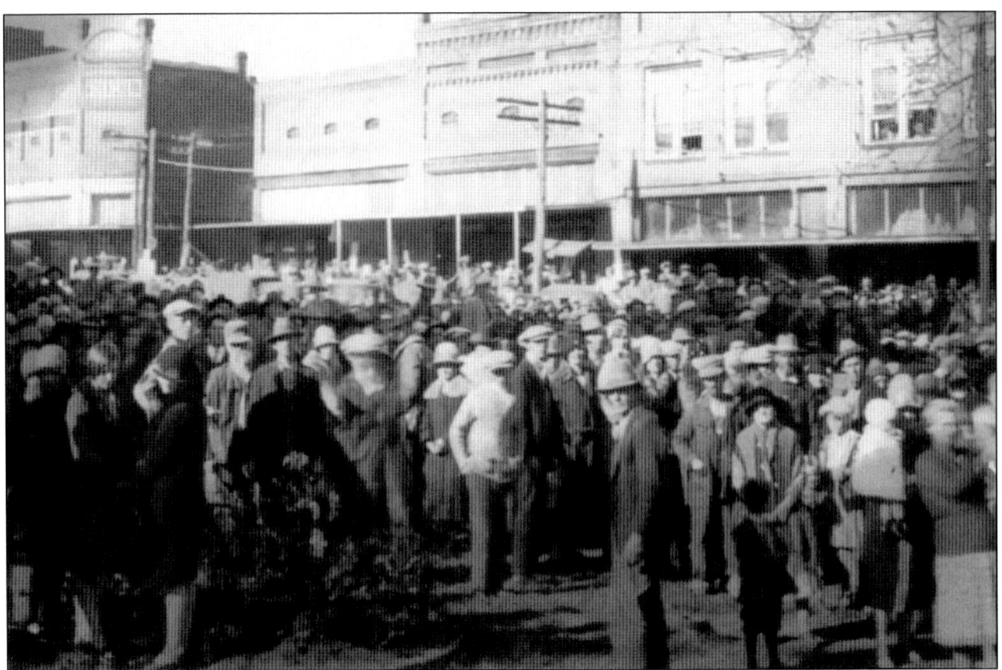

A group of Pocahontas citizens gather on the court square for Dairy Day on November 21, 1929. In the background, the Hamil Building, Turners Saloon, and the structure that currently houses the Randolph County Heritage Museum can be seen. The streets appear to still be dirt.

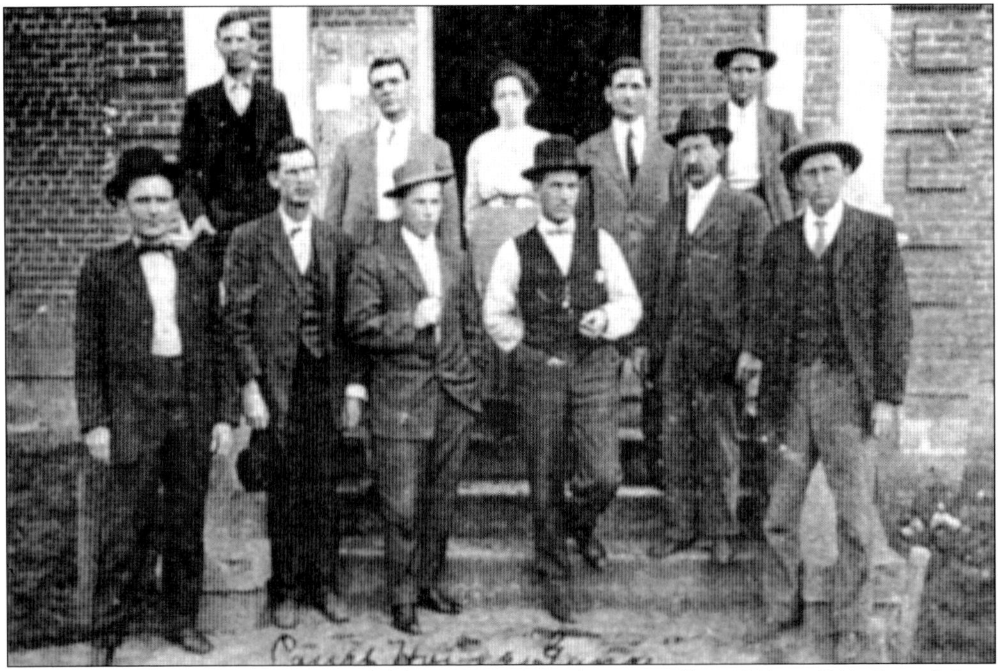

This photograph features the Randolph County Courthouse staff in 1910 or 1911. From left to right are (first row) Hubert Hollowell, Ben Johnson, unidentified, Jack Lewis, Mont Armstrong, and Sam Brown; (second row) Alec Parker, Dee Mock, Mag Johnston Carroll, Oscar Mock, and Herbert Schoonover.

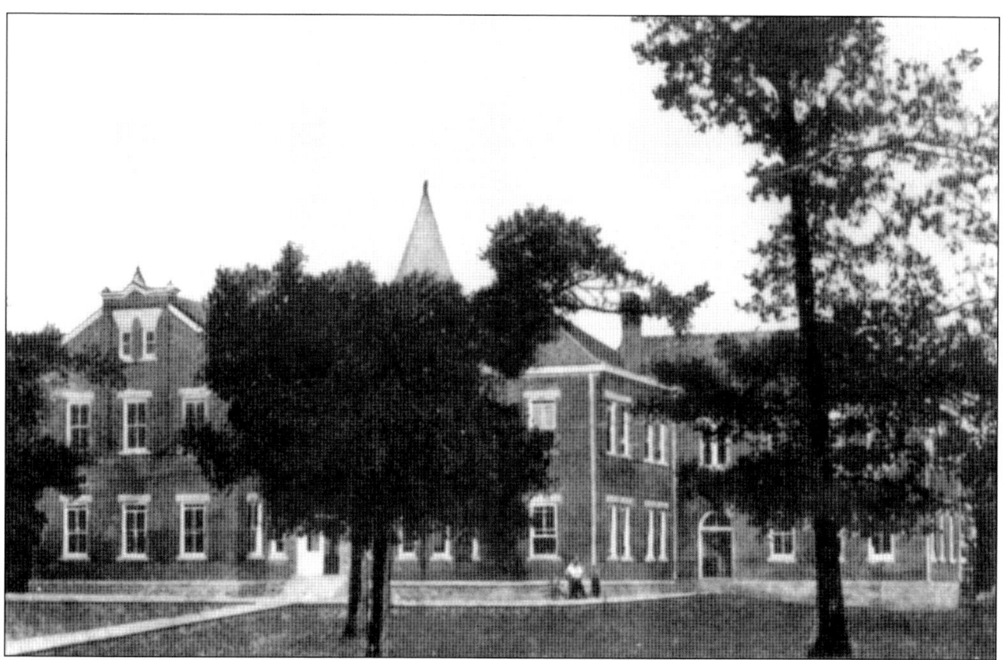
The Pocahontas School on North Marr Street is seen in this undated photograph. Pocahontas Public Schools was organized in 1880 but used various buildings in the early years. The school first used the former Masonic lodge building on the property before erecting this structure.

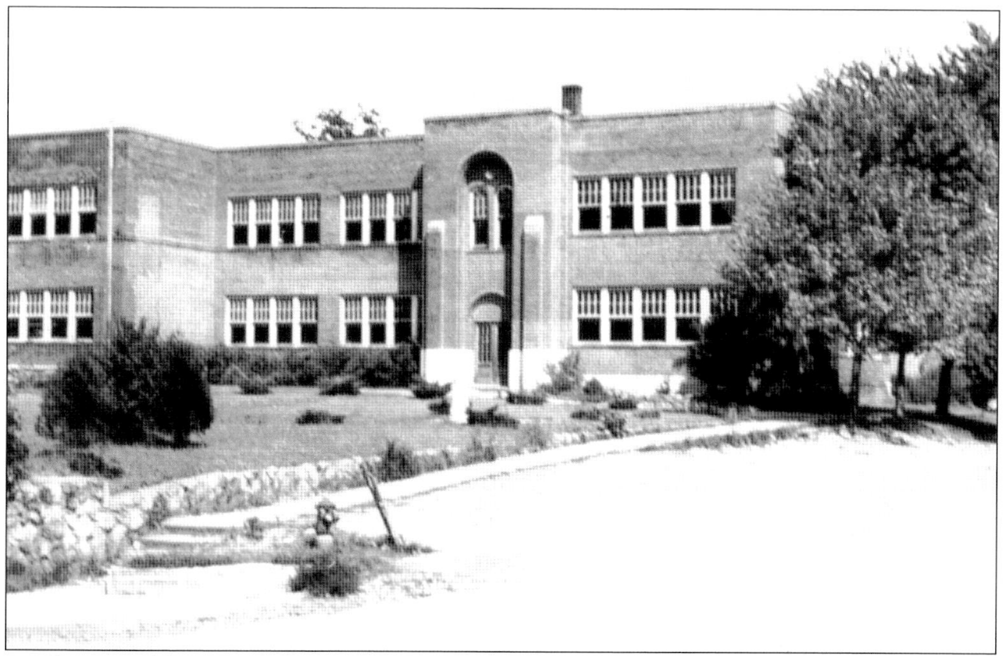
Pocahontas Public Schools's new building was at North Marr and Mason Streets. When constructed, it was a two-story modern building. In later years, the second floor was removed. The school district used the first floor until around 1963, when a new school was constructed. Following construction of the new Alma Spikes Elementary School, most of the school was torn down.

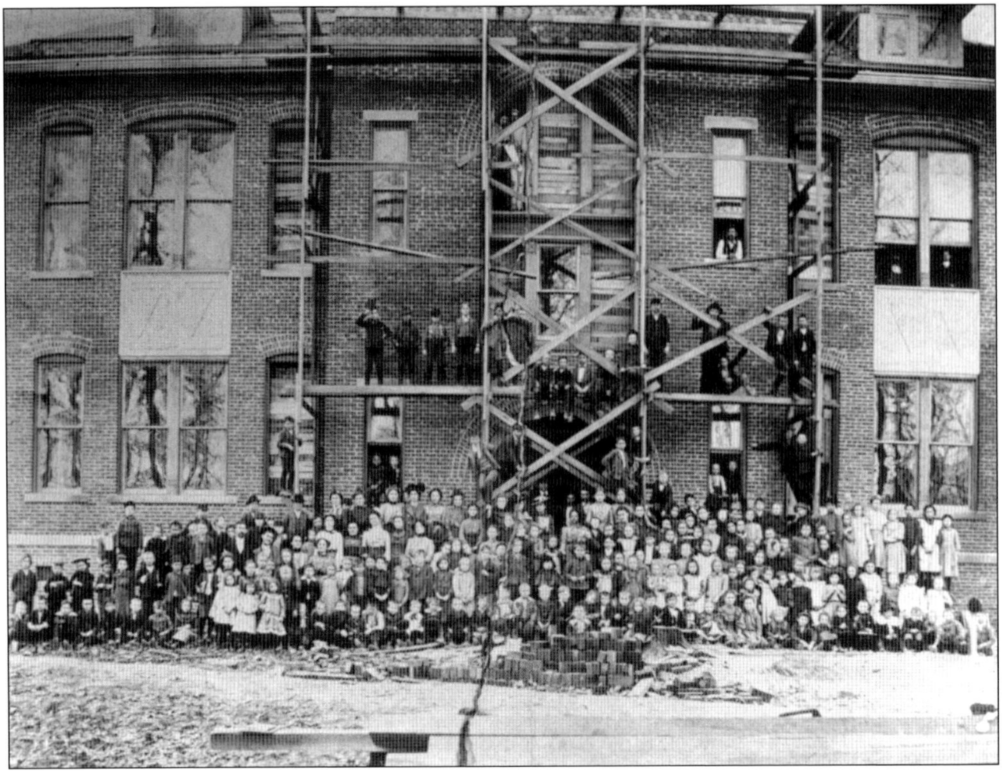

The Pocahontas School is seen under construction on North Marr Street. Based on the large number of people in the photograph, the building may have been used prior to completion. This location served as the school until the new high school was built on Thomasville Street.

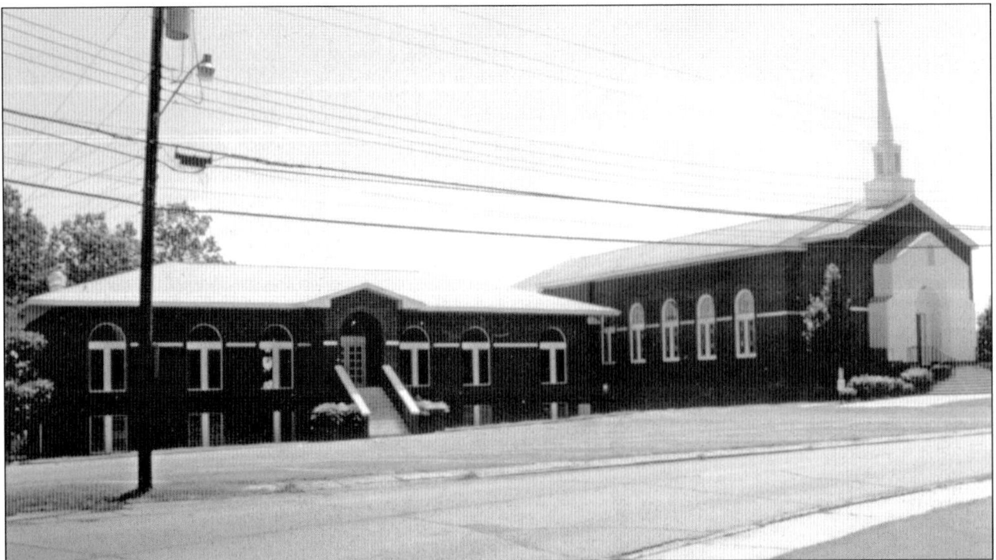

From 1843 to 1853, the Pocahontas Methodist Church congregation met in the courthouse. In 1852, the congregation agreed to erect a new building where the Methodist church stands today. The church did not officially organize until 1877. By 1908, the congregation had outgrown their present building and erected a new structure.

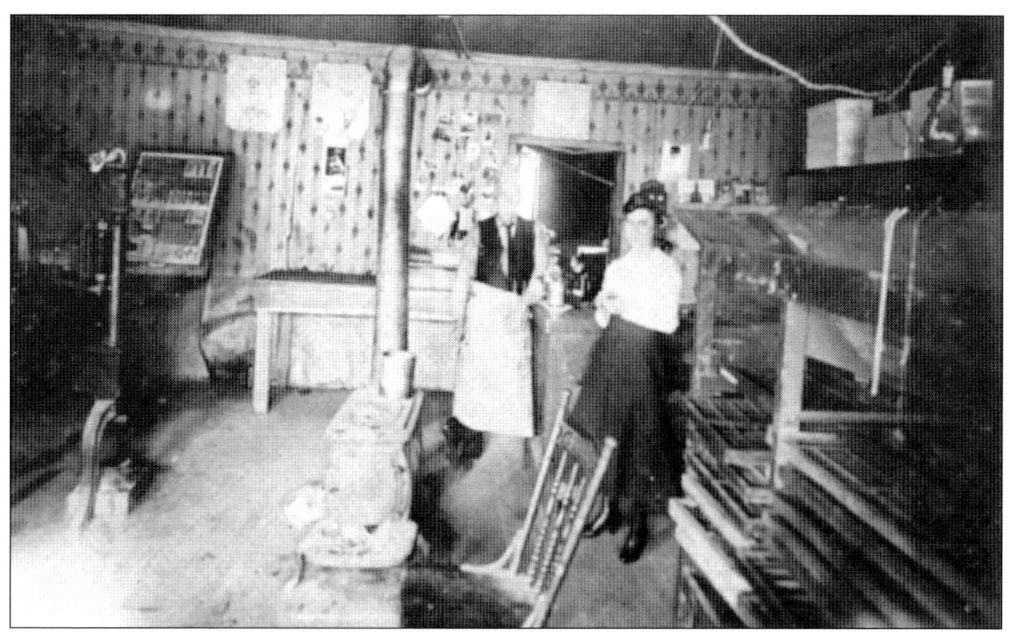

The *Pocahontas Star Herald* is the oldest continuous business in Pocahontas. It was started in 1880 and operated under various owners. By 1915, the Blankenship family had acquired the paper. The family had been partial owners since 1902. In 1935, Eunice B O'Baugh became partial owner and editor.

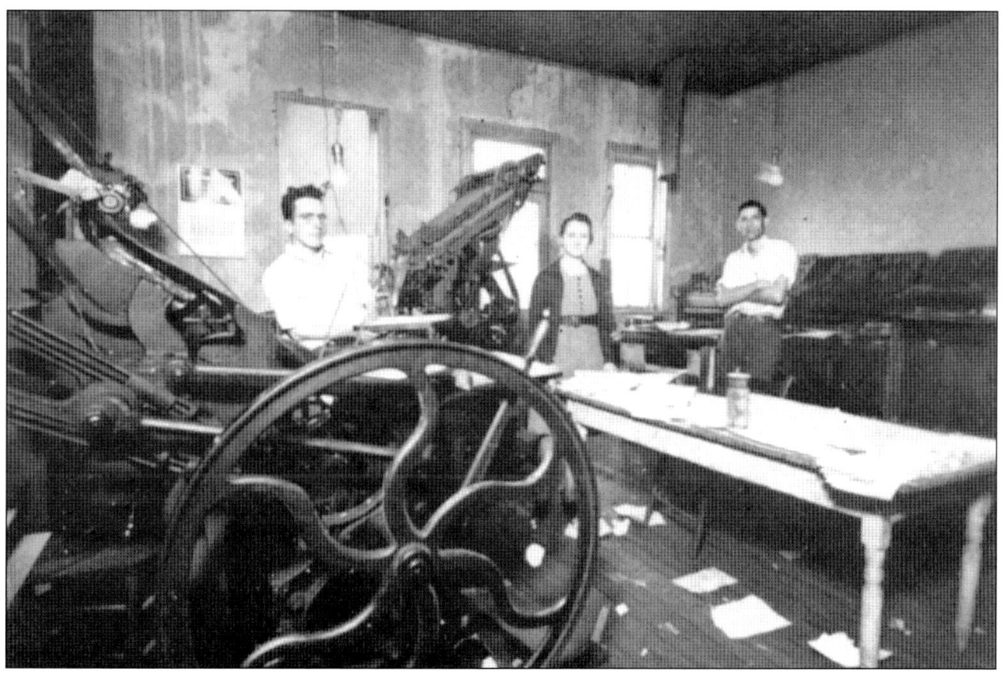

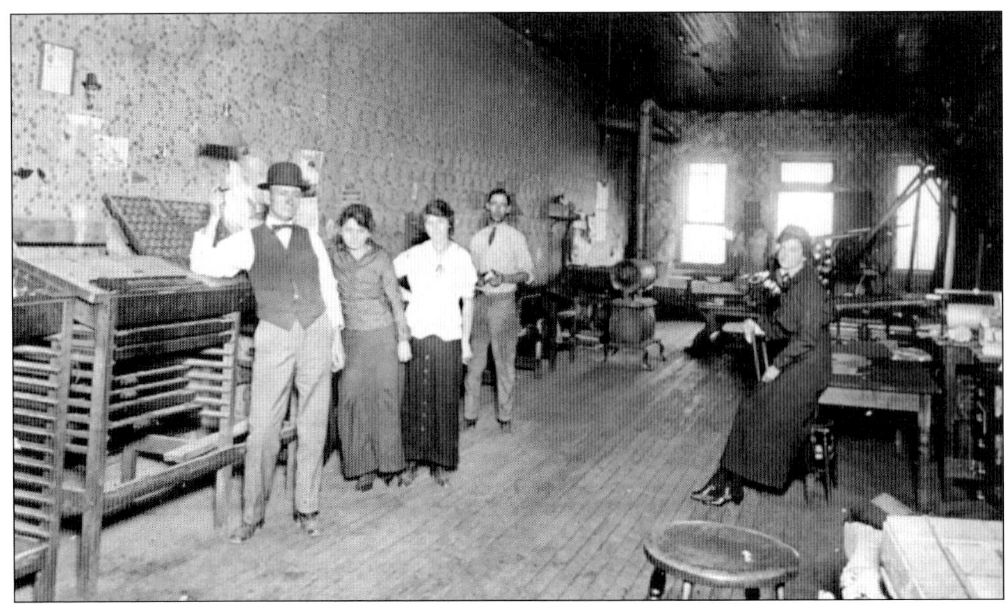

The newspaper has been housed in various buildings in Pocahontas, including on the court square and Everett Street east of the square. When the US Post Office moved out of the building on Van Bibber Street, the paper purchased the old post office and called the building home for years. The paper recently moved to a building on Thomasville Street near the Pocahontas High School campus. It remains in business today.

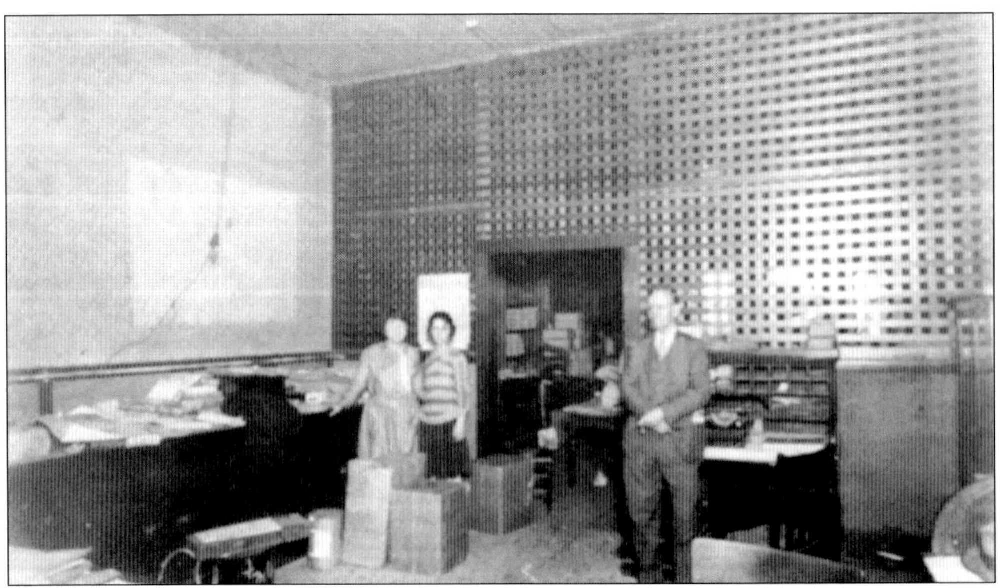

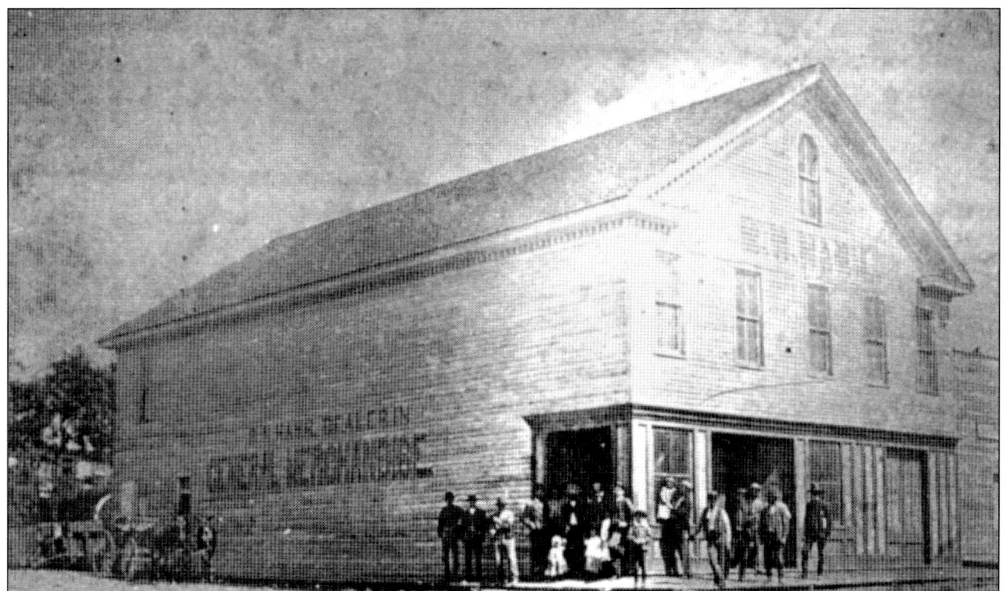

This photograph from 1910 shows the R.N. Hamil general store at the corner of Marr and Everett Streets. Hamil later built a larger brick building that remains today. The building later served as Kings Department Store.

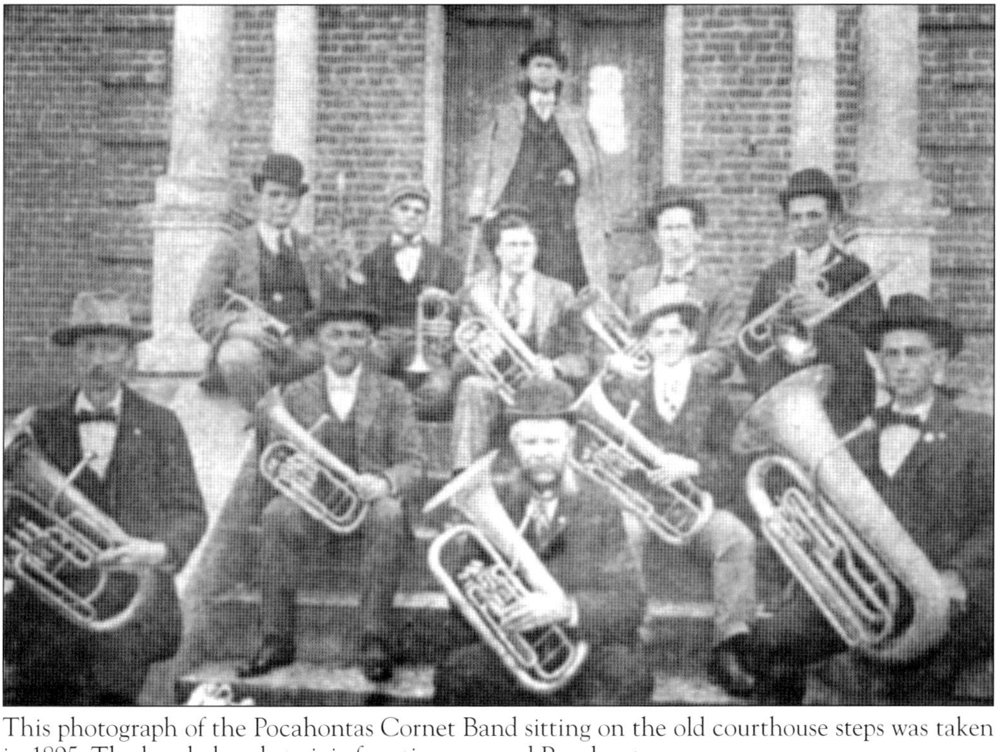

This photograph of the Pocahontas Cornet Band sitting on the old courthouse steps was taken in 1895. The band played at civic functions around Pocahontas.

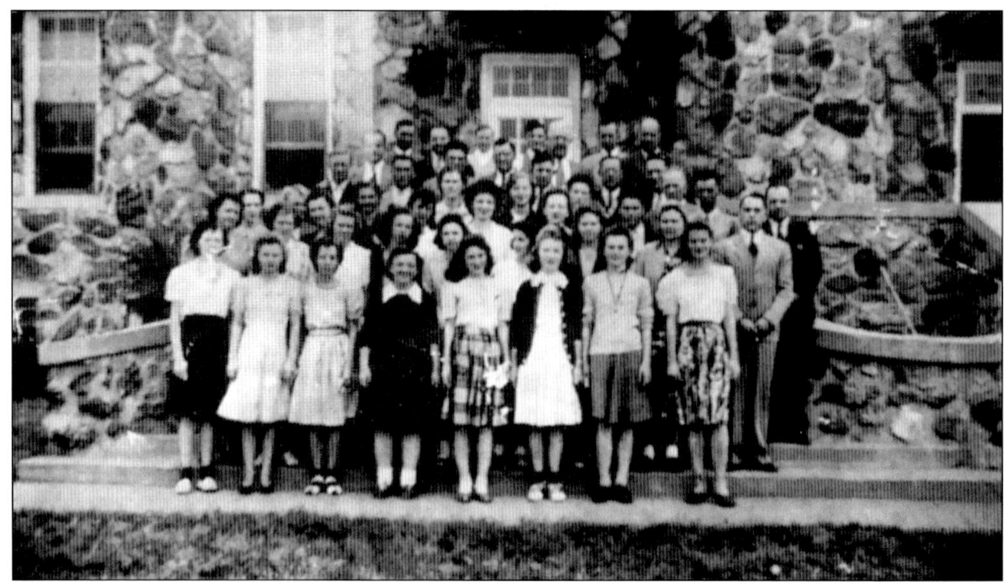

Southern Baptist College students pose in front of the Old Rock Building in 1943. The building served as classroom space and administrative offices, and at least for a short while, Dr. Williams lived in a small apartment here. A fire later gutted the building.

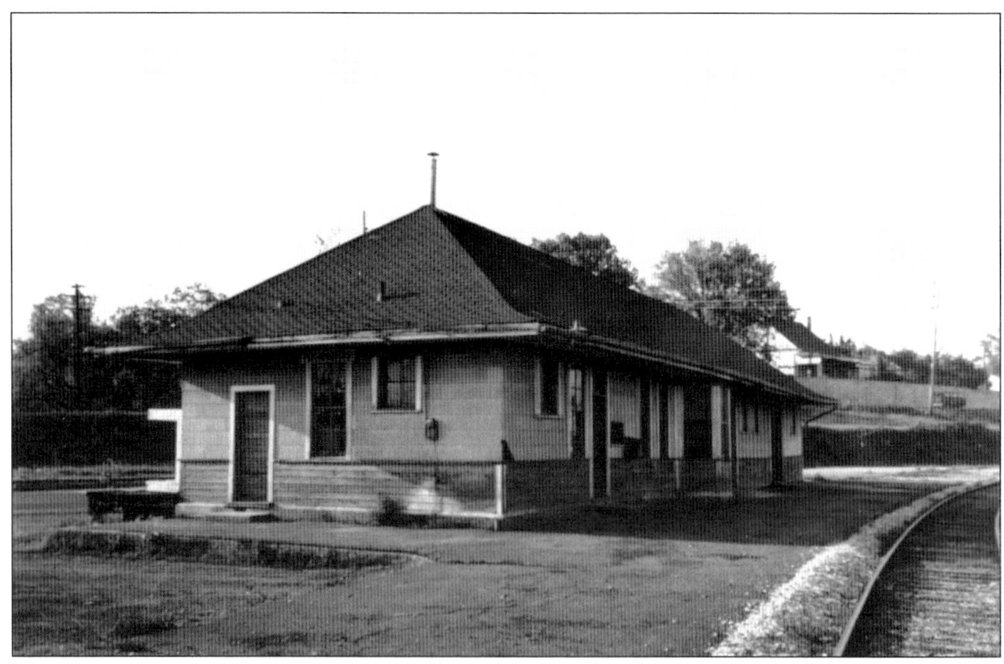

This train depot replaced the earlier building. The new building was east of the older structure. This depot continued to serve Pocahontas until approximately 1970. After the depot ceased to serve the railroad, the property was a used car lot and a church and was later restored and used as a visitor information center and transportation museum.

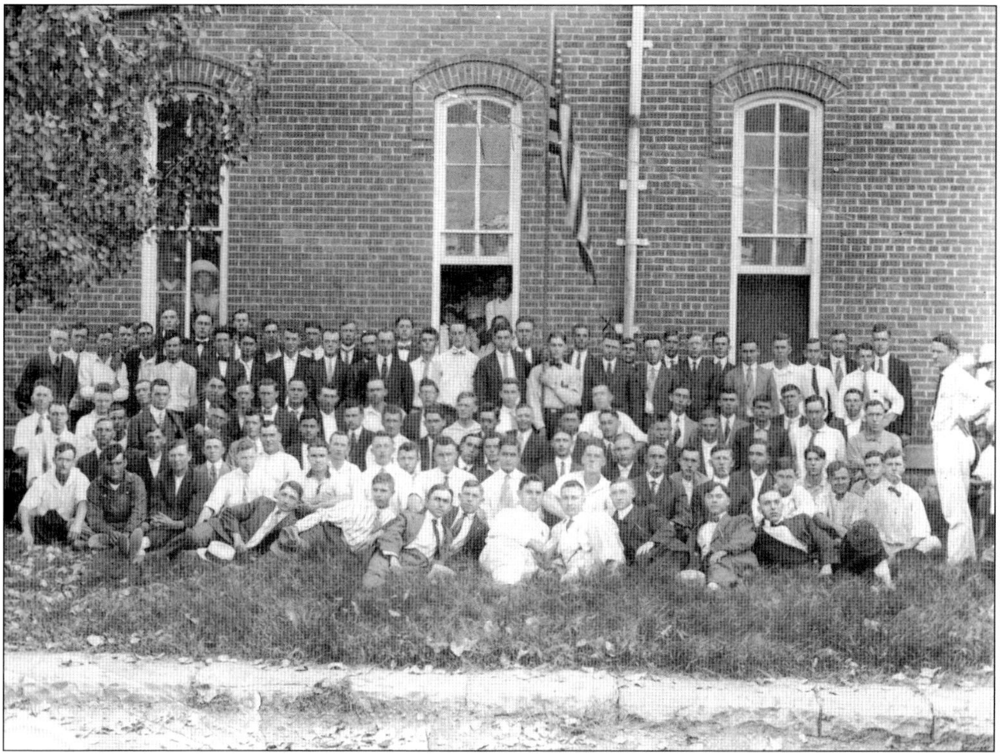

In this image, more than 100 young men are getting ready to leave Randolph County on September 18, 1917, for service in World War I. The photograph was taken in front of the old courthouse. Some people can also be seen inside the building.

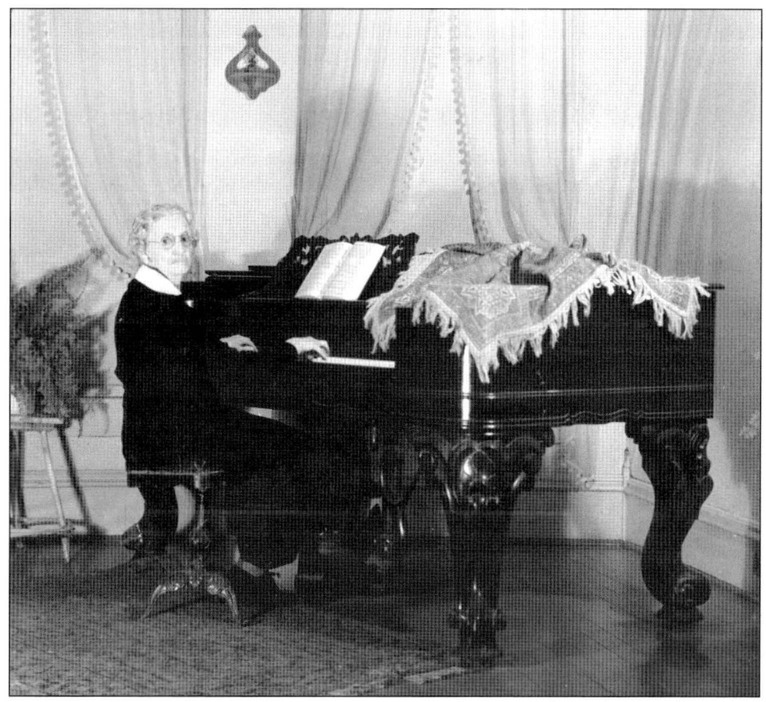

Anne Reynolds Martin is playing a piano that is currently part of the Randolph County Heritage Museum collection. It was purchased in 1883 by Dennis W. Reynolds in New Orleans and shipped by boat up the Mississippi, the White, the Black, and the Current Rivers to Shewmaker's landing between Biggers and Reyno.

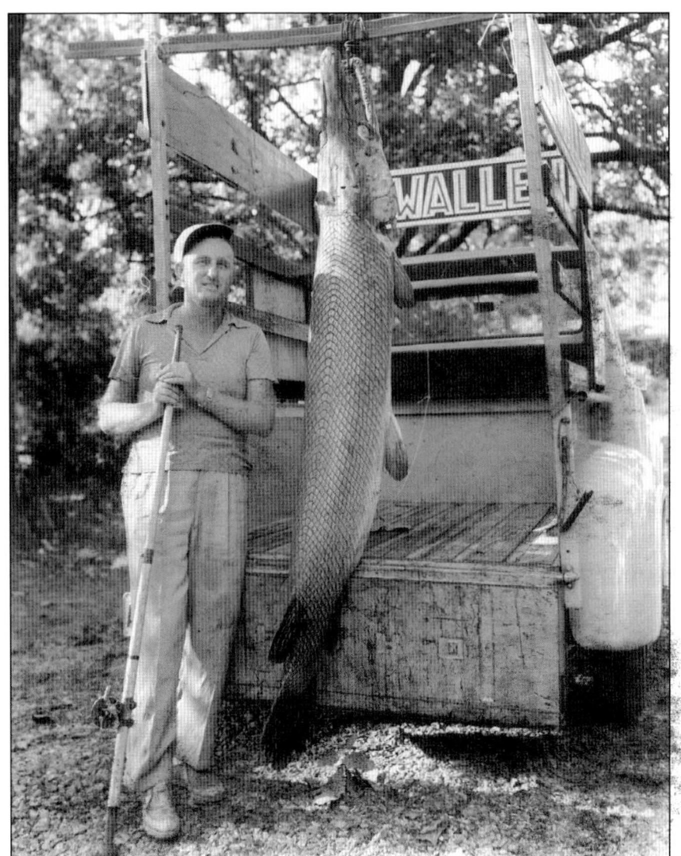

This alligator gar was caught in Randolph County by Rudolph Gazaway Sr. at Shaver's Eddy on the Black River on August 30, 1955. Weighing in at 164 pounds and measuring seven feet and three inches long, Gazaway eventually shot the gar to land it. This photograph was featured on the show *River Monsters* in 2009.

The J.G. Voohers Lumber Company was on the northeast corner of the court square at the corner of Bettis and Everett Streets. The building later housed Pocahontas City Hall and other businesses and served as the event headquarters for the Pocahontas centennial in 1956.

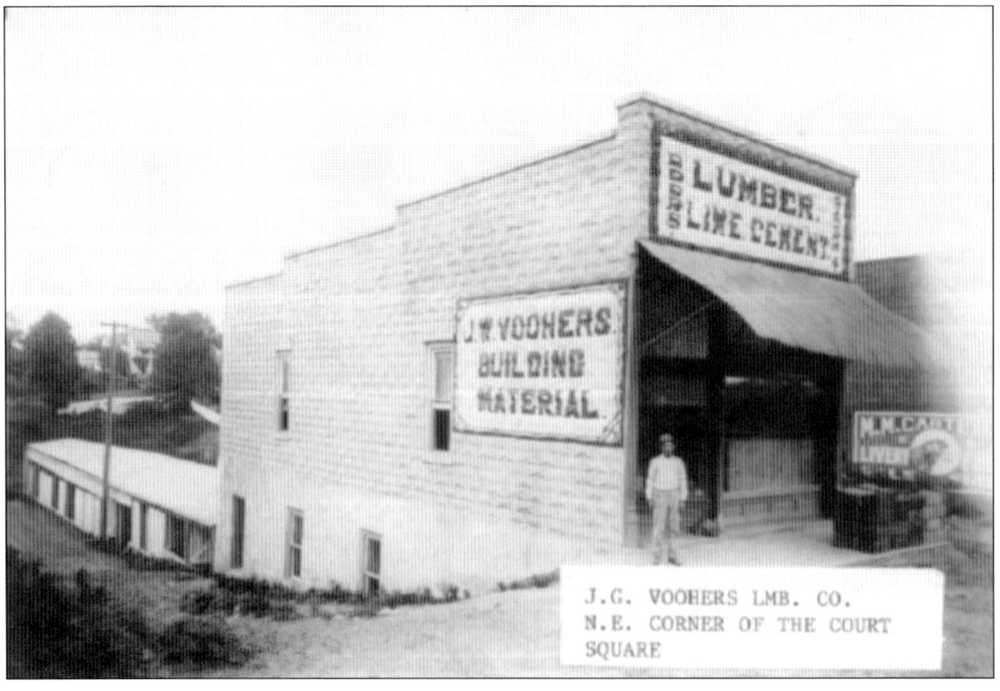

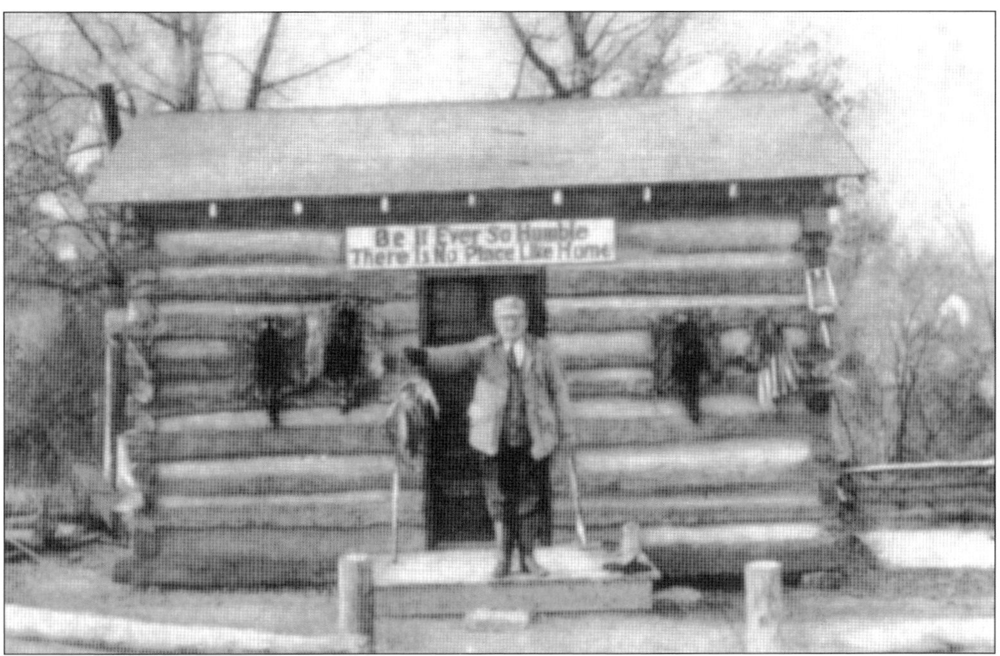

This is a postcard of Joe Decker's hunting and fishing lodge. Decker was a county judge more than once. He was also a local businessman and instrumental in advancing Randolph County. The cabin was in Ravenden Springs.

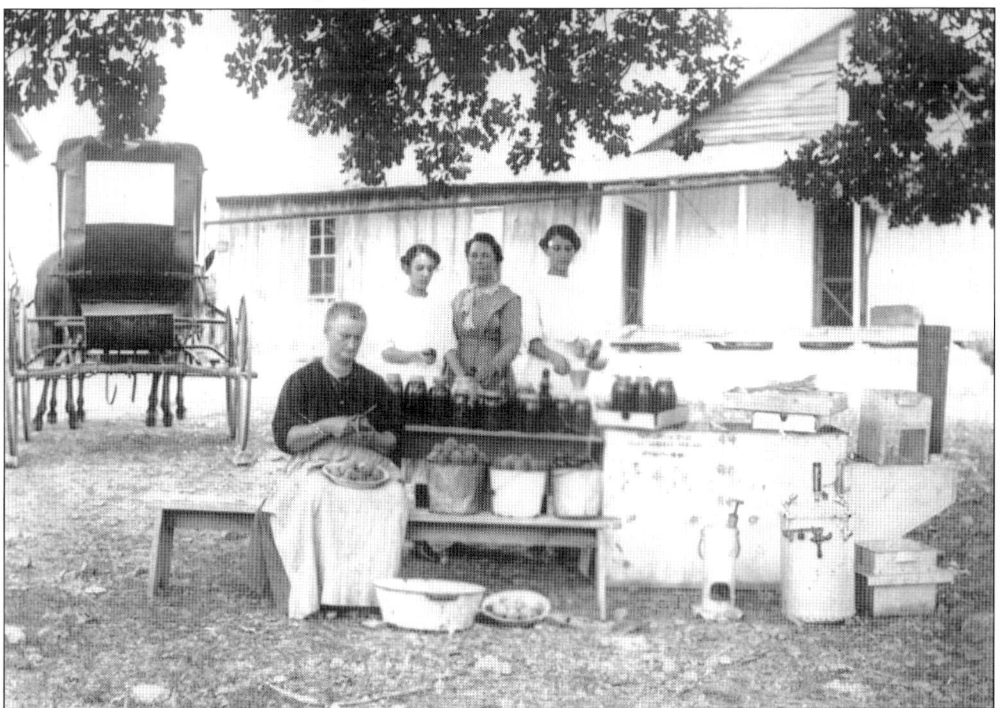

This photograph is of a Home Demonstration Club canning demo held at the home of George and Catherine Baltz near Birdell in 1914. From left to right are Catherine Baltz and her daughters Anna and Lena. Also pictured is Birdie Kizer, the club agent and John Kizer's wife.

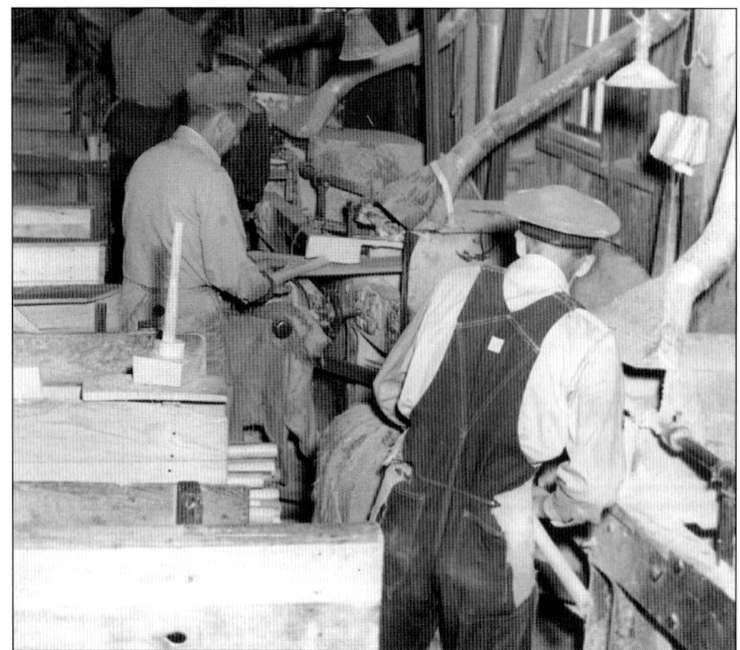

Workers are seen inside the Sallee Handle Mill in Pocahontas. The mill was located along the riverfront. In the early years, logs were floated down the river from sawmills on the Current and Black Rivers. The mill then turned the logs into staves, ties, and other items, such as ax handles and baseball bats. Clearing the forests along the rivers allowed the agricultural economy to flourish today.

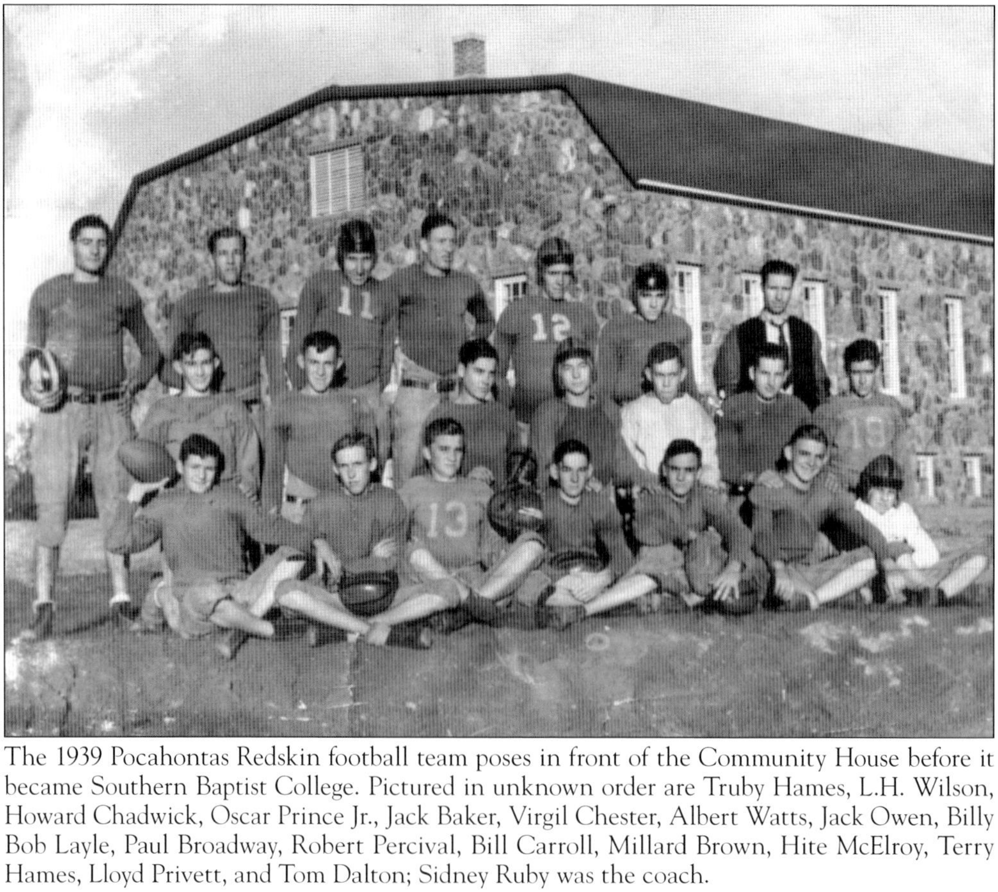

The 1939 Pocahontas Redskin football team poses in front of the Community House before it became Southern Baptist College. Pictured in unknown order are Truby Hames, L.H. Wilson, Howard Chadwick, Oscar Prince Jr., Jack Baker, Virgil Chester, Albert Watts, Jack Owen, Billy Bob Layle, Paul Broadway, Robert Percival, Bill Carroll, Millard Brown, Hite McElroy, Terry Hames, Lloyd Privett, and Tom Dalton; Sidney Ruby was the coach.

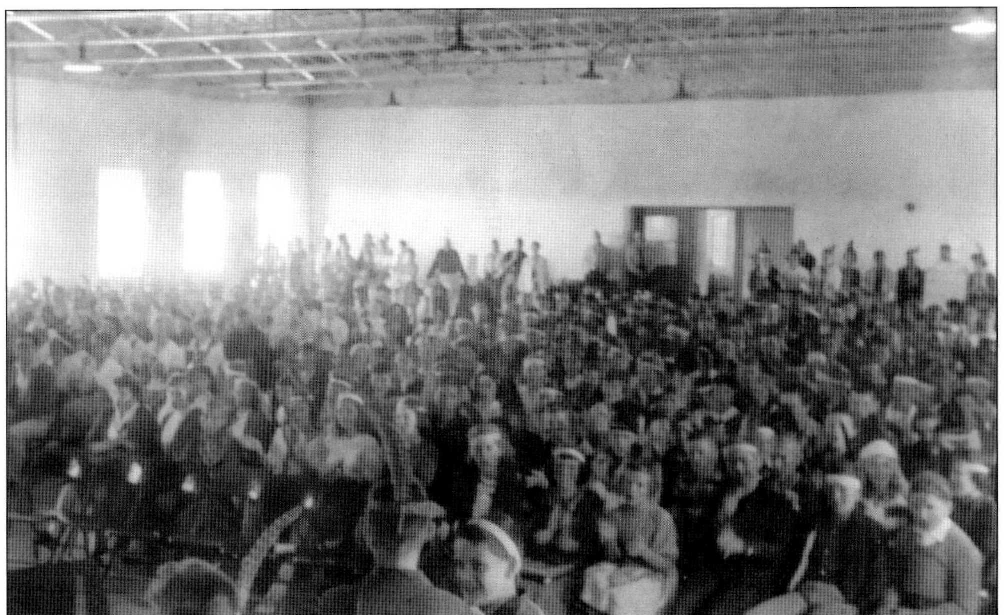

Pocahontas public school students are pictured at an assembly in the 1950s in the old rock building after it was converted to an auditorium. After Pocahontas High School moved to its present location on North Thomasville Street in the 1950s, the district rehabilitated the Old Rock Building, gutted by fire in the 1940s, forcing Southern Baptist College to move.

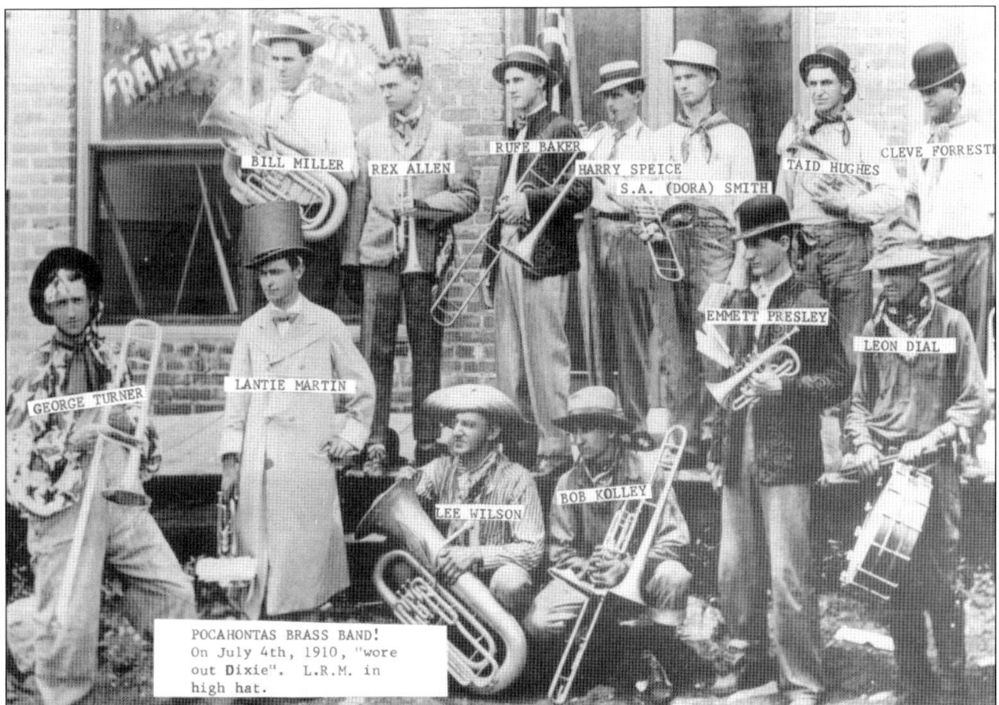

Lantie Martin, noted citizen and business leader, is in the top hat in this photograph of a Pocahontas band. Other members include George Turner, C. Lee Wilson, Bob Kolley, Emmet Presley, Leon Dial, Bill Millar, Rex Allen, Rufe Baker, Harry Spiece, Doris Smith, Ted Hughes, and Cleve Forrester.

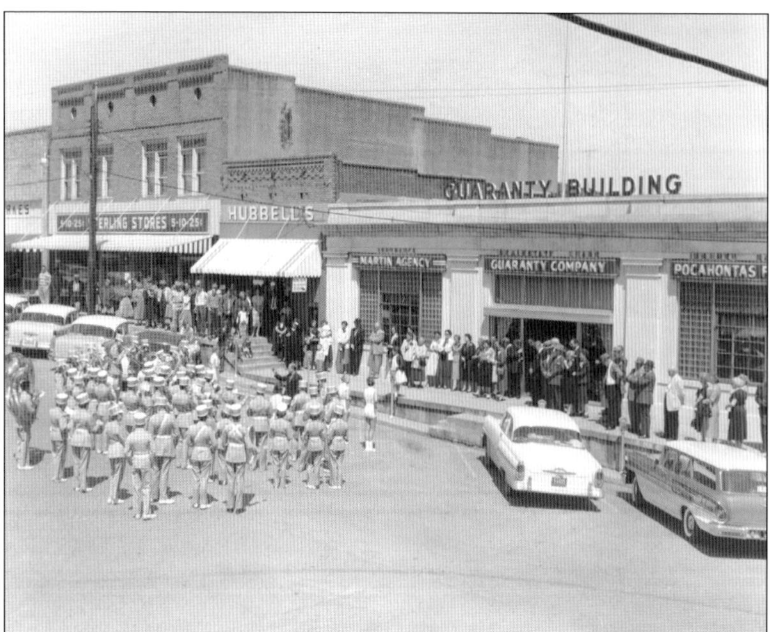

The Pocahontas High School Band is performing on Everett Street in front of Pocahontas Federal Savings and Loan in the 1950s or 1960s. The building that currently houses the Randolph County Heritage Museum can be seen in the background.

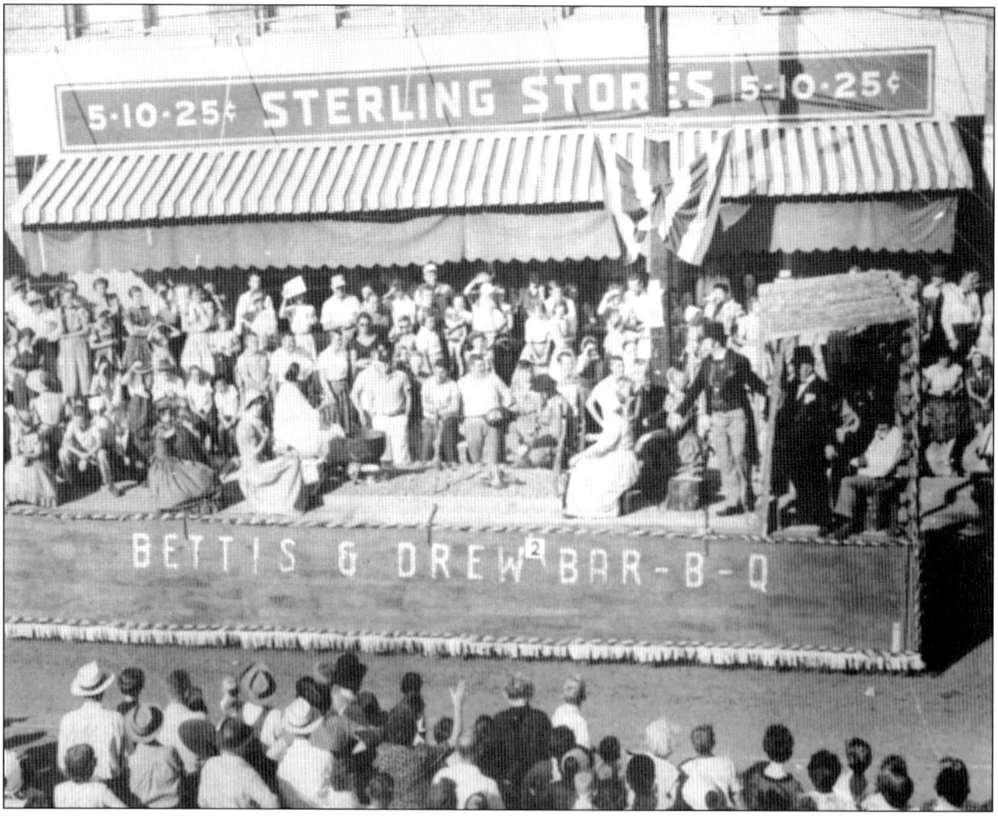

In 1956, Pocahontas celebrated its centennial. This Pocahontas Kiwanis Club float depicts the "Bettis & Drew Bar-B-Q," in which Ransom Bettis and Thomas Drew hosted a barbecue with free whiskey on the day of the election to determine the county seat.

The women of the Pocahontas Garden Club pose in 1942. Pictured are Anne Martin, Nellie Childs, Ana Martin, Mrs. Clarence Stubblefield, Tala Cox, Lena Black, Pauline Blankenship, Mrs. Joe Crittenden, Edena Amos, Mrs. Jesse Phipps, Evelyn Throgmarton, Ora Pace, Elizabeth Bauer, Mrs. Fender, Ella Bristow, Mrs. L.W. Cox, Anna Peters, Mrs. George Lewallen, Mrs. George Reid, Leona Hite, Agnes James, Mrs. Mack Archer, and Mrs. George Promberger.

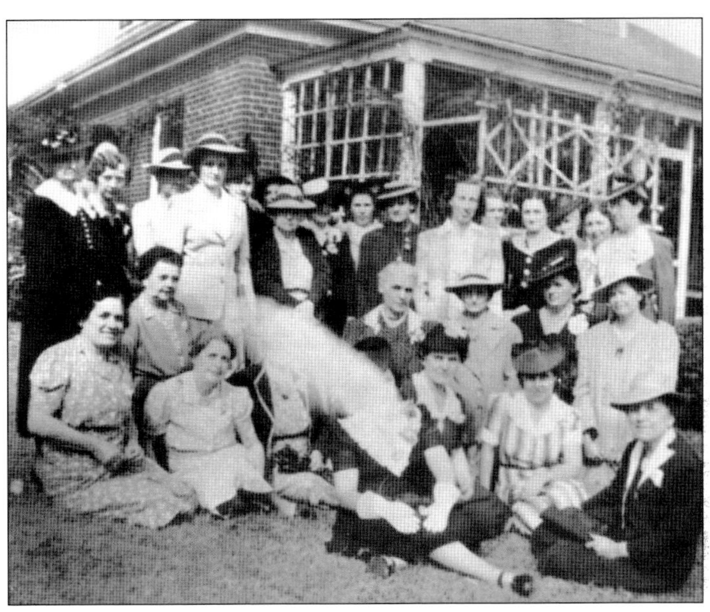

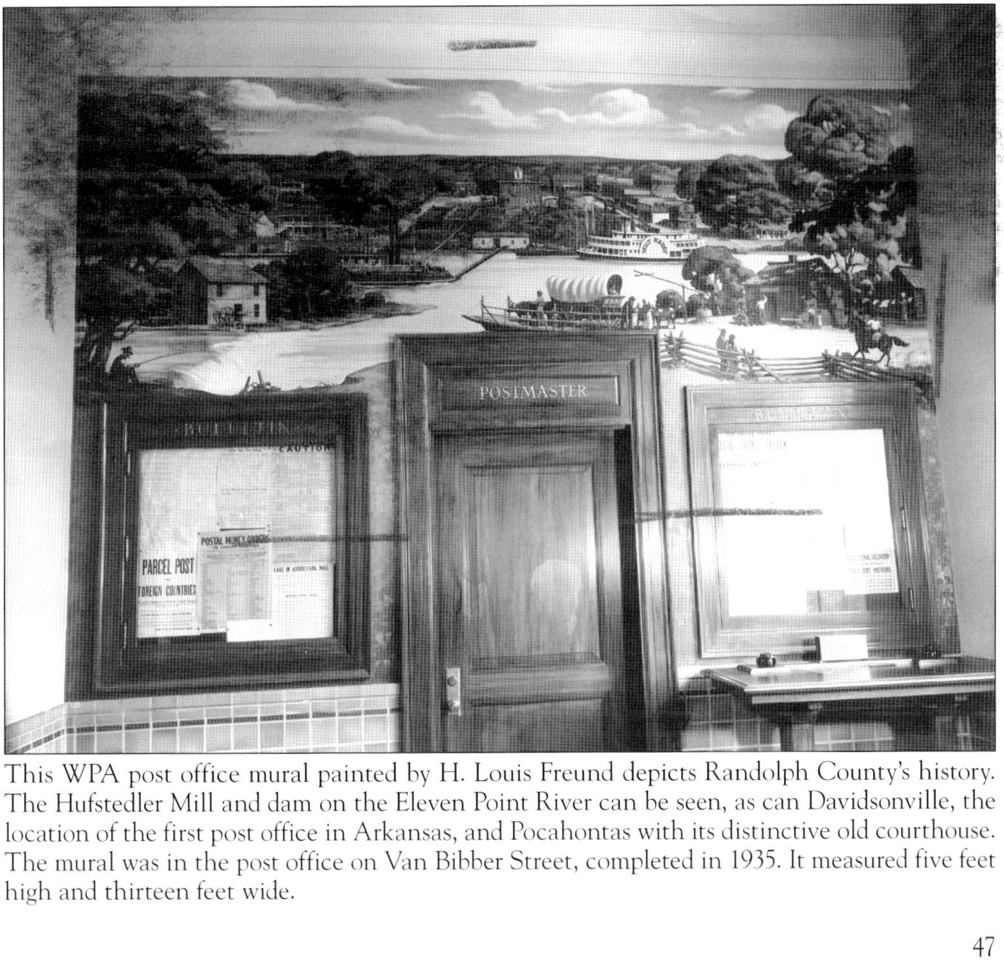

This WPA post office mural painted by H. Louis Freund depicts Randolph County's history. The Hufstedler Mill and dam on the Eleven Point River can be seen, as can Davidsonville, the location of the first post office in Arkansas, and Pocahontas with its distinctive old courthouse. The mural was in the post office on Van Bibber Street, completed in 1935. It measured five feet high and thirteen feet wide.

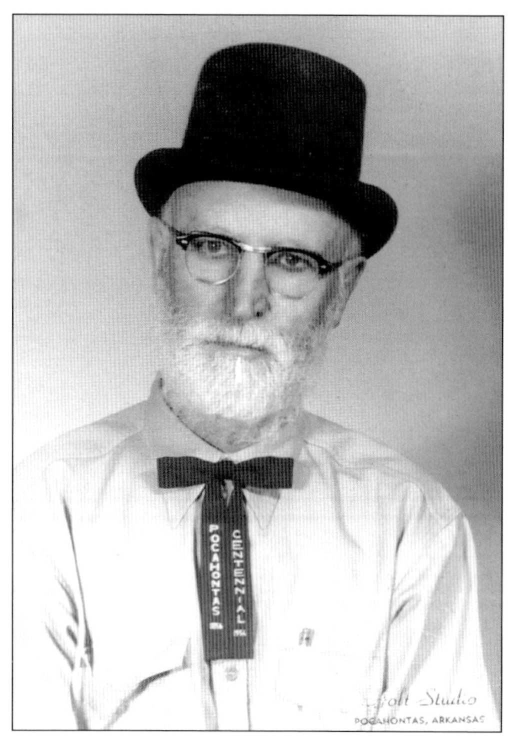

William "Bill" Baltz invented the Wonder Horse in 1939 as a Christmas present for his son Billy. He removed the rockers from a rocking horse and suspended the horse from springs held by a wooden frame. The Wonder Horse was invented in Baltz's workshop at the corner of Bettis and Rice Streets near the court square. Baltz eventually filed a patent for the toy and partnered with a manufacturing firm in Memphis to produce and market it.

This is a photograph of the Pocahontas Modern Woodmen Camp No. 13600 taken April 17, 1910. Modern Woodmen of America was one of several fraternal organizations active in Pocahontas over the years and is still active in the community today.

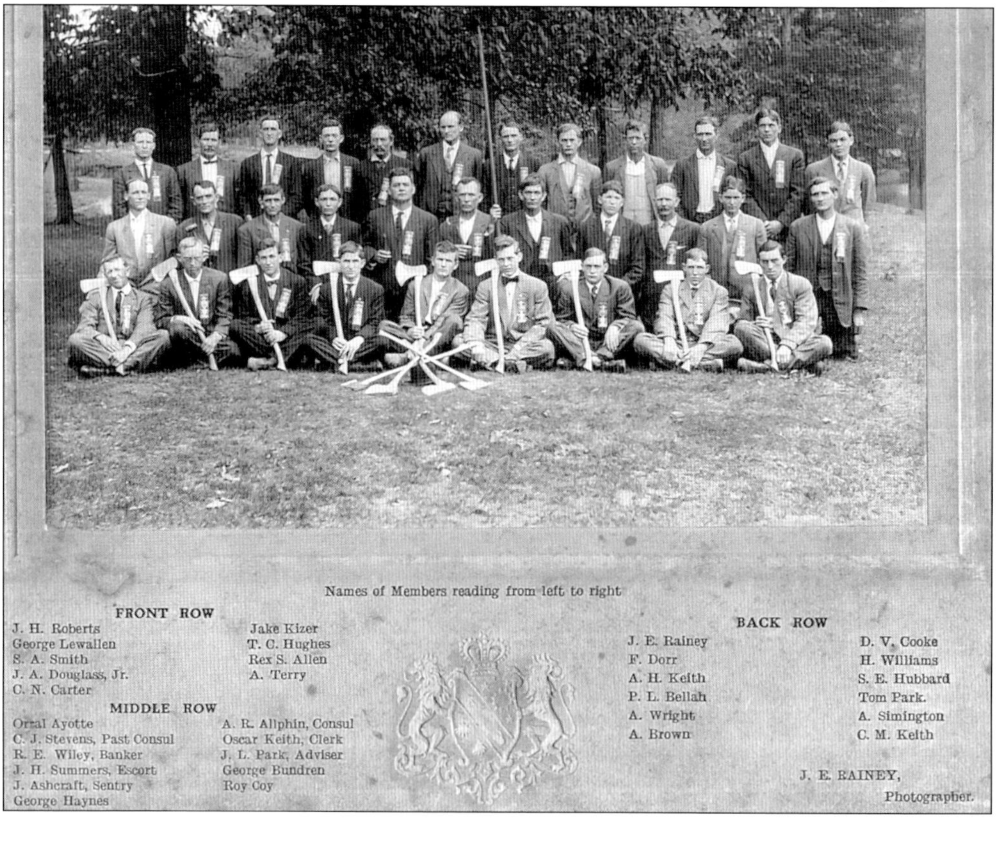

Names of Members reading from left to right

FRONT ROW

J. H. Roberts
George Lewallen
S. A. Smith
J. A. Douglass, Jr.
C. N. Carter
Jake Kizer
T. C. Hughes
Rex S. Allen
A. Terry

MIDDLE ROW

Orral Ayotte
C. J. Stevens, Past Consul
R. E. Wiley, Banker
J. H. Summers, Escort
J. Ashcraft, Sentry
George Haynes
A. R. Allphin, Consul
Oscar Keith, Clerk
J. L. Park, Adviser
George Bundren
Roy Coy

BACK ROW

J. E. Rainey
F. Dorr
A. H. Keith
P. L. Bellah
A. Wright
A. Brown
D. V. Cooke
H. Williams
S. E. Hubbard
Tom Park.
A. Simington
C. M. Keith

J. E. RAINEY,
Photographer.

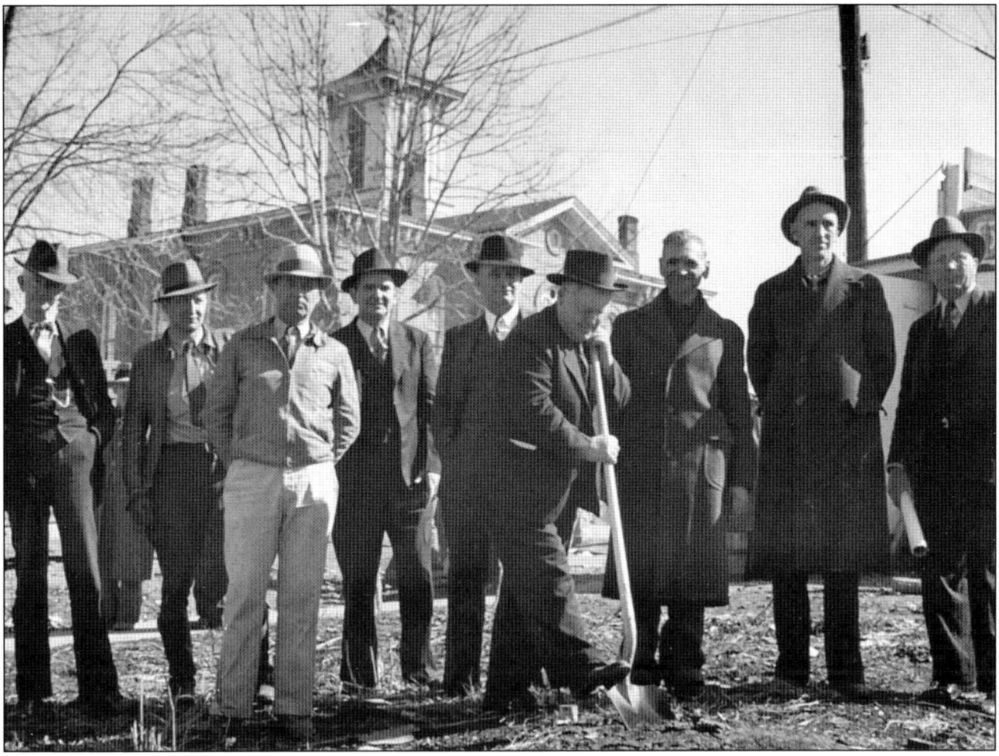

By 1940, the government of Randolph County had outgrown the old courthouse. On February 17, the county held a groundbreaking ceremony for the new courthouse southwest of the court square. Pictured from left to right are Ben A. Brown, chairman of the commission; Fred Schroeder, WPA engineer; Carl H. Brooks, commissioner; Joe P. Randolph, contractor; E.V. Bird, contractor; Dee Mock, commissioner; Will Baltz, county surveyor; Carl Bird, superintendent of construction; and Joe S. Decker, county judge.

The Randolph County Bank building was erected in 1910 at the corner of Bettis and Broadway Streets. The streets around the square were not yet paved. The Martin Insurance Agency that remains in business began in this building. After the building ceased to be a bank, it became Futrell's Western Auto Hardware Store, which remained until 2022, when it closed.

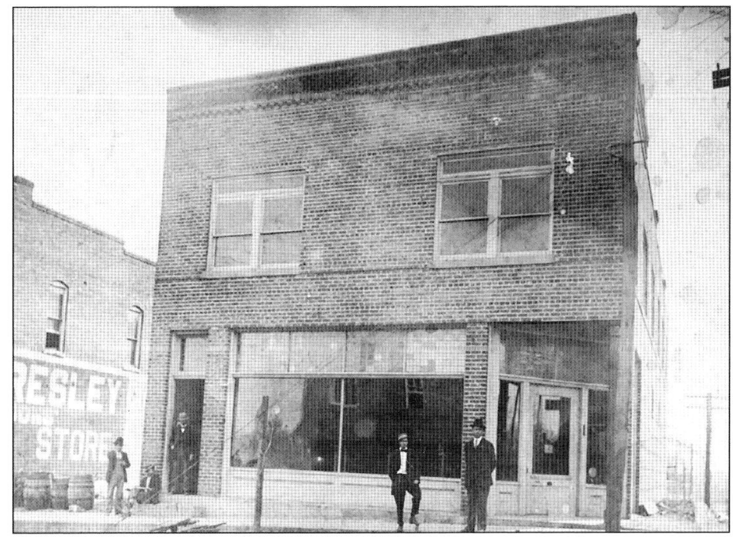

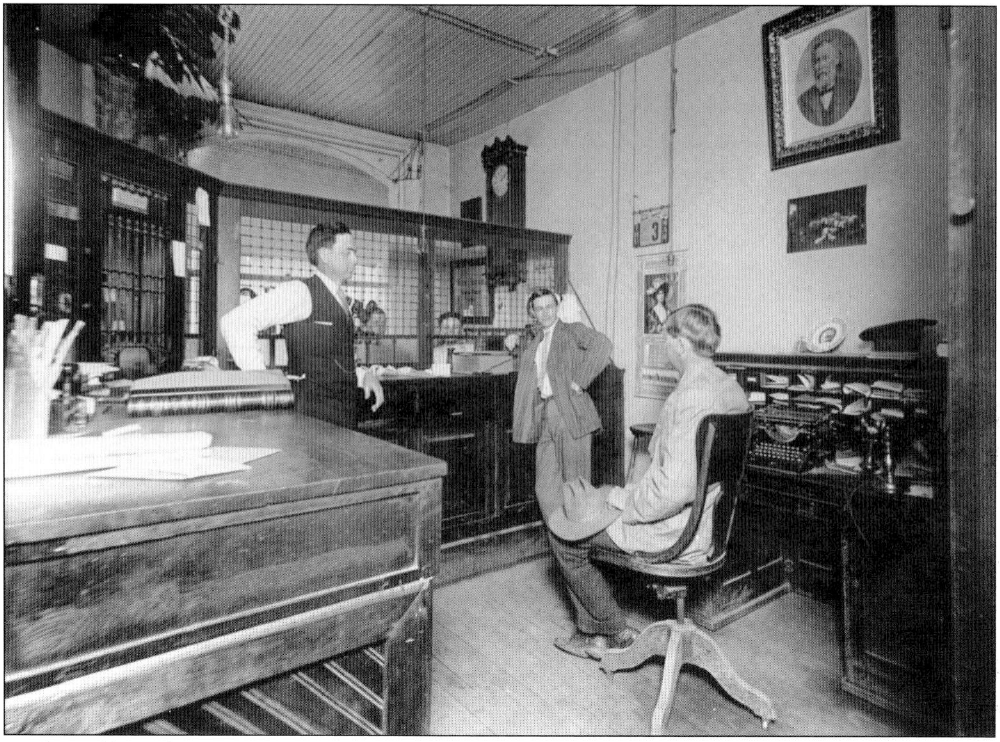

Daily Wells and Lantie Martin are pictured in the lobby of the Randolph County Bank at the corner of Broadway and Bettis Streets. This building later housed Futrell Western Auto. Martin was the youngest bank cashier in the state at the time. At the time, the cashier was one of the most important officers of the bank. Martin later founded Pocahontas Federal Savings and Loan and the Martin Agency insurance company, which is still in business today.

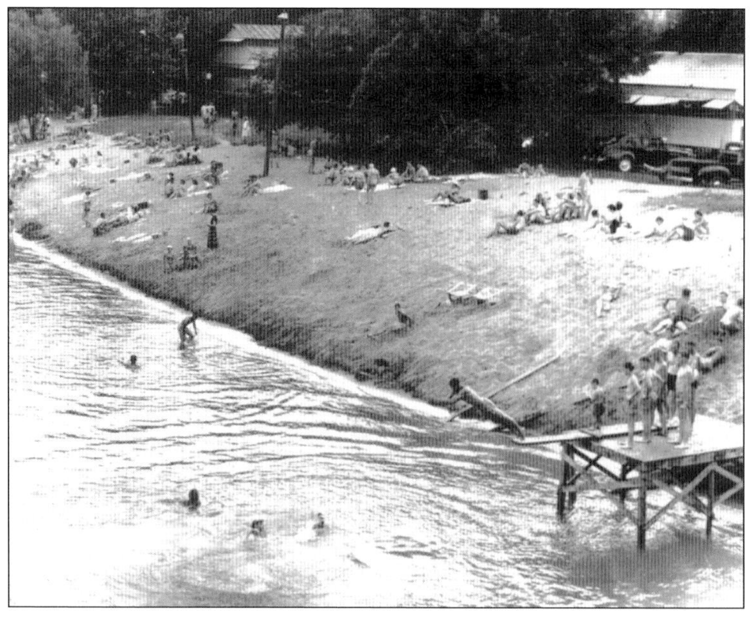

This photograph shows a busy Current River Beach Club around 1941. The beach club was near where Highway 67 North crosses the Current River. The beach was a popular place in the summer. People of all ages came from miles around to swim, water ski, camp, and dance.

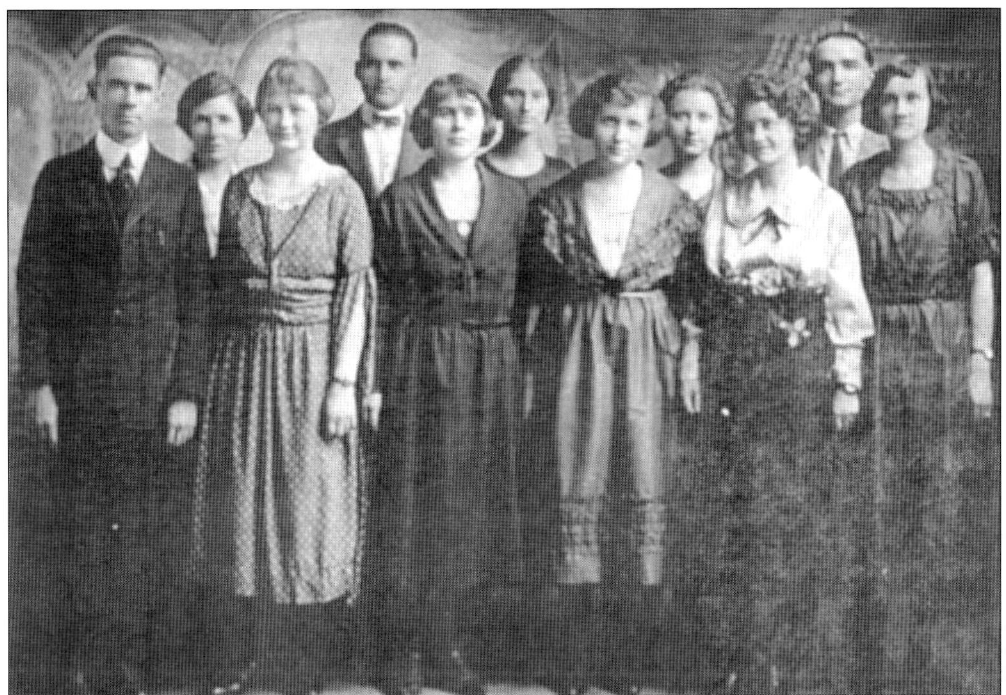

The faculty of Pocahontas Public Schools pose around 1920. From left to right are (first row) H.H. Price, Verda Robbins, Grace Haynes, Clara Wells, and Bertha Mock; (second row) Zadie Smith, Charles Baker, Nell Hufstedler, Micky Halton, and Jim Spikes.

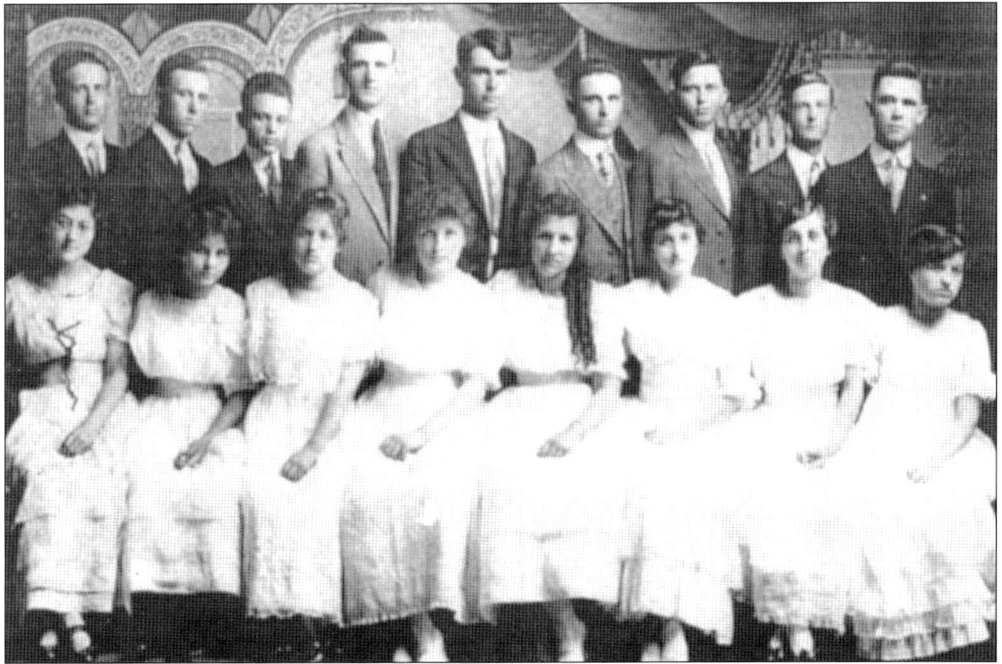

The Pocahontas High School graduating class of 1917 is pictured here. This class was the first to graduate from the new high school. The photograph was taken by George Lemmons, who owned Lemmons Studio.

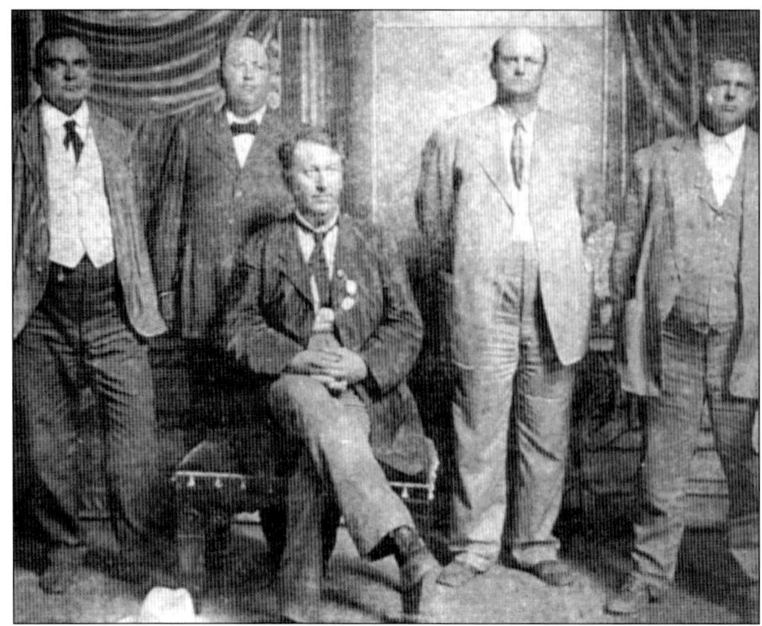

The "Big Five" of the Randolph County Circuit Court pose for a photograph, most likely at Lemmons Studio. From left to right are James Louis Robinson, Clarence Henderson, Circuit Judge J.W. Meeks (seated), Harry Hite, and Charles Bode. Robinson and Henderson were local attorneys.

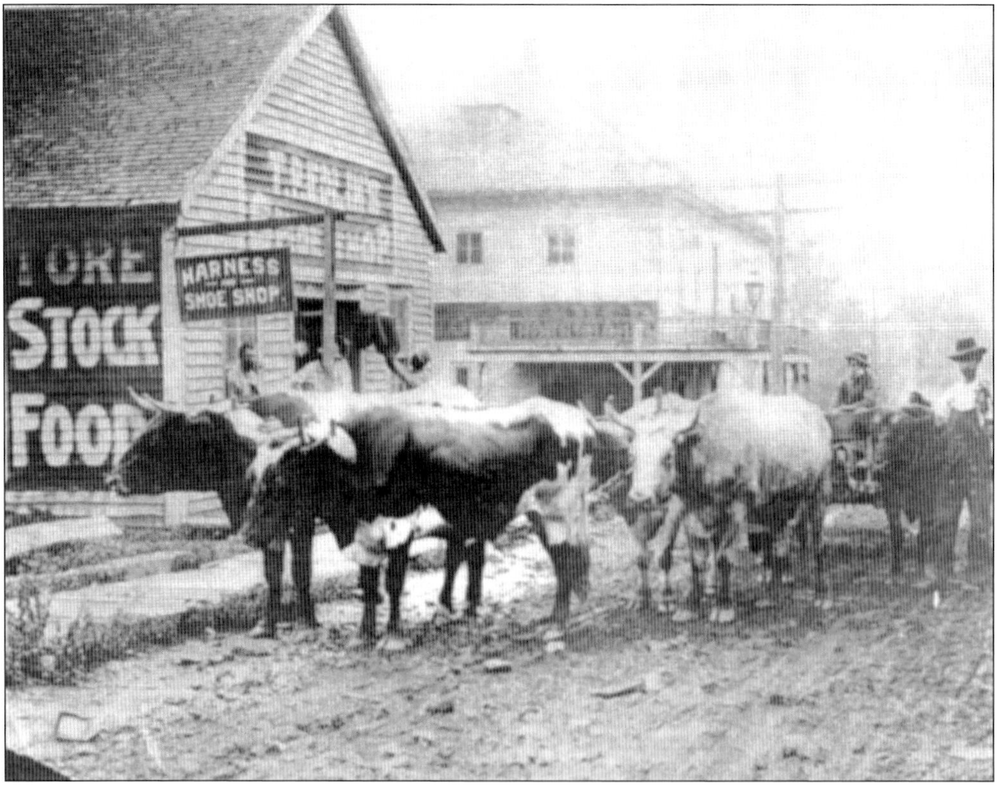

This photograph is looking south on Bettis Street. Bettis Street from Broadway South contained some of the homes of Pocahontas's leading citizens, such as Joe P. Baltz and Ray Sallee. A team of eight oxen can be seen pulling a wagon. The streets are dirt and appear muddy.

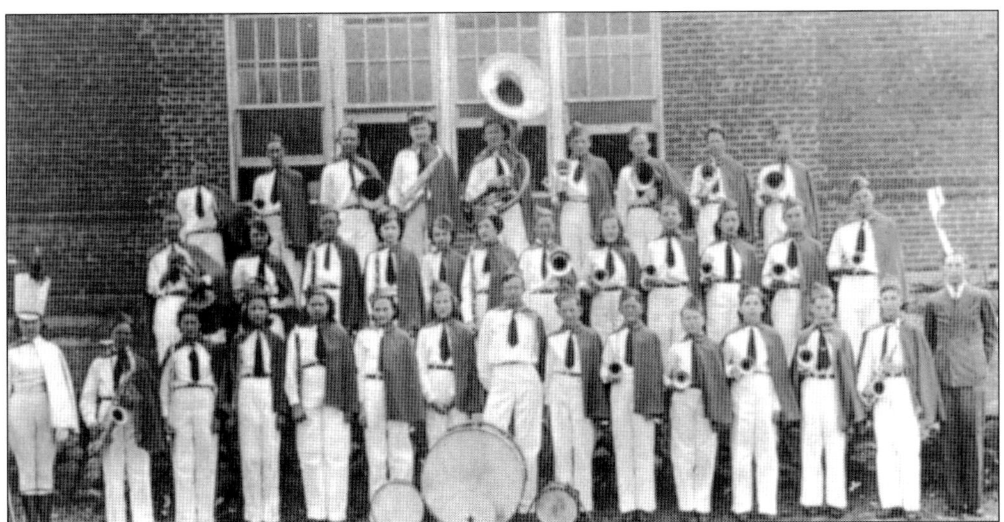

The Randolph County Band poses in their uniforms in 1939. The band was made up of students from Pocahontas and Maynard public schools. They were under the direction of Coulter Cunningham and led by drum major Yvonne Ingram of Maynard. Notable members included Lena Mae Abbott, Helen Carnes, Clem Cox, Joe Martin, Virginia McNabb, and Raymond Sallee.

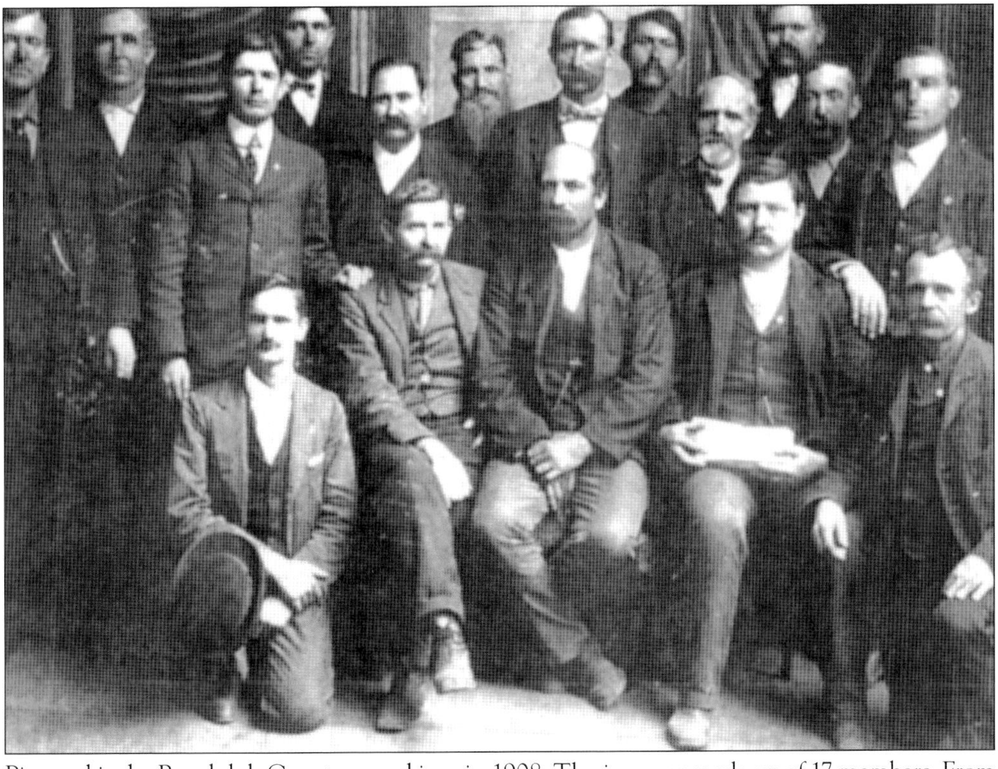

Pictured is the Randolph County grand jury in 1908. The jury was made up of 17 members. From left to right are Larkin Johnson, W.A. Brooks, John L. Fry, Joe DeClerk, D.C. Fowler, Frank Harrison, Tom Wells, Charley Dixon, Andrew McCarroll, T. Jesse Redwine, Joseph Hufstedler, John R. Holt, J.E. Hufstedler, W.C. Brown, John R. Ray, W.A. Taylor, and Green Davis.

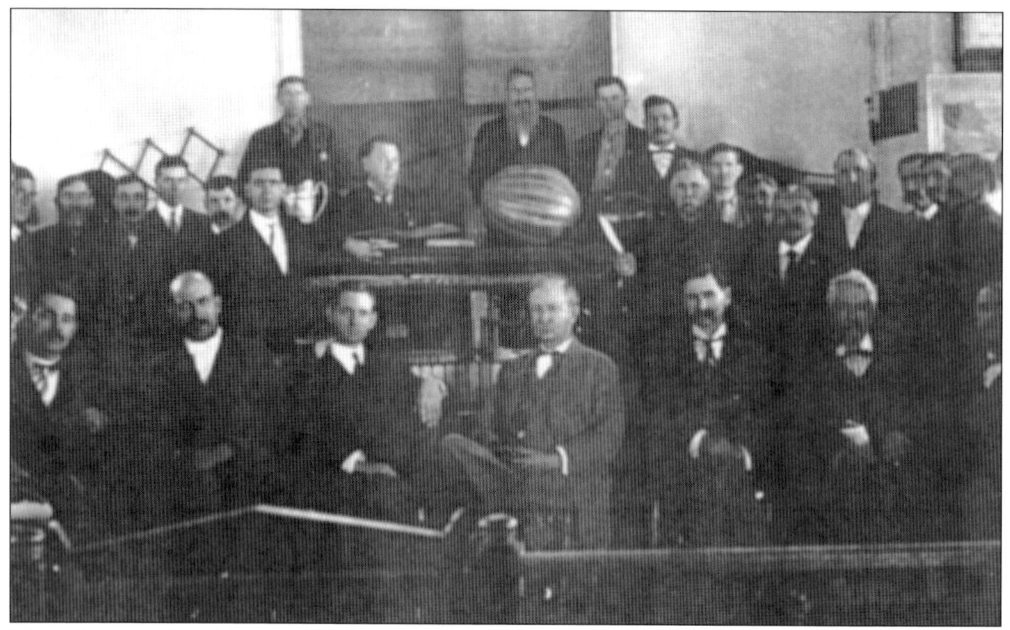

This photograph of the Randolph County grand jury in 1911 was taken in the old courthouse in the upstairs courtroom. Circuit Judge J.W. Meets is seated. The others include John Lomax, Jon L. Fry, Tom Campbell, George Black, H.M. Bishop, A.J. Witt, and prosecuting attorney C.E. Elmore. It is unknown why there was a giant pumpkin on the judge's bench.

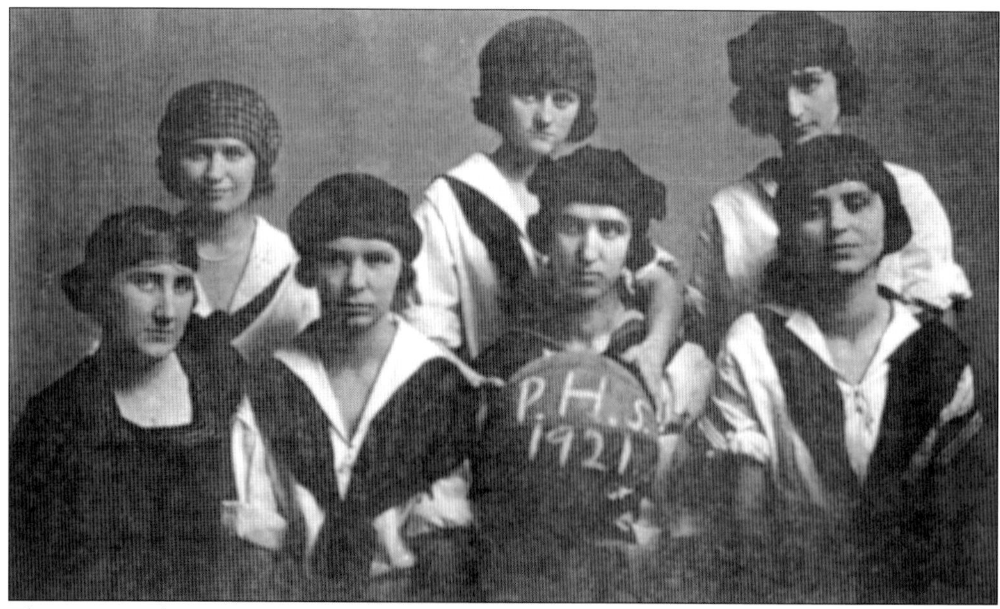

The 1921 Pocahontas High School girls basketball team poses for a team photograph. The team won 9 of 12 games during the season. Edith Johnson Hughes coached them. From left to right are (first row) Mary Knotts, Anna Baltz, and Senna Lemmons Henley; (second row) Rheta Price Jackson, Pauline Bishop, and Ouida Blankenship Thompson.

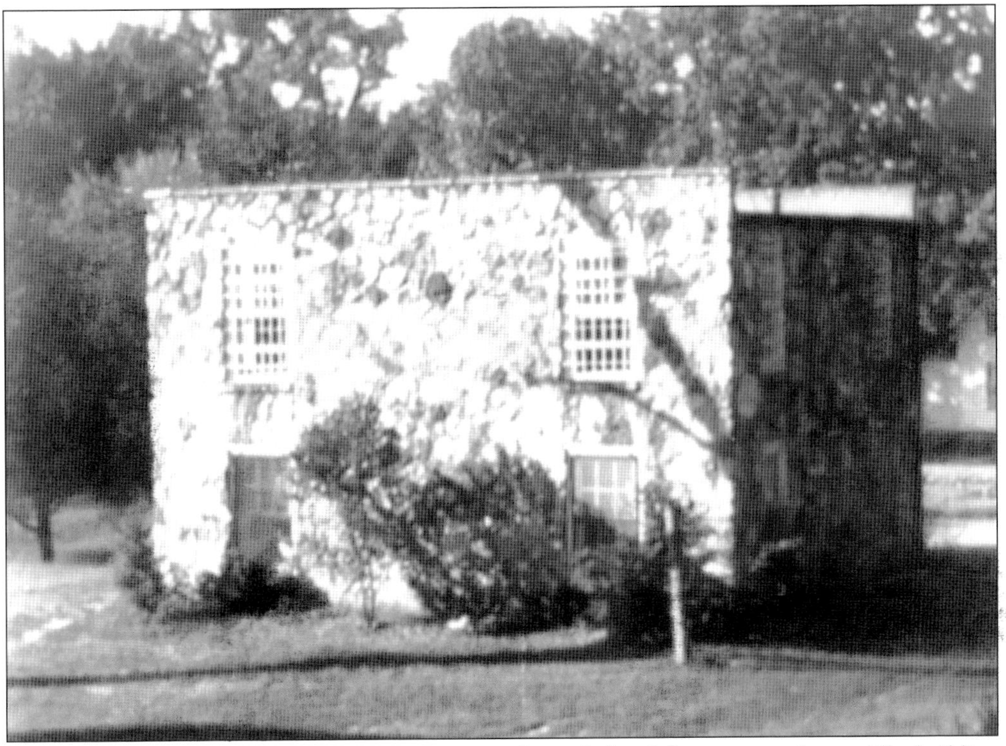

Henry Dust built the rock jail in the 1940s on Marr Street behind the new courthouse. The building housed the county jail for several years. After the jail moved, the building was used for multiple other purposes, including county offices. For many years, it served as the office for the Arkansas State Revenue service, where many people remember getting their car tags and driver's licenses.

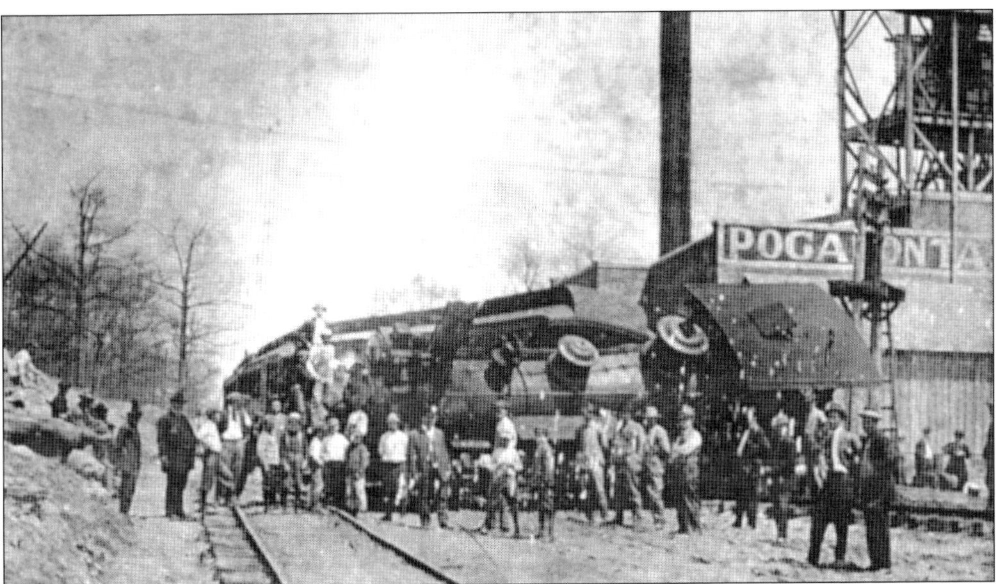

This train derailment happened in April 1915 near the present train depot in Pocahontas. The passenger train derailment did not lead to serious injuries or deaths.

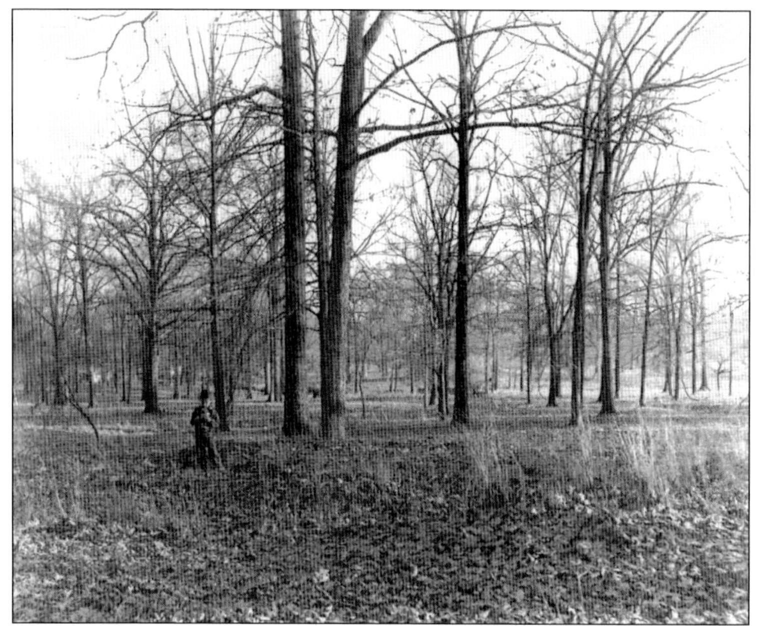

This is the site of the old town of Davidsonville on the Black River in the 1950s. The town was the location of the first post office in Arkansas and the first land office in the state. The town declined in importance and was eventually overtaken by Bettis Bluff, which became Pocahontas. In 1957, Arkansas established a state park here to preserve and protect the site.

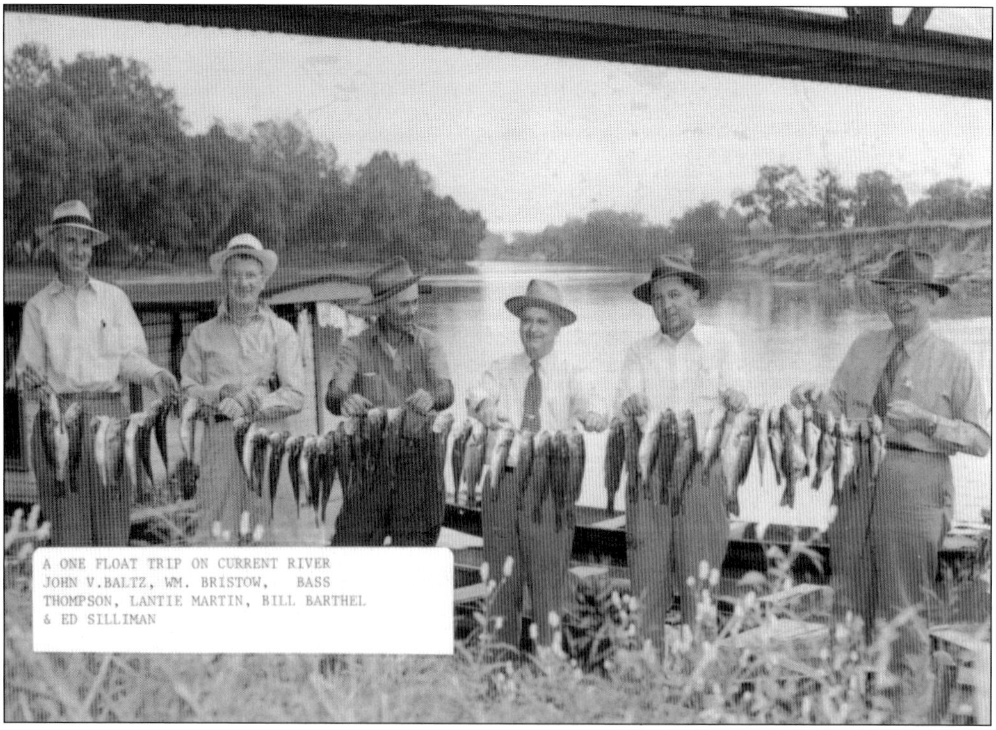

A ONE FLOAT TRIP ON CURRENT RIVER
JOHN V.BALTZ, WM. BRISTOW, BASS
THOMPSON, LANTIE MARTIN, BILL BARTHEL
& ED SILLIMAN

In this undated photograph, some of Pocahontas's leading businessmen can be seen after a successful fishing trip on the Current River. From left to right are John V. Baltz, W.M. Bristow, Bass Thompson, Lantie Martin, Bill Barthel, and Ed Sillman.

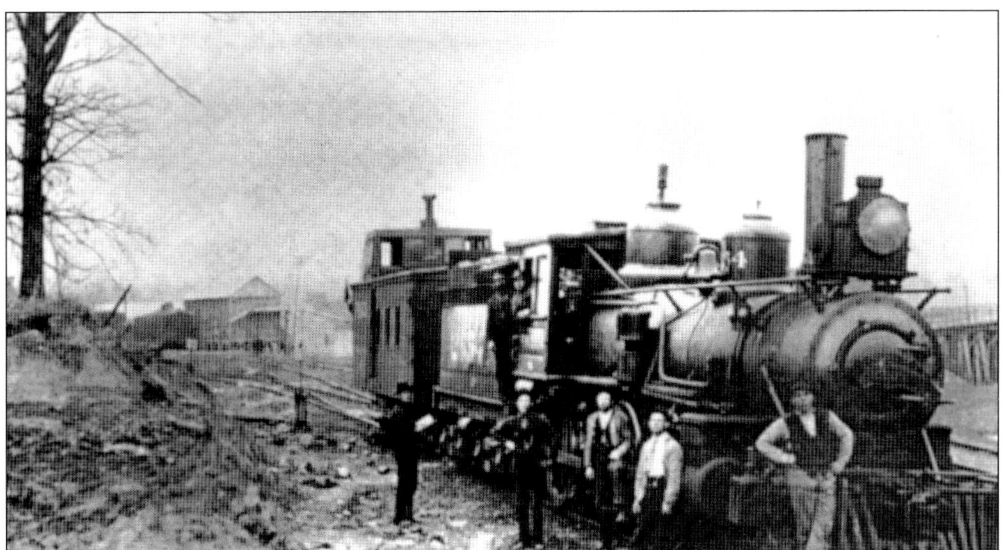

This image features a railroad crew in Pocahontas around 1909. Trains operating from Hoxie to Cape Girardeau passed through Pocahontas.

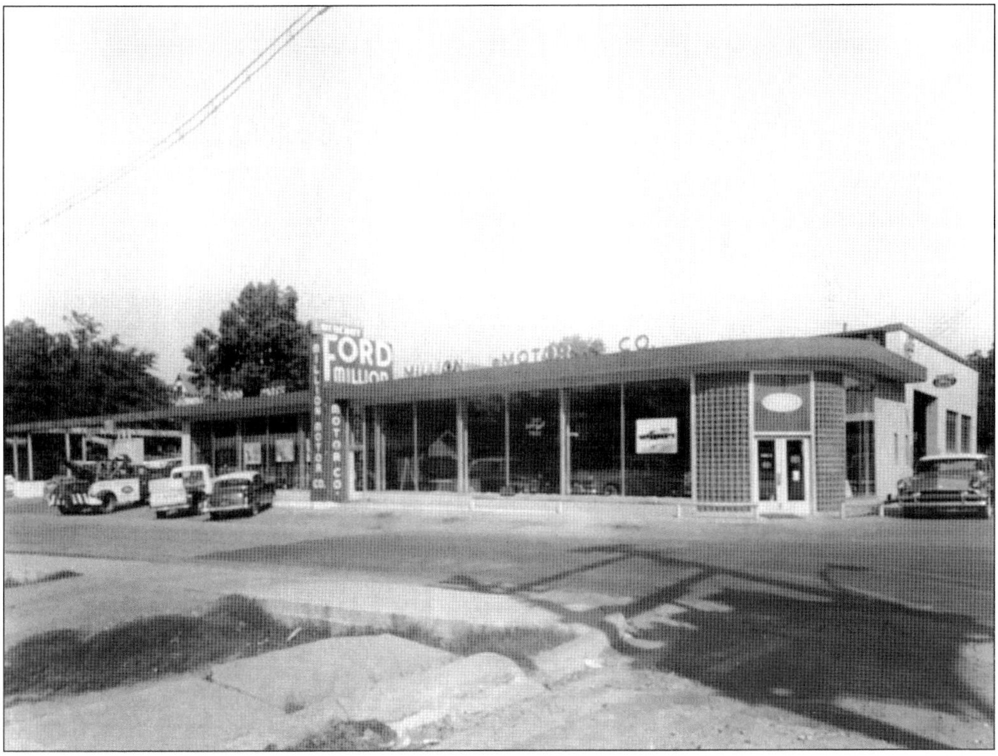

Pocahontas boasted multiple car dealerships, including Chevrolet, Dodge, Oldsmobile, and Ford. Pictured here is Million Motor Company, the Ford dealership. It remained in business in Pocahontas until the late 1990s. This modern building had a large showroom and a parts department. A gas pump in the showroom was used to fill the tanks of newly sold cars. The lot for the dealership was across Broadway Street.

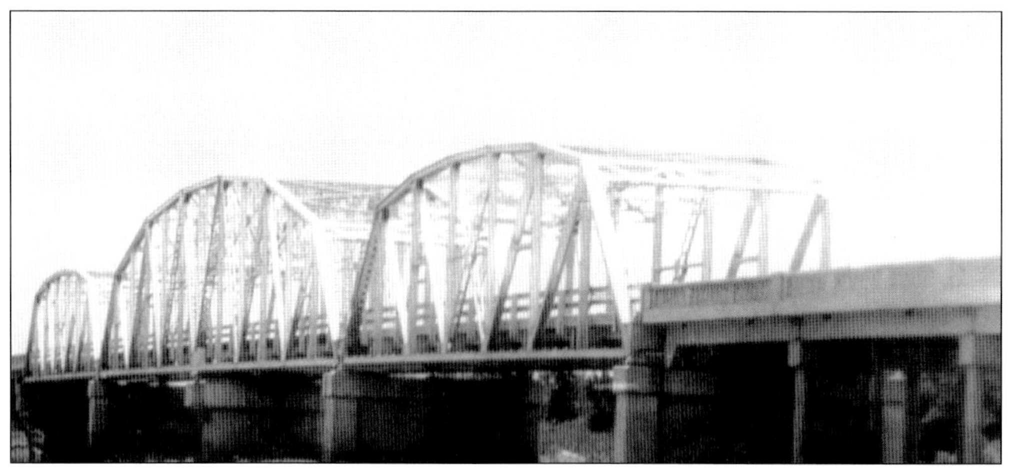

The "new bridge" was built across the Black River at Pocahontas in 1934 by the Pittsburgh–Des Moines Steel Company. The bridge initially turned on a center pedestal to allow river traffic to pass. The bridge carried US Highway 67 across the Black River. It was listed in the National Register of Historic Places but was demolished by the Arkansas Department of Transportation in 2016.

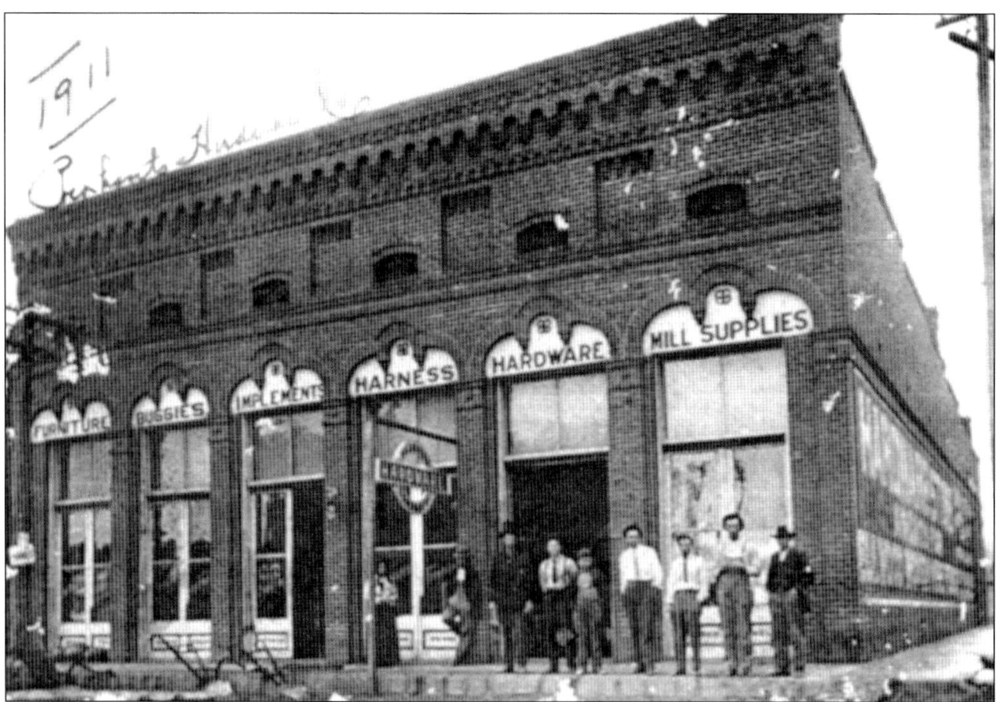

George Promberger Sr. operated Pocahontas Hardware for many years. The hardware store was at the corner of Marr and Everett Streets in the building now occupied by Marr Street Productions. This photograph was taken in 1911.

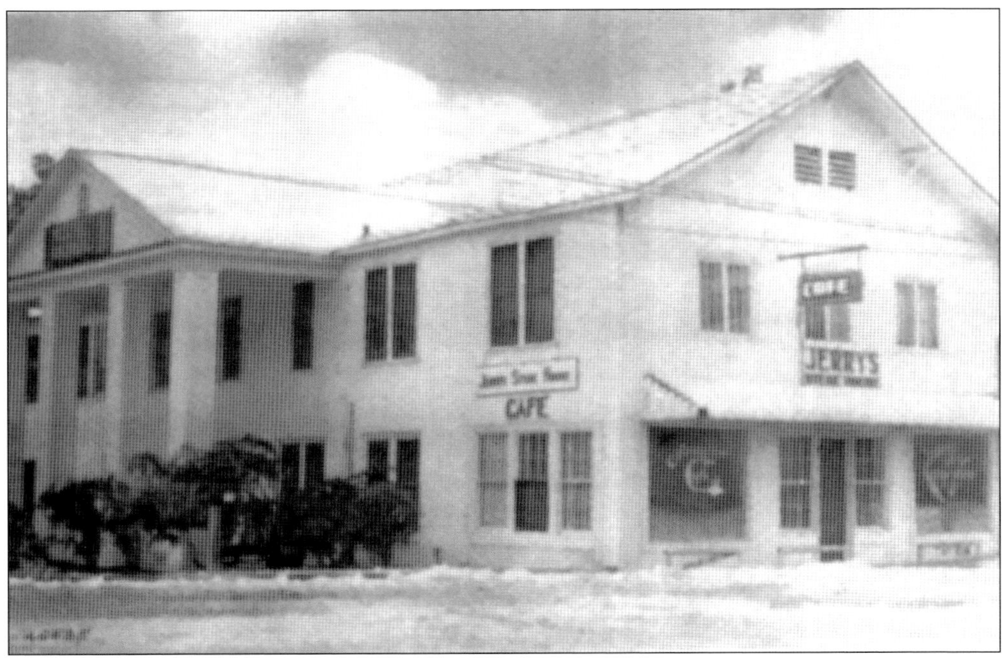

The Colonial House Hotel and Jerry's Steak House were at the Corner of Van Bibber and Broadway Streets, where Pocahontas Federal Savings and Loan later built its new building. The hotel was owned by Joe Decker, who served as county judge and owned several businesses. It faced Van Bibber Street and was just across the street from the new courthouse.

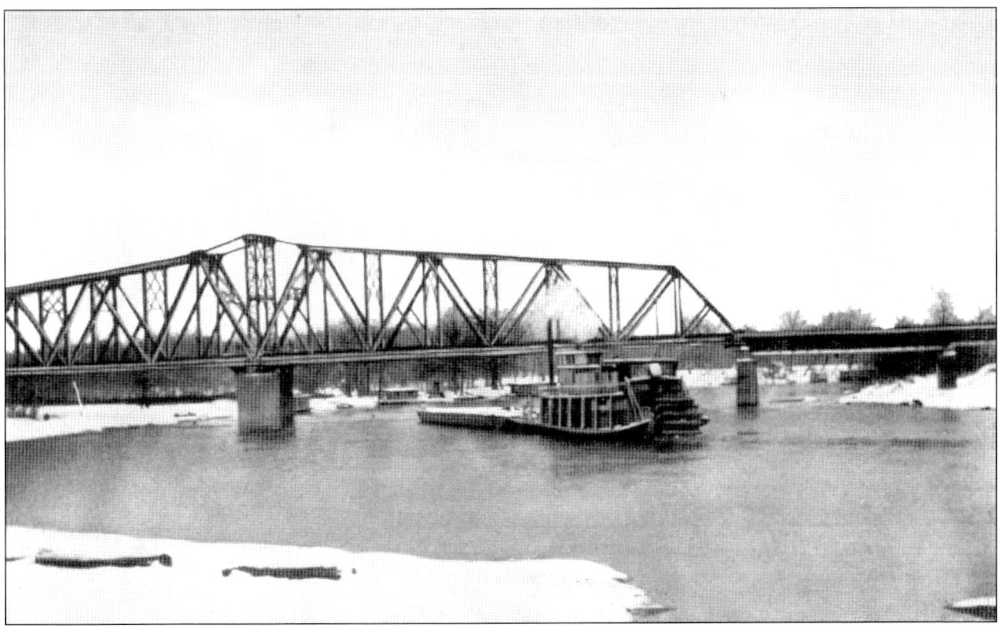
The Frisco railroad bridge was built in 1912. It was designed to turn on a central pillar to allow river traffic to pass and was one of the country's longest spans. Following the railroad abandoning the line, the bridge was demolished in 1986. While the bridge itself was demolished, the piers remain.

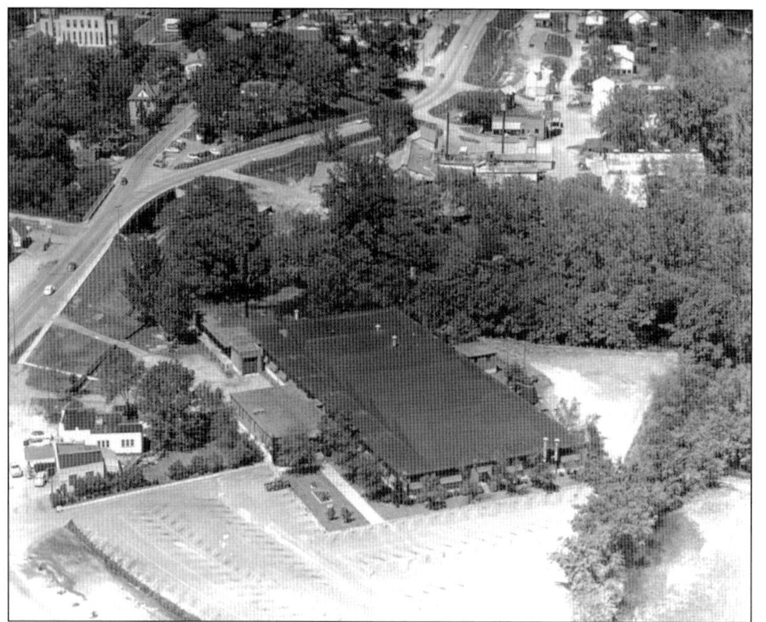
The Brown Shoe Company operated in Pocahontas for many years and employed multiple generations of families. For many years, Brown Shoe was the most prominent industry operating in Pocahontas. The factory opened in 1945 and had doubled in size by 1955. Unfortunately, it closed in the mid-1990s.

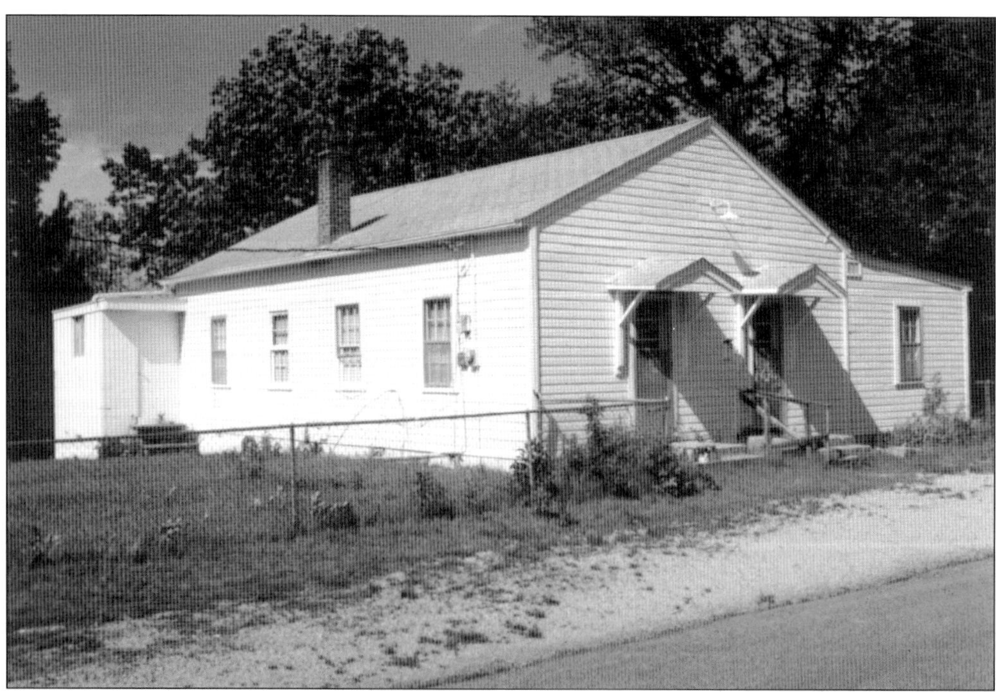
The Eddie Mae Herron Center is on Archer Street in a former African Methodist Episcopal church that also served as the segregated elementary school for the Pocahontas school district. The building was constructed in 1919 and is listed in the National Register of Historic Places. Today, it hosts educational events, houses a small museum, and serves as an African American cultural center.

Sheriff W. Hunter Perrin poses with one of five stills destroyed in one day in Randolph County. Perrin served as sheriff from 1925 to 1926. Randolph County appears to have been a hotbed of bootlegging during Prohibition.

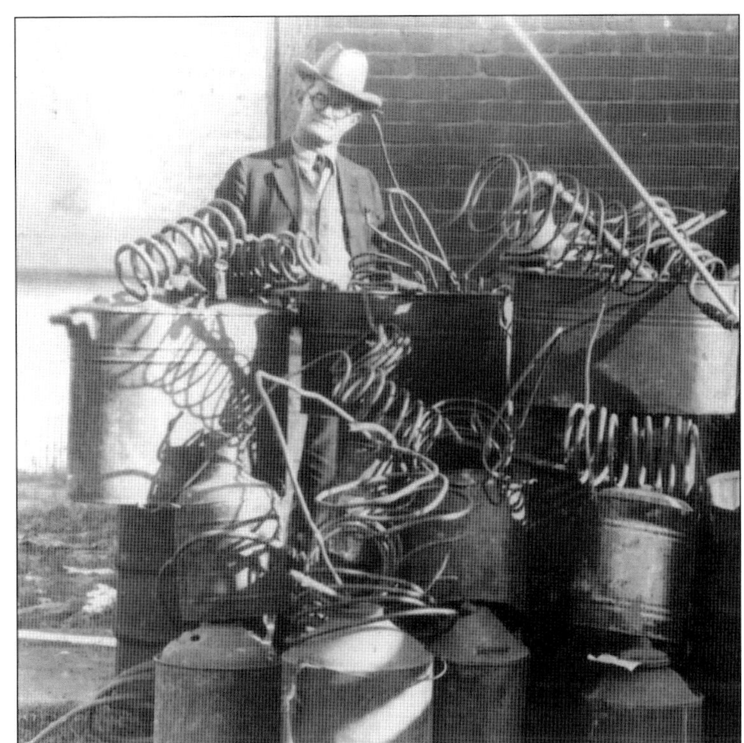

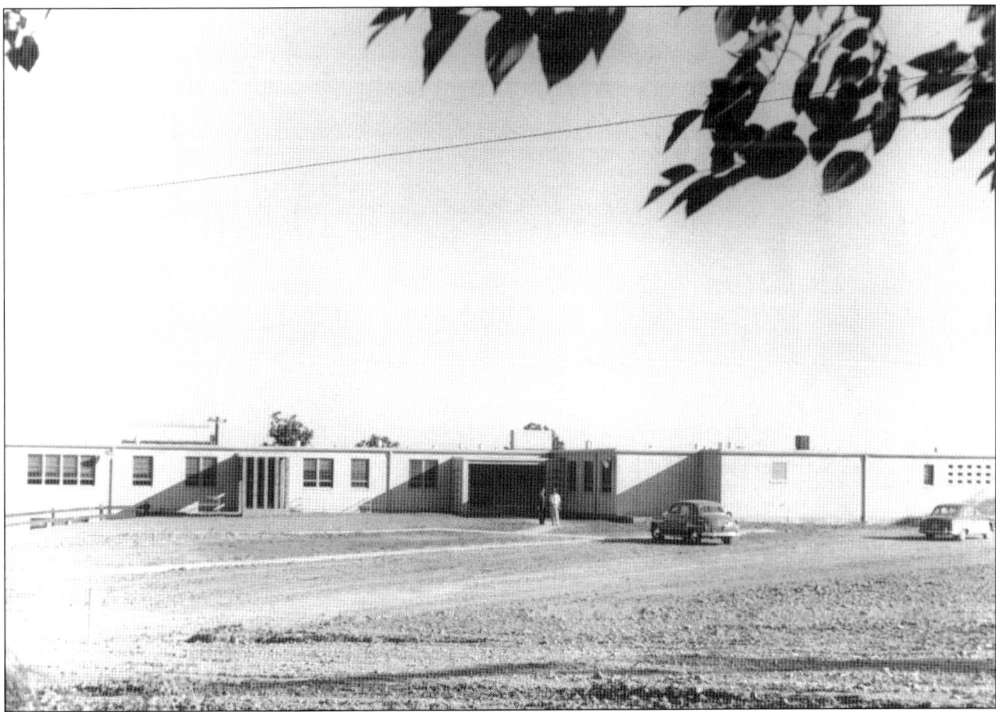

The old hospital is on Hospital Drive in Pocahontas. It was constructed in the 1950s and served the community until the new hospital was built on Country Club Road. Following the opening of the new hospital, the building became the home of the Black River Area Development Agency.

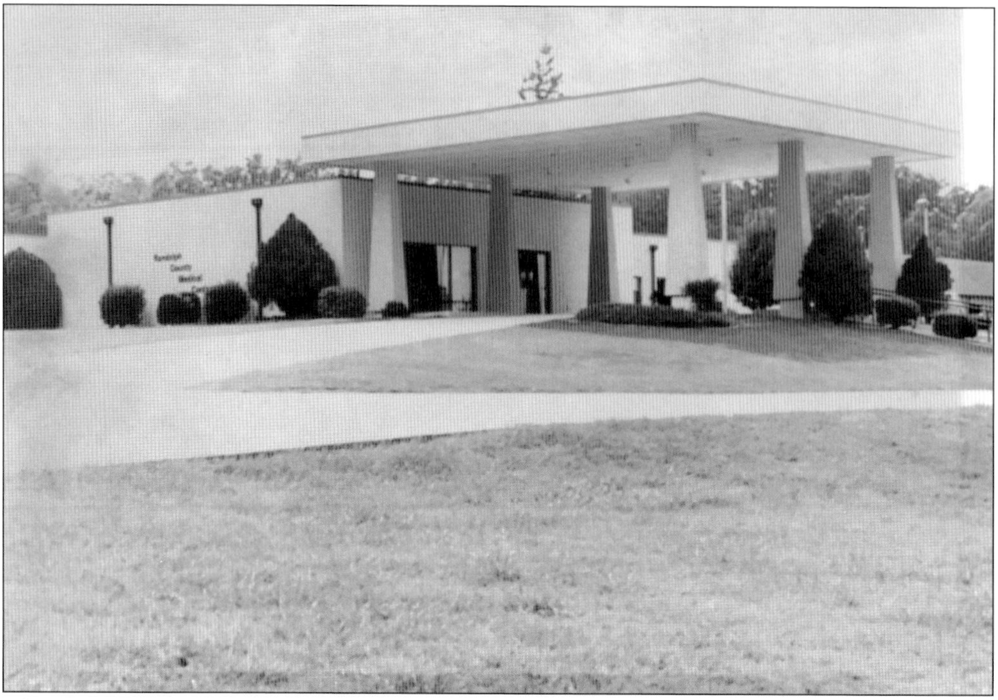

The new hospital is located in what has become a medical district. The facility was constructed in the 1980s. St. Bernard's Medical Center now operates the hospital out of Jonesboro, Arkansas. The new facility was considered state of the art. The image below shows a technician operating a CT scanner at the hospital. After the hospital was built, other medical facilities located nearby, including nursing homes, doctors' offices, and dental offices.

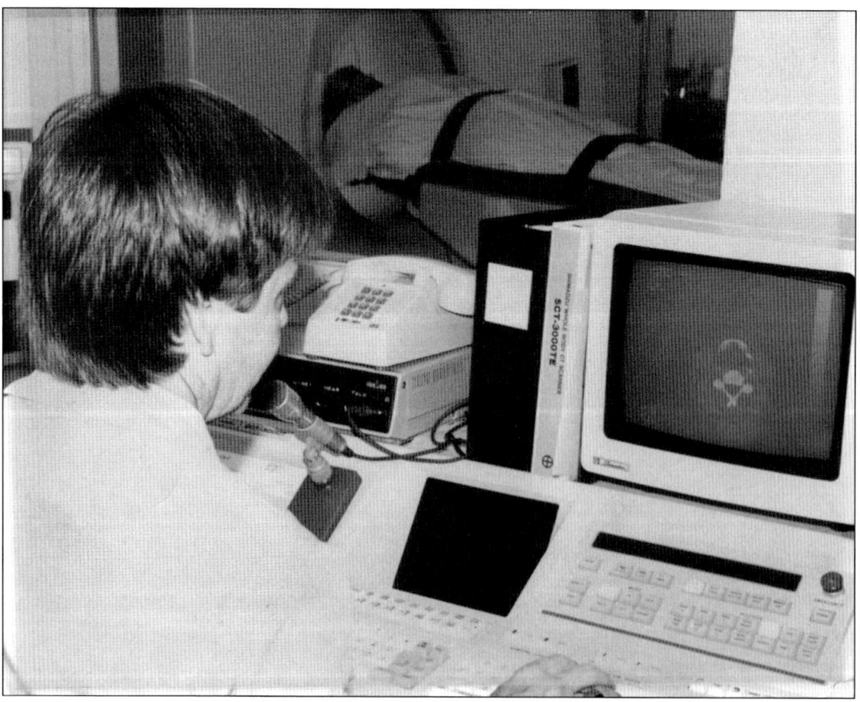

Three

Crossroads, Communities, and Towns

Randolph County boasts remarkable communities that have played significant roles in the history of the region. These communities, towns, and crossroads have unique histories. Some of them are older than Pocahontas, such as Columbia and Davidsonville. Others, such as Pitman, once boasted large business districts that have since faded away, with only remnants left to be seen. Some grew out of specific industries and agriculture, while others emerged as centers of commerce. Many were centered around local schools, often of one or two rooms. Other communities were centered around churches or other social institutions, such as Mt. Pleasant Baptist Church at Pitman, which also served as the Odd Fellows hall for many years. While many of these communities have ceased to be, they remain a vital part of the county's heritage.

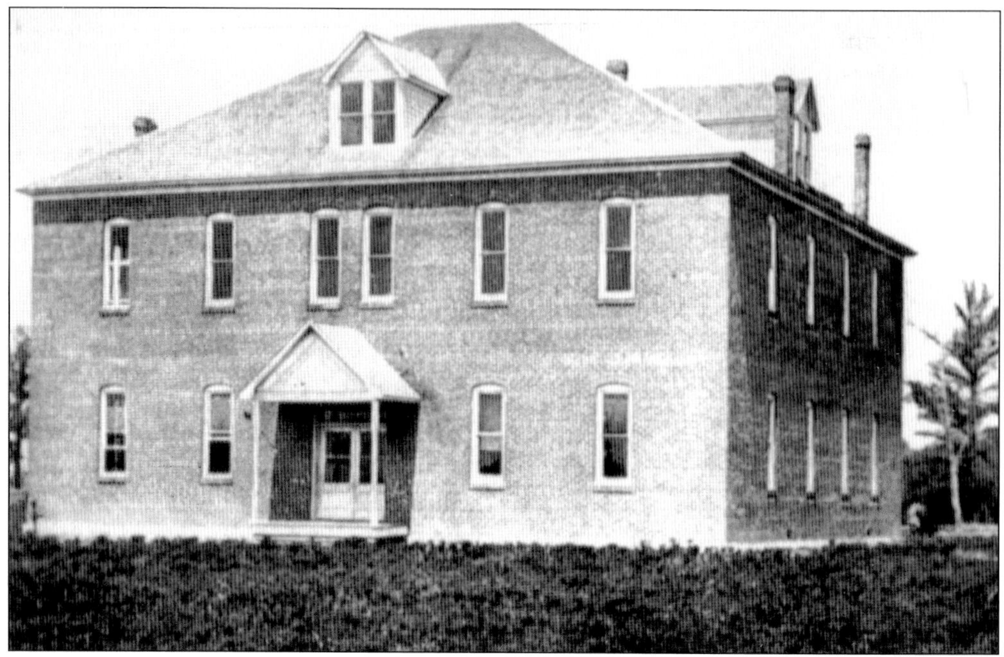

Masons have played a prominent role in the development of Randolph County. This is the Old Reyno Masonic lodge around 1895. Buildings such as this often served more than one purpose. In this case, the first floor served as the Old Reyno School, while the lodge met on the second floor.

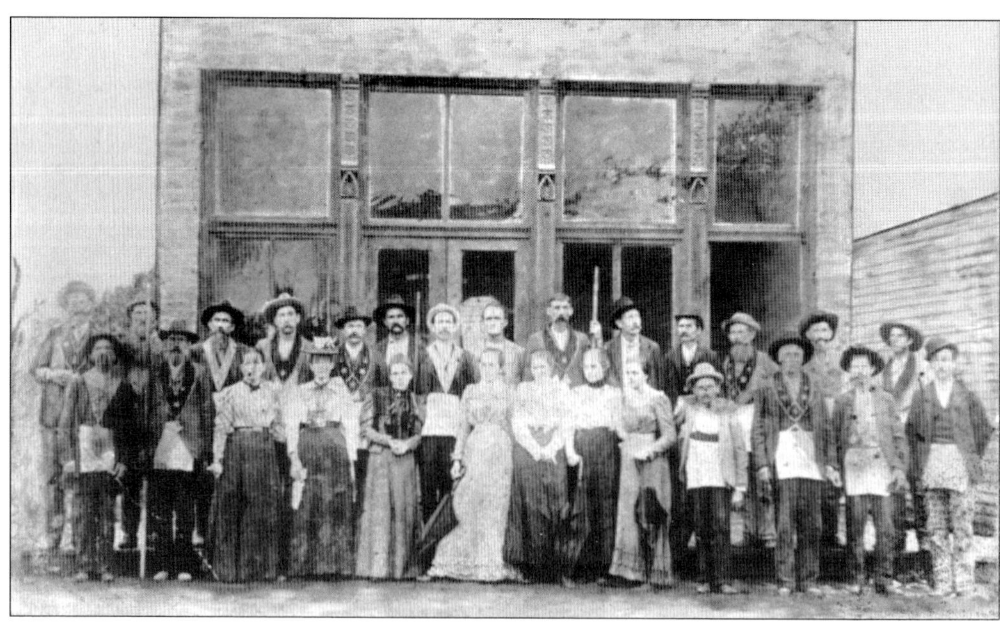

This undated photograph shows a group of men and women gathered outside the Maynard Masonic lodge. The image appears to have been taken around 1900. At the time, Maynard was home to various businesses and had a growing population.

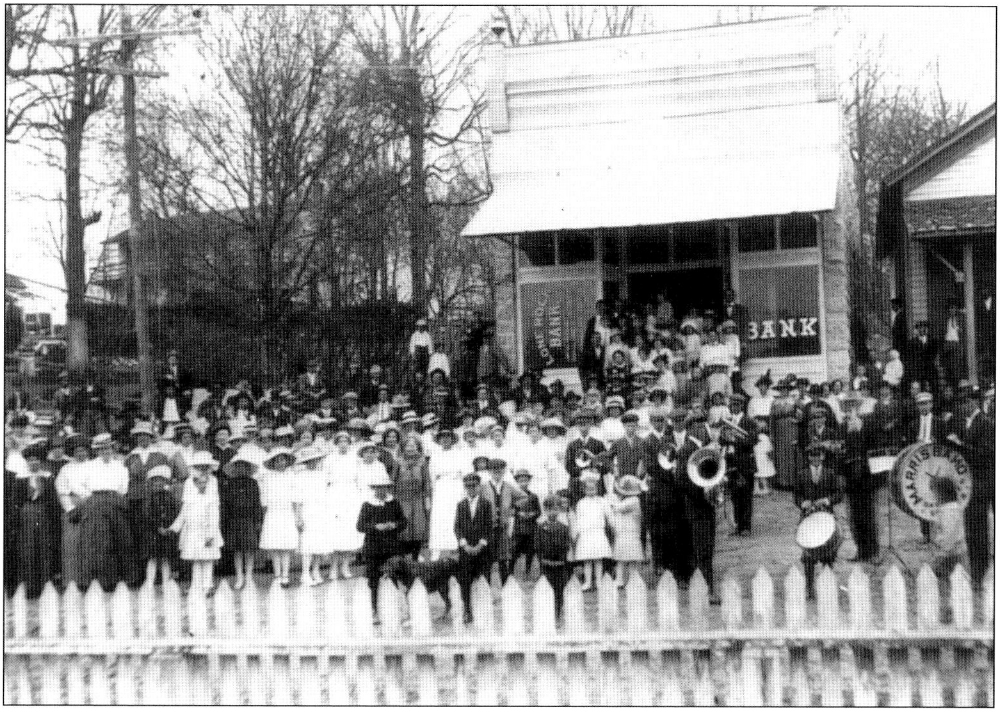

Pictured is the opening of the Lone Rock Bank at Ravenden Springs. The bank was built in 1903 and operated until the Depression in the 1930s. Frank Davis was the bank's first president. Ravenden Springs had a population of 1,500 at one time. The bank's left window has the sign painted sideways. The glass had been ordered pre-painted and came wrong, but was installed anyway.

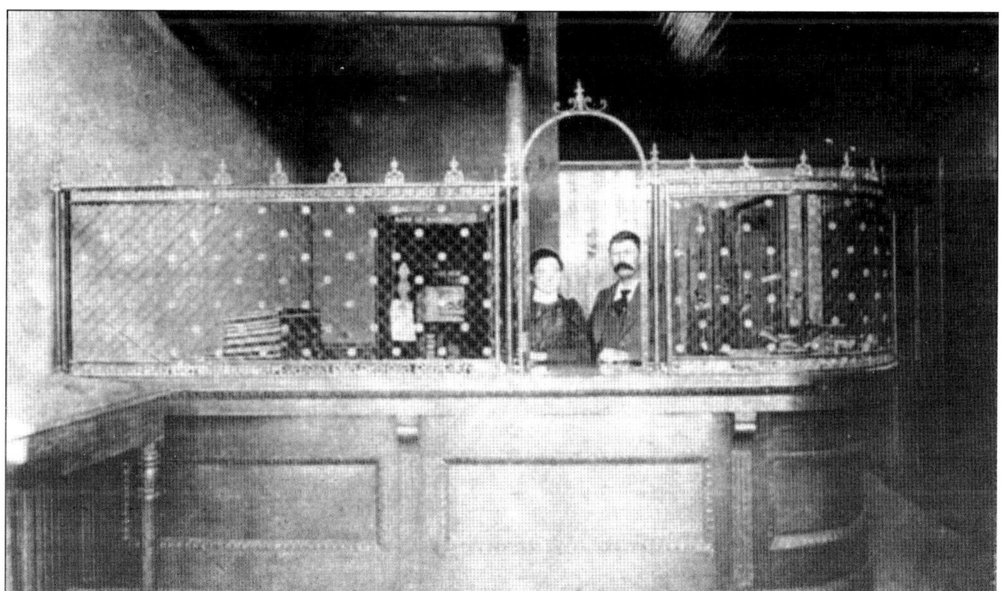

Pictured is the interior of the Bank of Maynard in 1900, when it opened for business. T. Jesse Redwine and Mrs. Abbott are standing in front of the teller window. Redwine served as the first cashier of the bank.

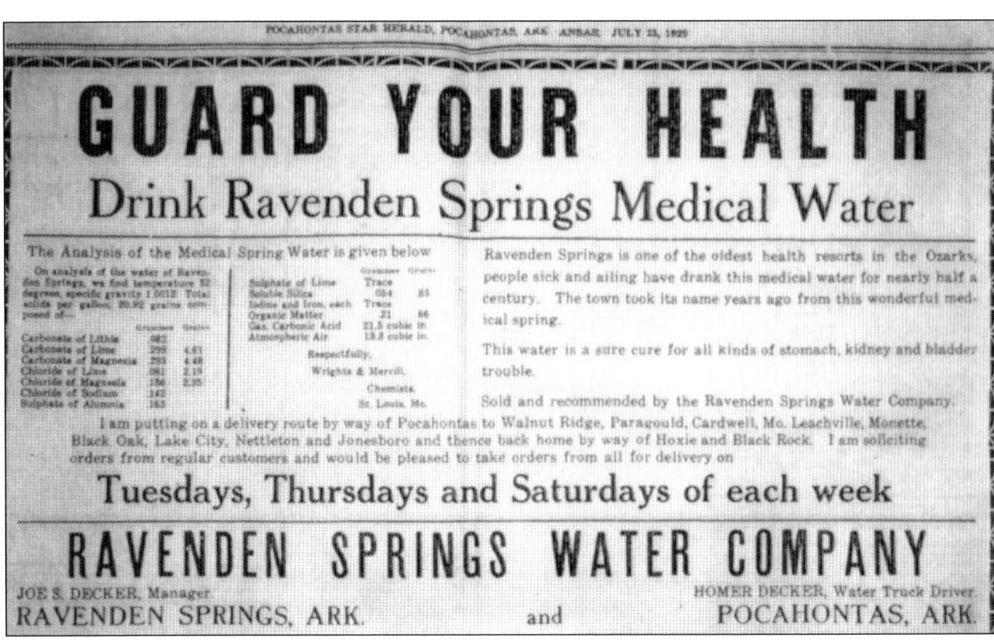

POCAHONTAS STAR HERALD, POCAHONTAS, ARK. JULY 25, 1929

GUARD YOUR HEALTH

Drink Ravenden Springs Medical Water

The Analysis of the Medical Spring Water is given below

On analysis of the water of Ravenden Springs, we find temperature 52 degrees, specific gravity 1.0012. Total solids per gallon, 20.92 grains composed of—

	Grammes	Grains
Carbonate of Lithia	.082	
Carbonate of Lime	.299	4.61
Carbonate of Magnesia	.293	4.48
Chloride of Lime	.061	2.19
Chloride of Magnesia	.156	2.35
Chloride of Sodium	.142	
Sulphate of Alumina	.163	
Sulphate of Lime	Trace	
Soluble Silica	.054	.83
Iodine and Iron, each	Trace	
Organic Matter	.21	.86
Gas, Carbonic Acid	21.5 cubic in.	
Atmospheric Air	13.3 cubic in.	

Respectfully,
Wrights & Merrill,
Chemists,
St. Louis, Mo.

Ravenden Springs is one of the oldest health resorts in the Ozarks, people sick and ailing have drank this medical water for nearly half a century. The town took its name years ago from this wonderful medical spring.

This water is a sure cure for all kinds of stomach, kidney and bladder trouble.

Sold and recommended by the Ravenden Springs Water Company.

I am putting on a delivery route by way of Pocahontas to Walnut Ridge, Paragould, Cardwell, Mo. Leachville, Monette, Black Oak, Lake City, Nettleton and Jonesboro and thence back home by way of Hoxie and Black Rock. I am soliciting orders from regular customers and would be pleased to take orders from all for delivery on

Tuesdays, Thursdays and Saturdays of each week

RAVENDEN SPRINGS WATER COMPANY

JOE S. DECKER, Manager
RAVENDEN SPRINGS, ARK.
and
HOMER DECKER, Water Truck Driver
POCAHONTAS, ARK.

This advertisement for the Ravenden Springs Water Company appeared in the *Pocahontas Star Herald* on July 25, 1929. According to the ad, Ravenden Springs was one of the oldest health resorts in the Ozarks. The waters were supposed to cure stomach, kidney, and bladder ailments.

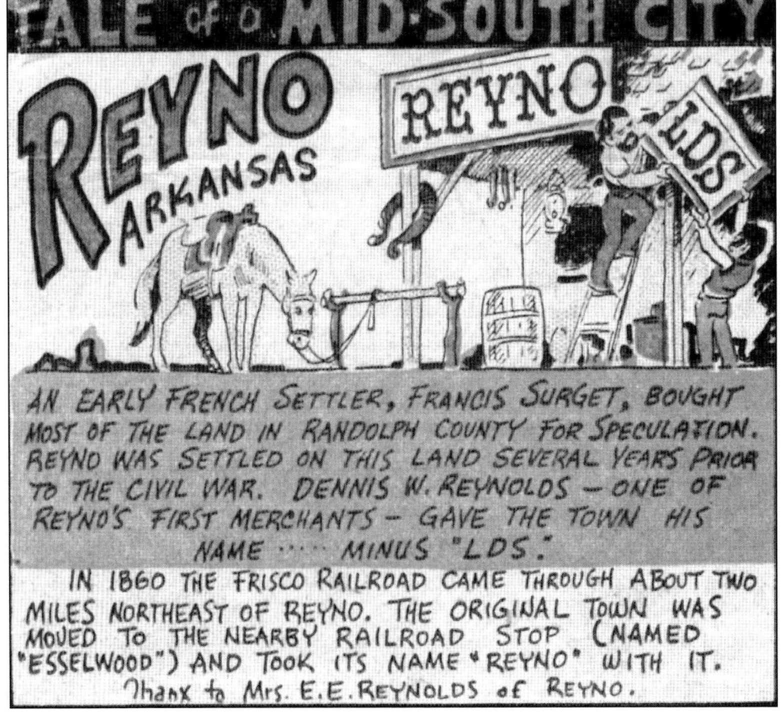

Reyno was officially platted and incorporated in 1886. The area boasted a ferry crossing the Current River until the 1970s, when a bridge was constructed. The area was home to several businesses and enterprises.

Vester's Store in Minarka, pictured around 1911, sold groceries, shoes, tobacco, and other goods to the local community. It was three miles north of Supply on the Missouri state line. Lemuel Vester and his son owned the store.

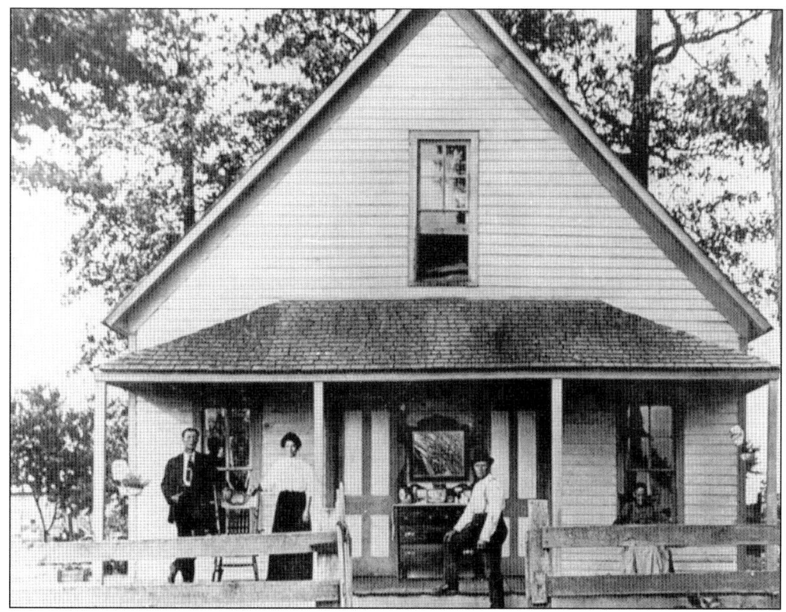

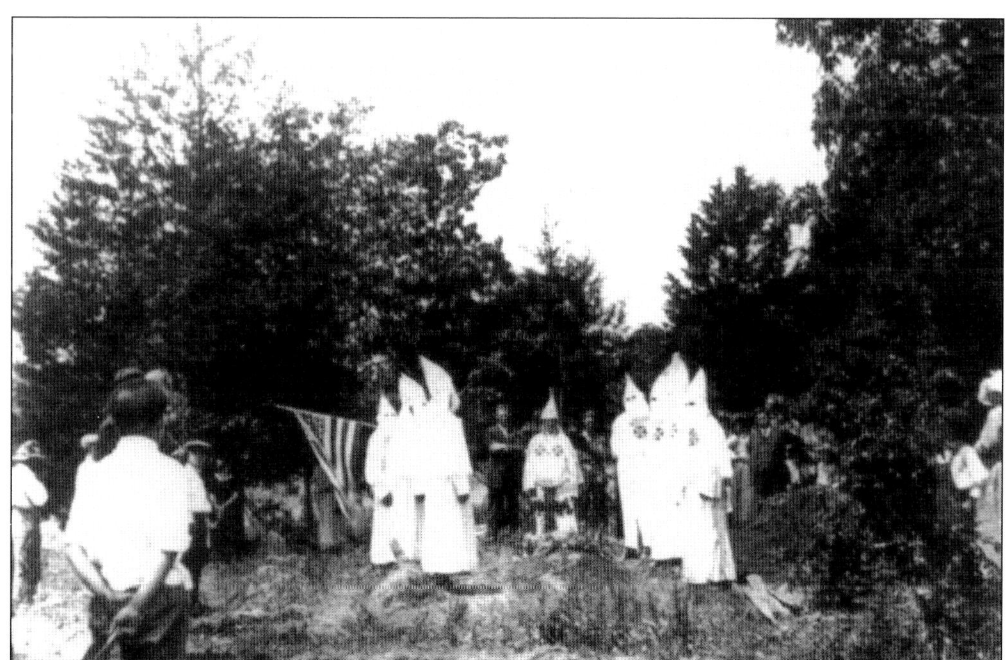

Pictured is a Ku Klux Klan funeral in Randolph County in 1923. The organization was active in the county during the 1920s, based on newspaper reports from the time. The KKK controlled much of the state's politics before its decline in the 1920s due to a number of scandals and internal issues. During this time, the women's auxiliary was based in Little Rock.

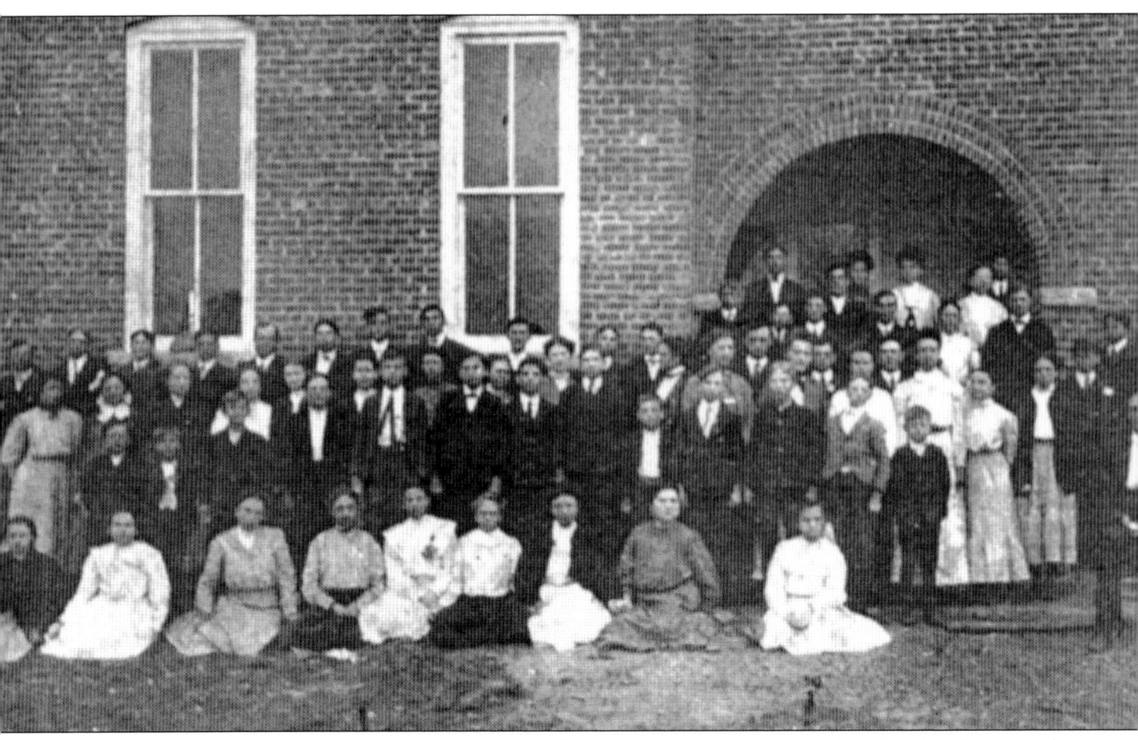

The Aurora Society is pictured at the Ouachita Academy in Maynard in 1904. The Ouachita Academy, sometimes called the Abbot Academy, was a private Baptist academy that served the region before a high school was reliably available. It was a boarding school with dormitories for women and young men in Maynard.

A group of women from Ravenden Springs pose around 1910. Pictured are Dona Holder, Permelia Poteet, Mrs. Hogan, Susan Barker, Mrs. Colbert, Lovella Garland, Mrs. Finney, Emily Lomax, Hannah Welch, and Eliza Edwards.

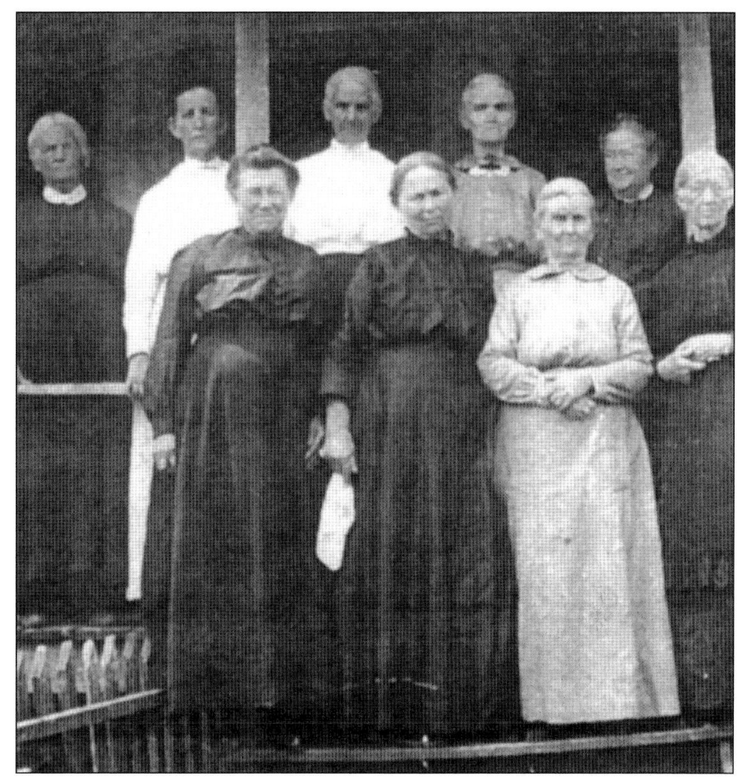

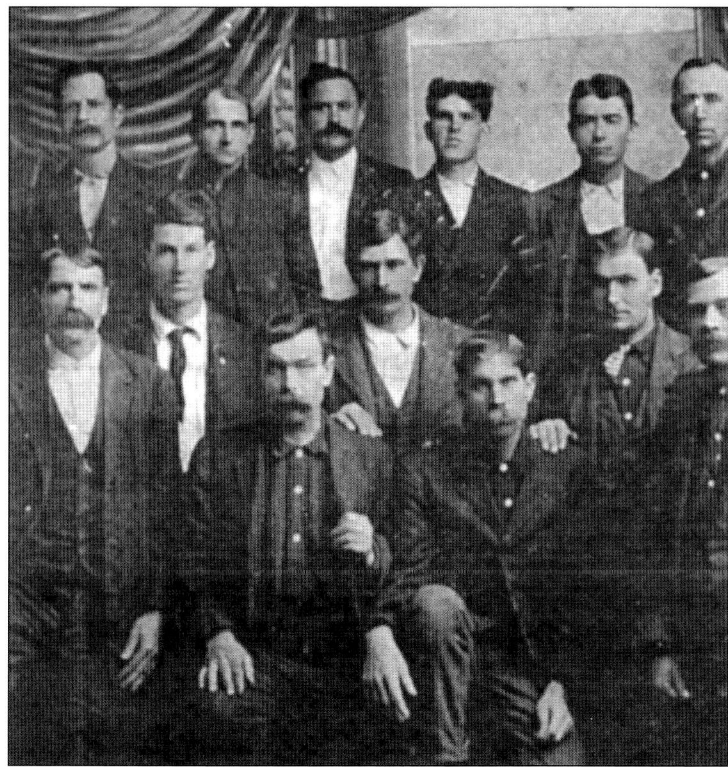

These men served as the petit jury for Supply in 1911. While today's Supply consists of a country store, at the time of this photograph, the community boasted multiple stores, a cotton gin, and other businesses.

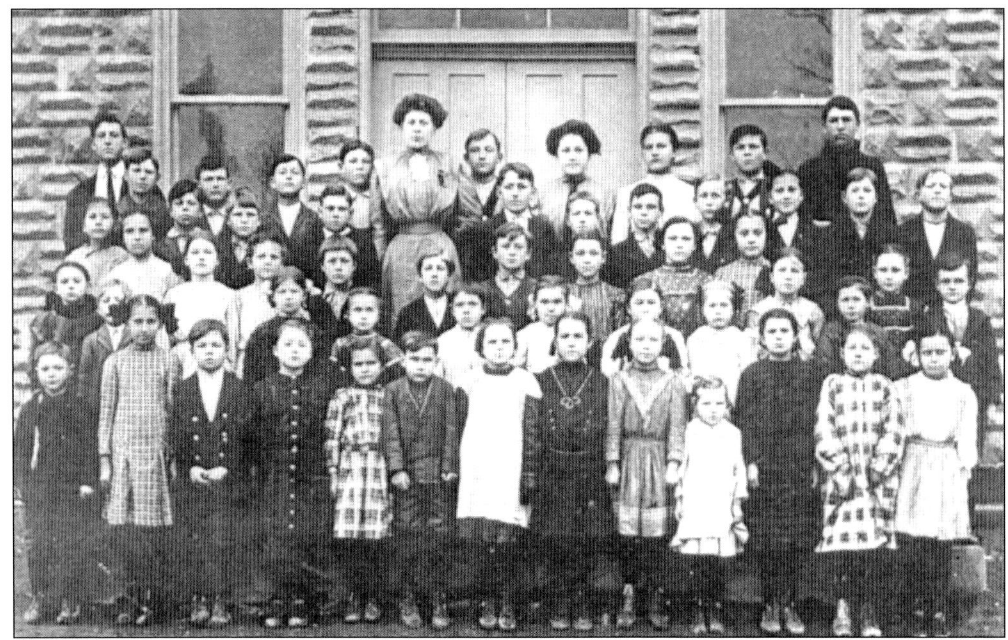

Pictured at Renyo School in 1909 are, from left to right, (first row) Ralph Brewer, Nellie Adams, Harry West, Mable Rice, Ruth Reed, Max Seymour, Gladys Cazey, Myrtle Jones, Clara Brewer, Irene Lamb, ? Wells, Priscilla Rhodes, and unidentified; (second row) unidentified, Lois Adams, Lorren Robinson, ? West, Manila Bellah, and Christine Lamb; (third row) Willie Robinson, Roy Glasco, Edna Totty, Pearl Hannaford, Loren Sparkman, Jay Sparkman, Dewey Bellah, Mayme Chorice, Iva Glasco, Eula Adams, Besse Rudd, Melzina Brown, Alma Glasco, and Harold Abbot; (fourth row) Viza Fry, Maud Totty, Victory Maynard, George Reed, Gilbert Hannaford, Ray Abbott, Horton Navy, unidentified, Harry Sparkman, Lexie Underwood, Bill Nance, and George Wells; (fifth row) Harry Blount, Loyd Butler, Vona Underwood, Nota Abbot, Alva Jones, teacher Myrtle Jackson, Ben Hannaford, Eli Abbot, John Hannaford, Clifton Wells, and unidentified.

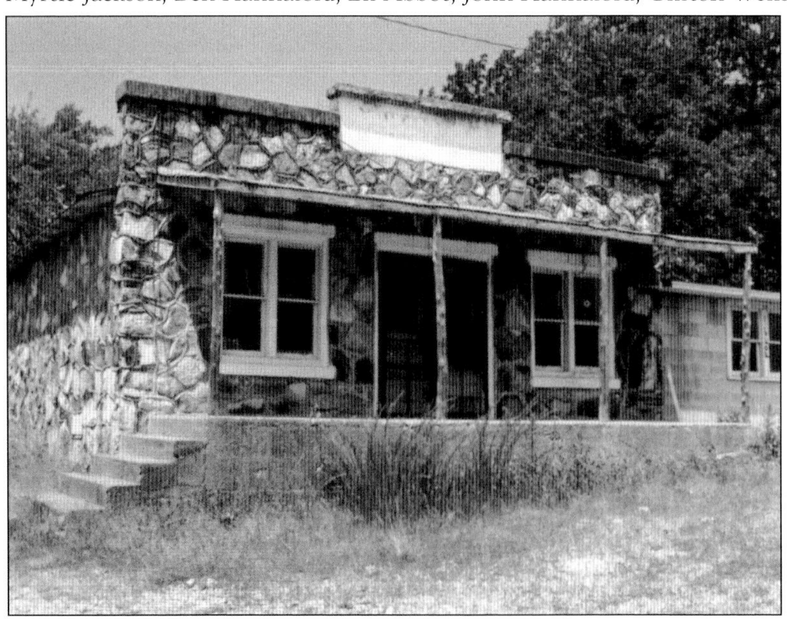

The small town of Middlebrook is north of Maynard on Highway 115. This is the Middlebrook store. The town also had a few churches, including a Methodist church.

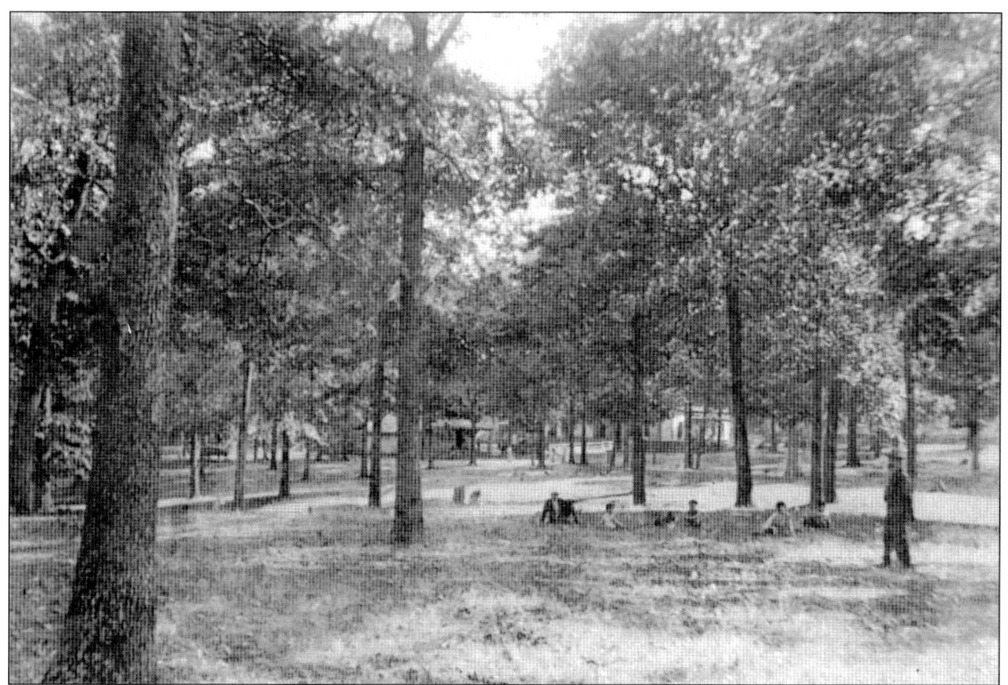

The Shemwell/Rham General Store was south of Mt. Pleasant Baptist Church at Pitman. It operated until 1928, when it closed its doors after a new store opened across the road from the church. The image above shows a park-like lawn in front of the store and the Shemwell home, with people walking and visiting. The image below shows the store today. The Randolph County Heritage Museum has part of the store on display.

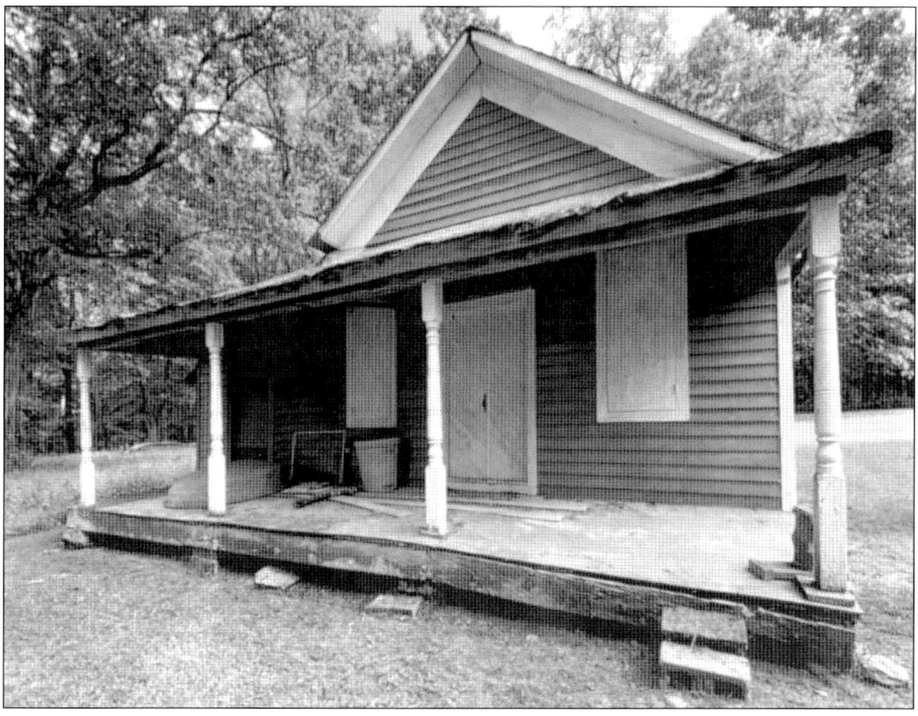

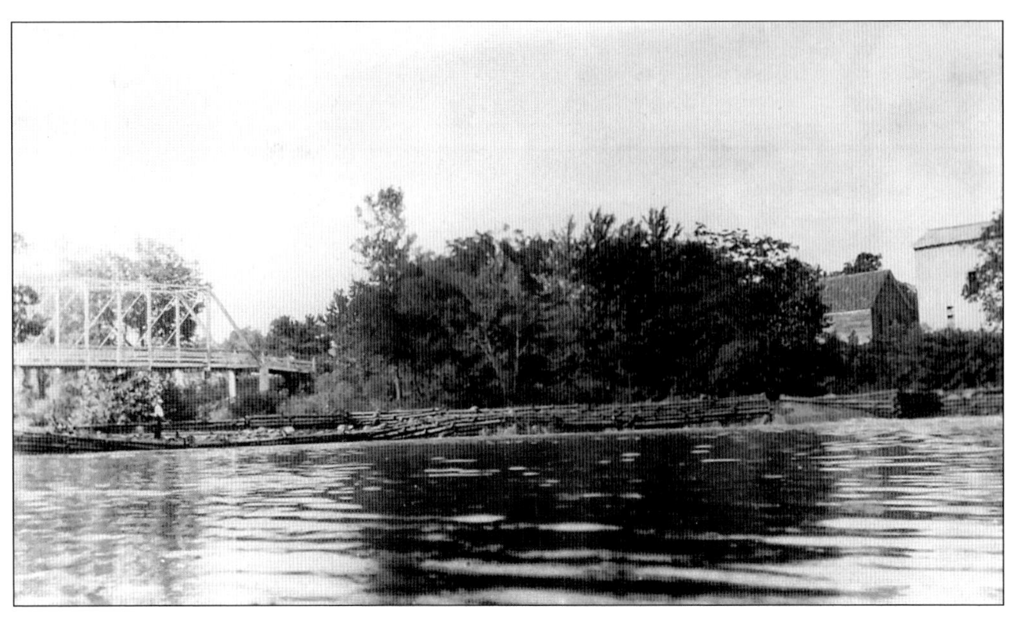

The town of Birdell had a post office near the Eleven Point River in western Randolph County. A bridge was built across the river in 1911. The town boasted a water-powered mill that operated until roughly 1880. The area also had a Church of Christ congregation and a school.

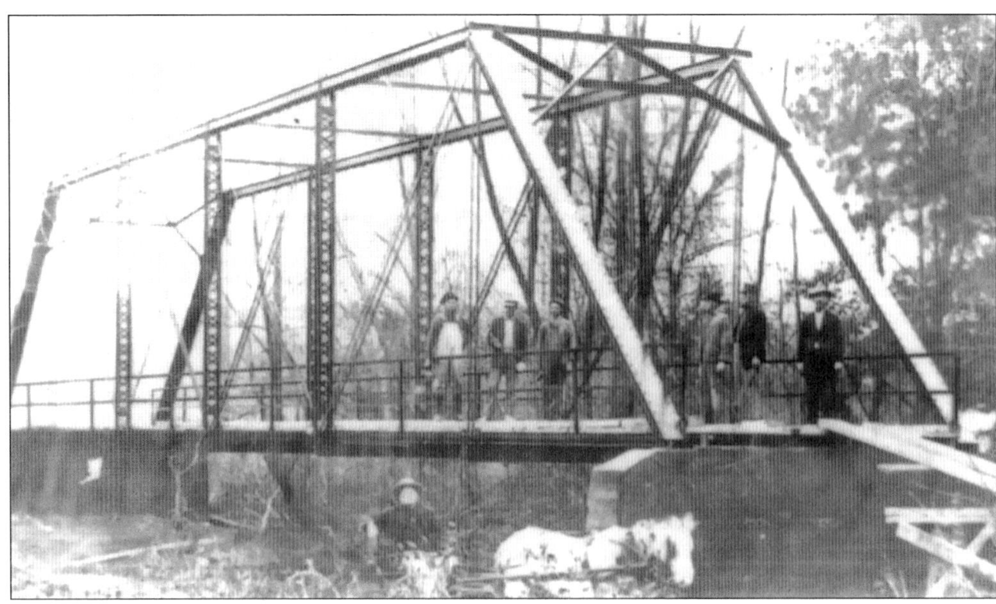

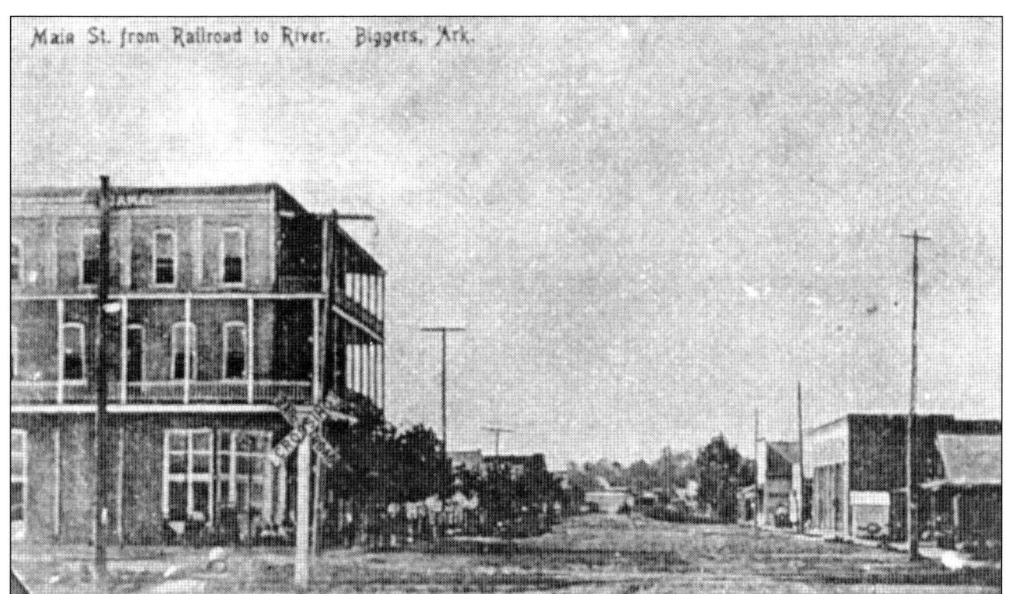

The town of Biggers grew around the Southern Missouri & Arkansas Railroad, which extended from Hoxie in Lawerence County to Poplar Bluff. B.F. Bigger and his wife constructed a large hotel in Biggers known for its hospitality and facilities. The hotel boasted 24 rooms and opened in 1906.

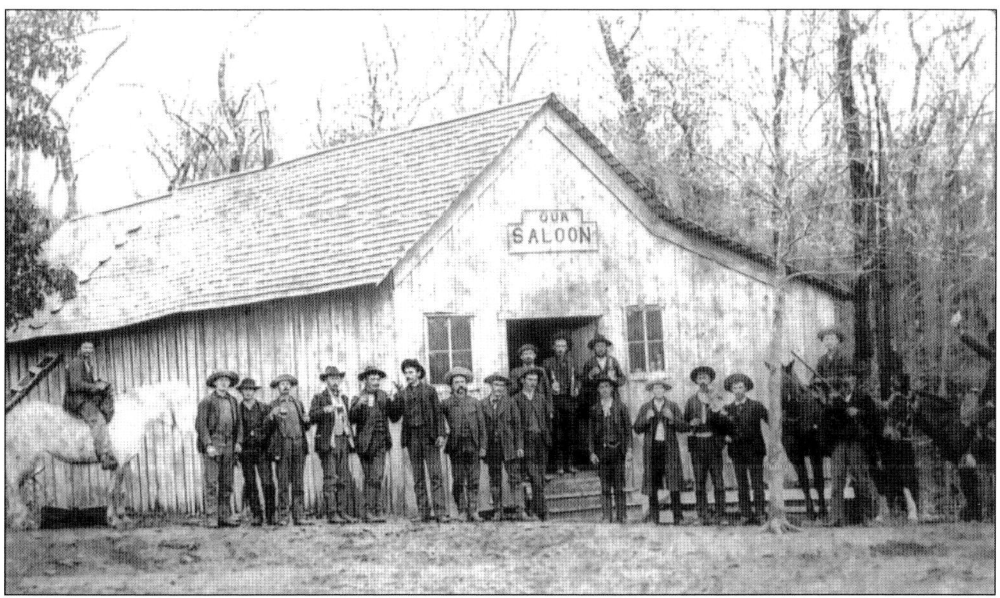

B.F. Biggers opened a distillery at Biggers around the turn of the 20th century. This undated photograph shows a group of men outside a rustic establishment in Biggers named Our Saloon.

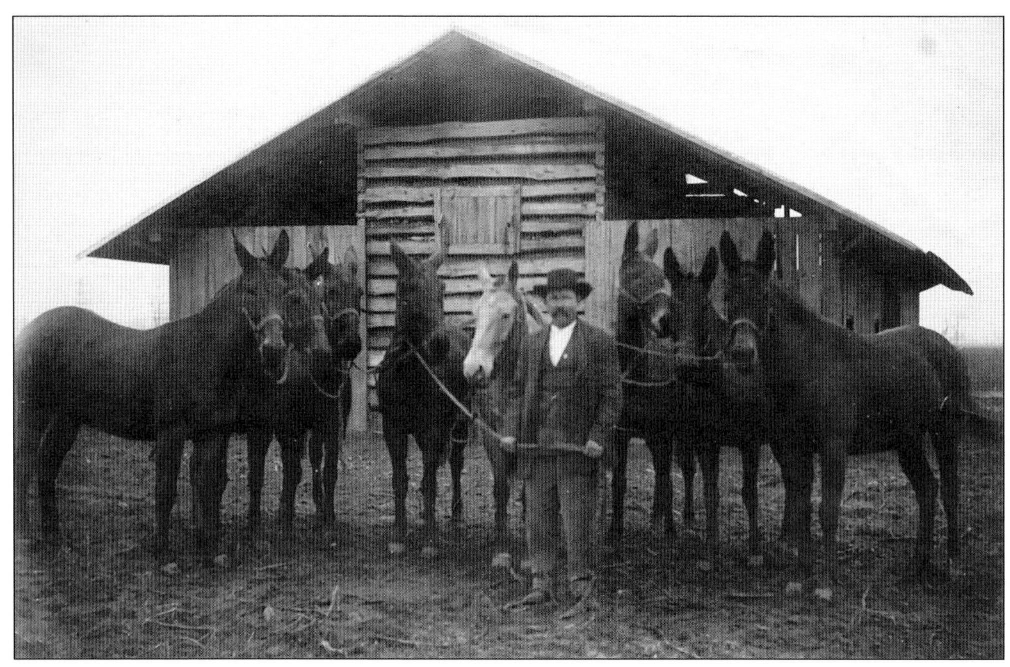

A man poses with a team of mules near Biggers in the early 20th century. Mules were vital in the work of clearing the region's forests.

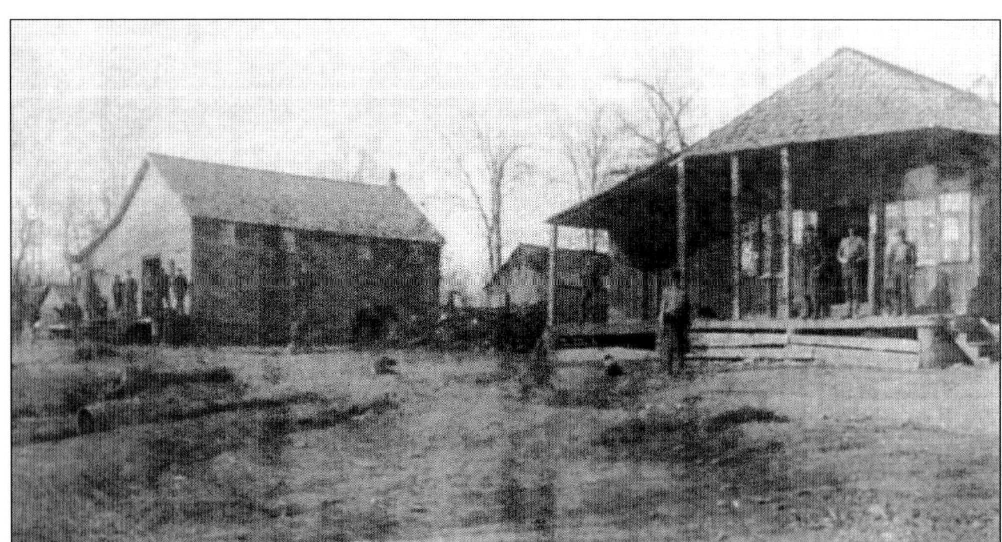

Dalton, Arkansas, is along the west bank of the Eleven Point River in northwest Randolph County. The town once had a general store, feed store, and other businesses. The Rice-Upshaw house is located nearby.

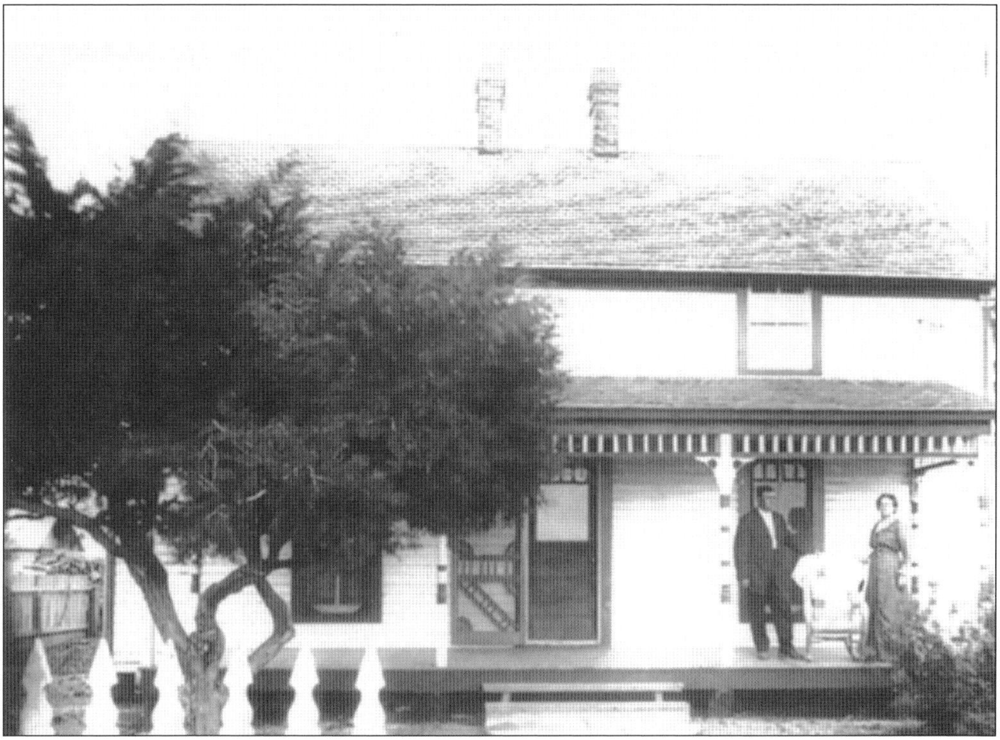

A descendant of the Rice family is pictured on the front porch of a home in the Dalton area.

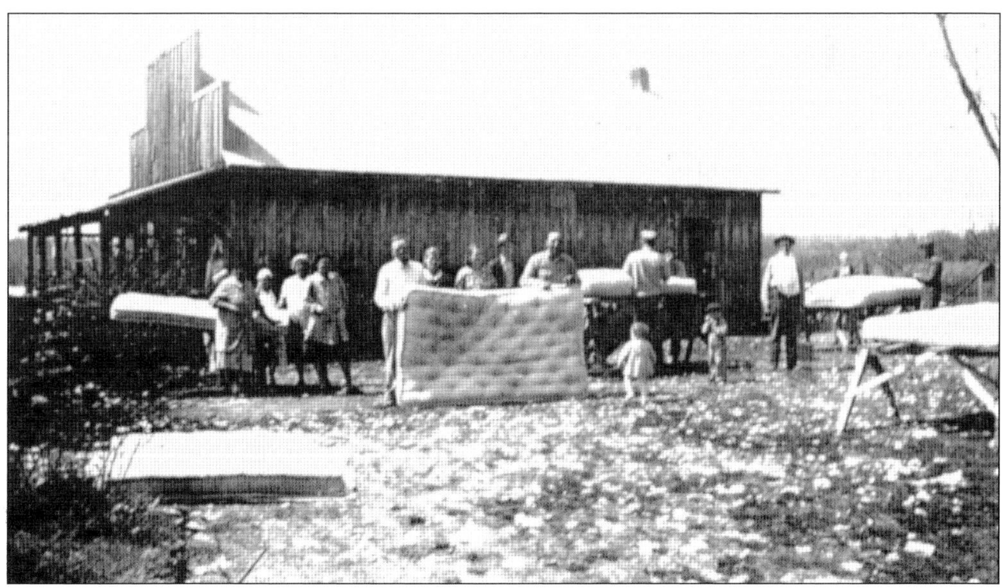

Here, people are making mattresses. They appear to be filled with feathers or possibly cotton. Mattresses were aired out in the sun often, and the filling replaced yearly.

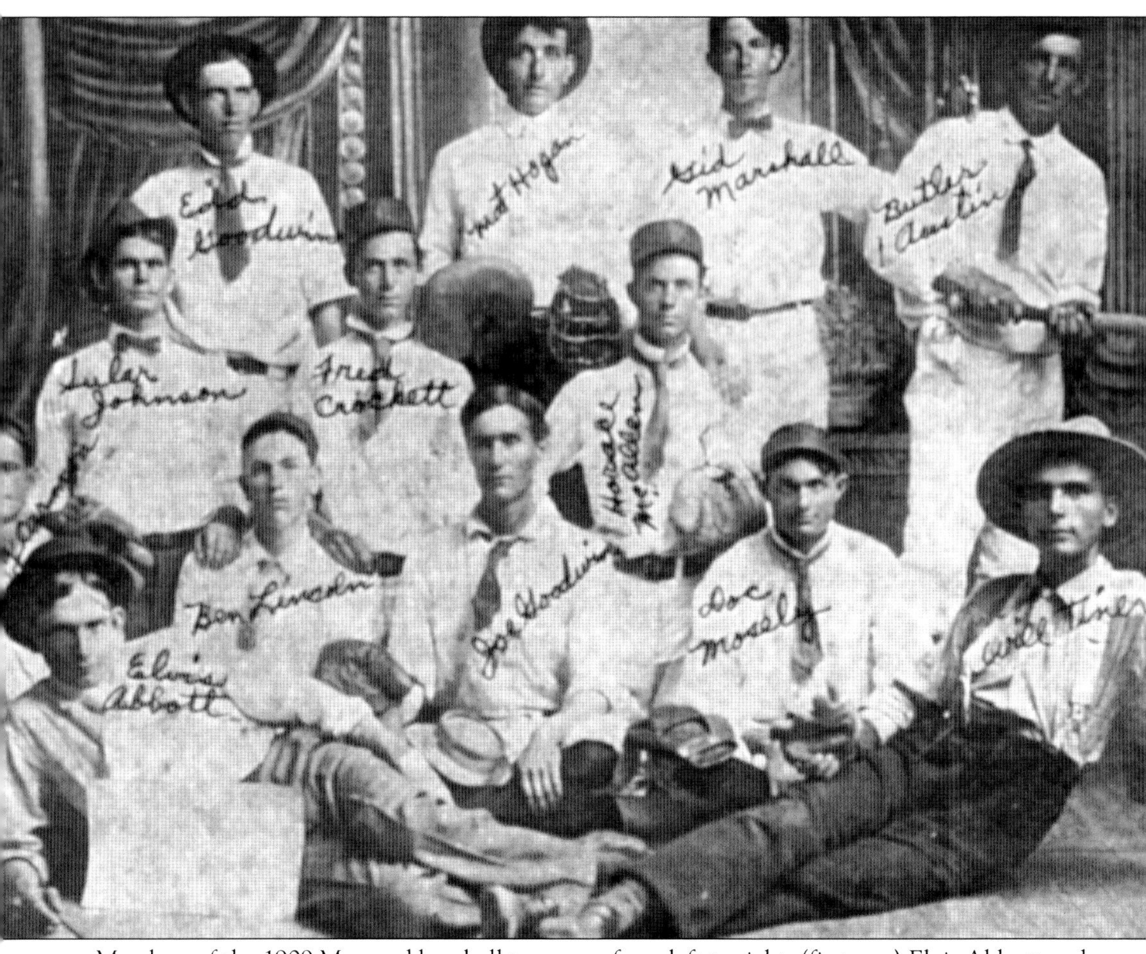

Members of the 1909 Maynard baseball team are, from left to right, (first row) Elvis Abbott and Will Tiner; (second row) Jerry Carmon, Ben Lincoln, Joe Goodwin, and Doc Mosely; (third row) Sular Johnson, Fred Crockett, and Herall McAllen; (fourth row) Edd Goodwin, Mat Hogan, Gid Marshall, and Butler Austin.

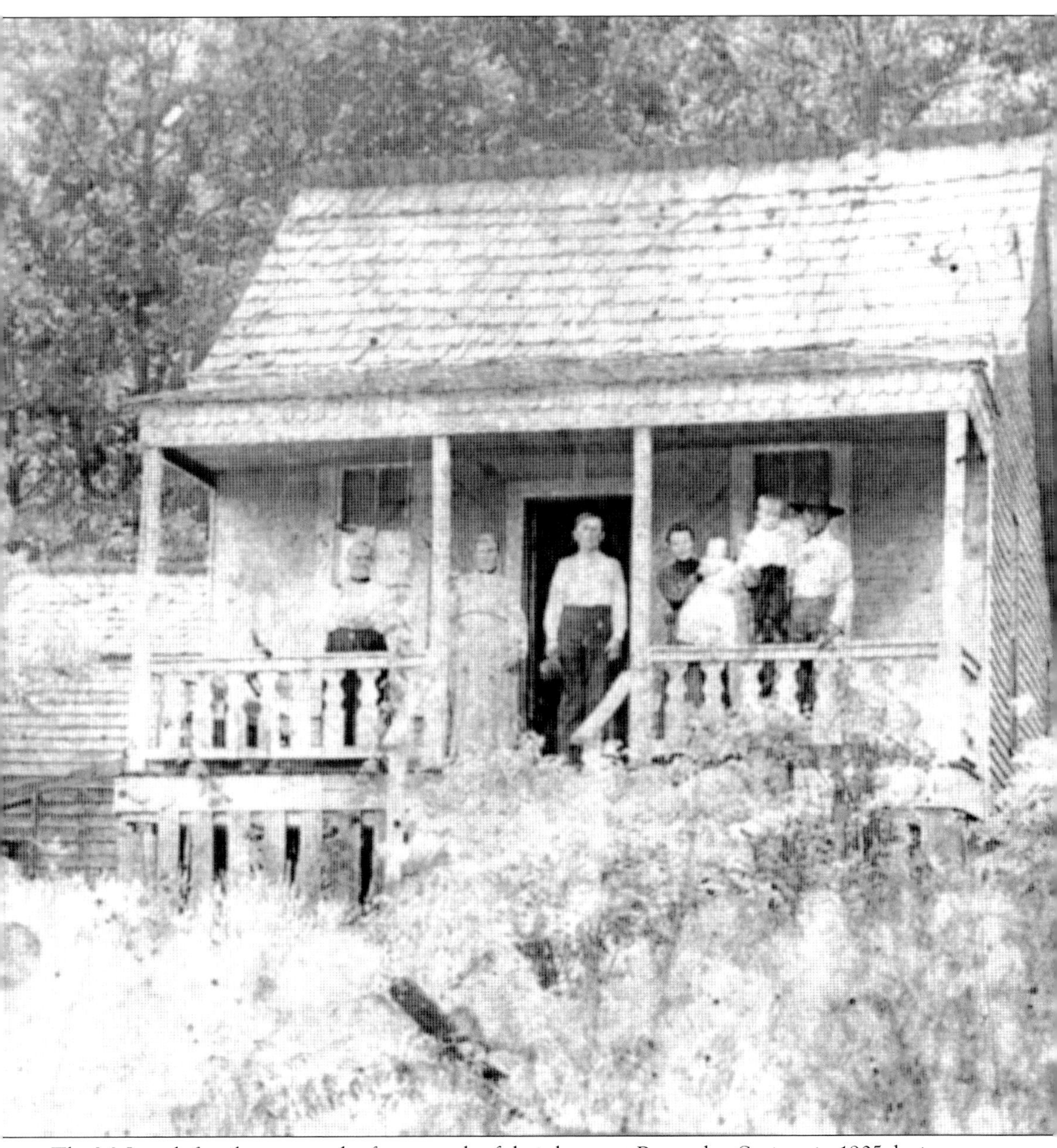

The McIntosh family pose on the front porch of their home at Ravenden Springs in 1905 during a family function. The home was constructed in 1899 by Mary McIntosh and her son Lon Sparlin.

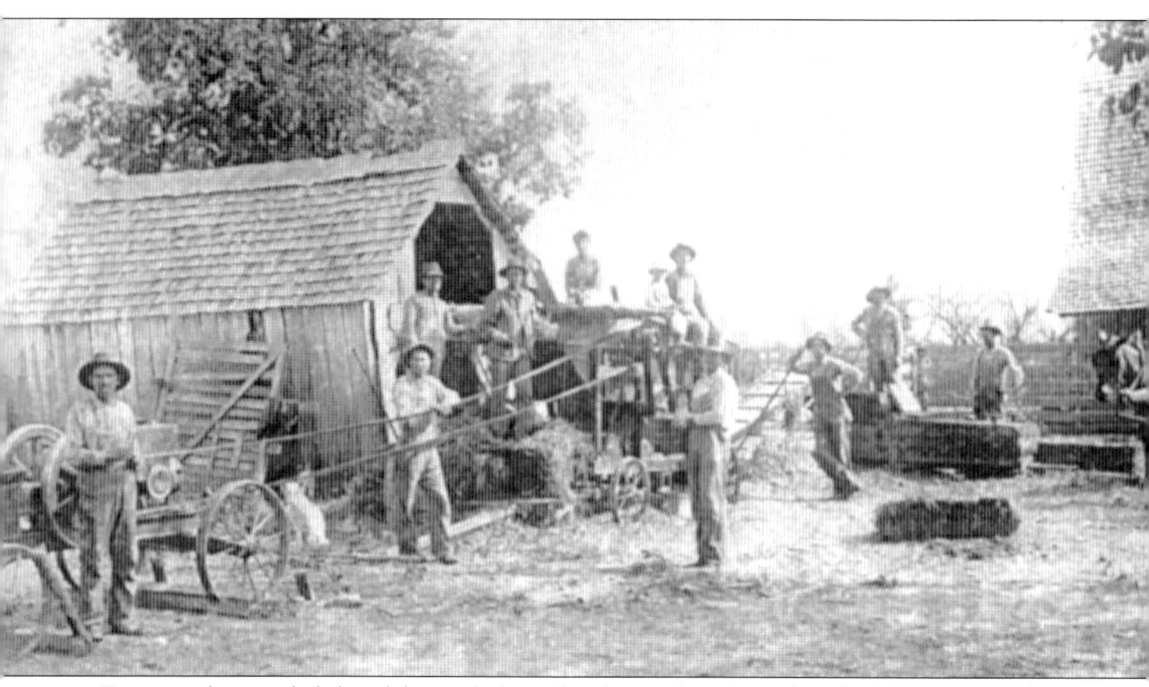

Farmers often pooled their labor to help each other with tasks such as building barns or baling hay. In this photograph from 1911, farmers are helping each other bale hay for the winter. The large Hite barn can be seen at right, along with a threshing machine and hay baler.

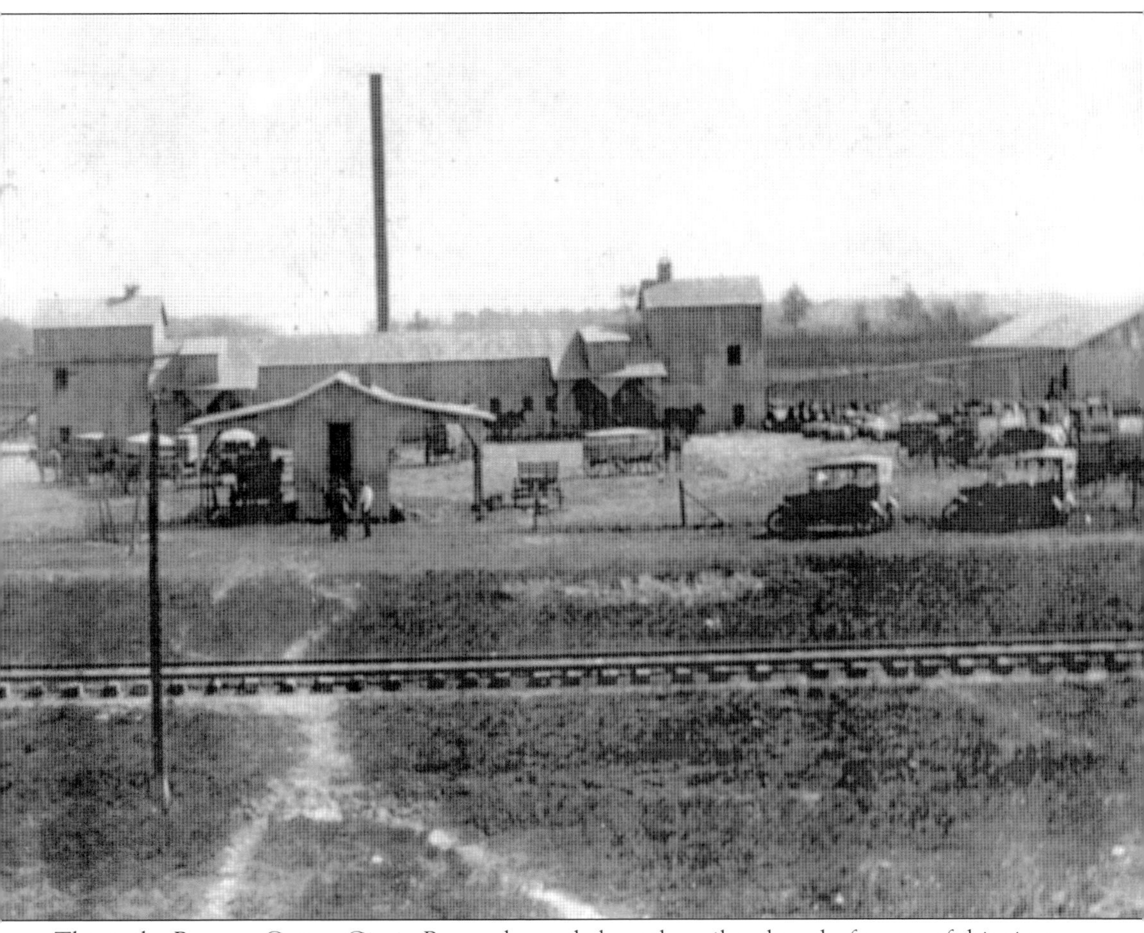

This is the Bennett Cotton Gin in Reyno, located along the railroad tracks for ease of shipping the cotton. Cotton gins were found in small towns and communities throughout Randoph County due to the number of small producers raising a substantial amount of cotton.

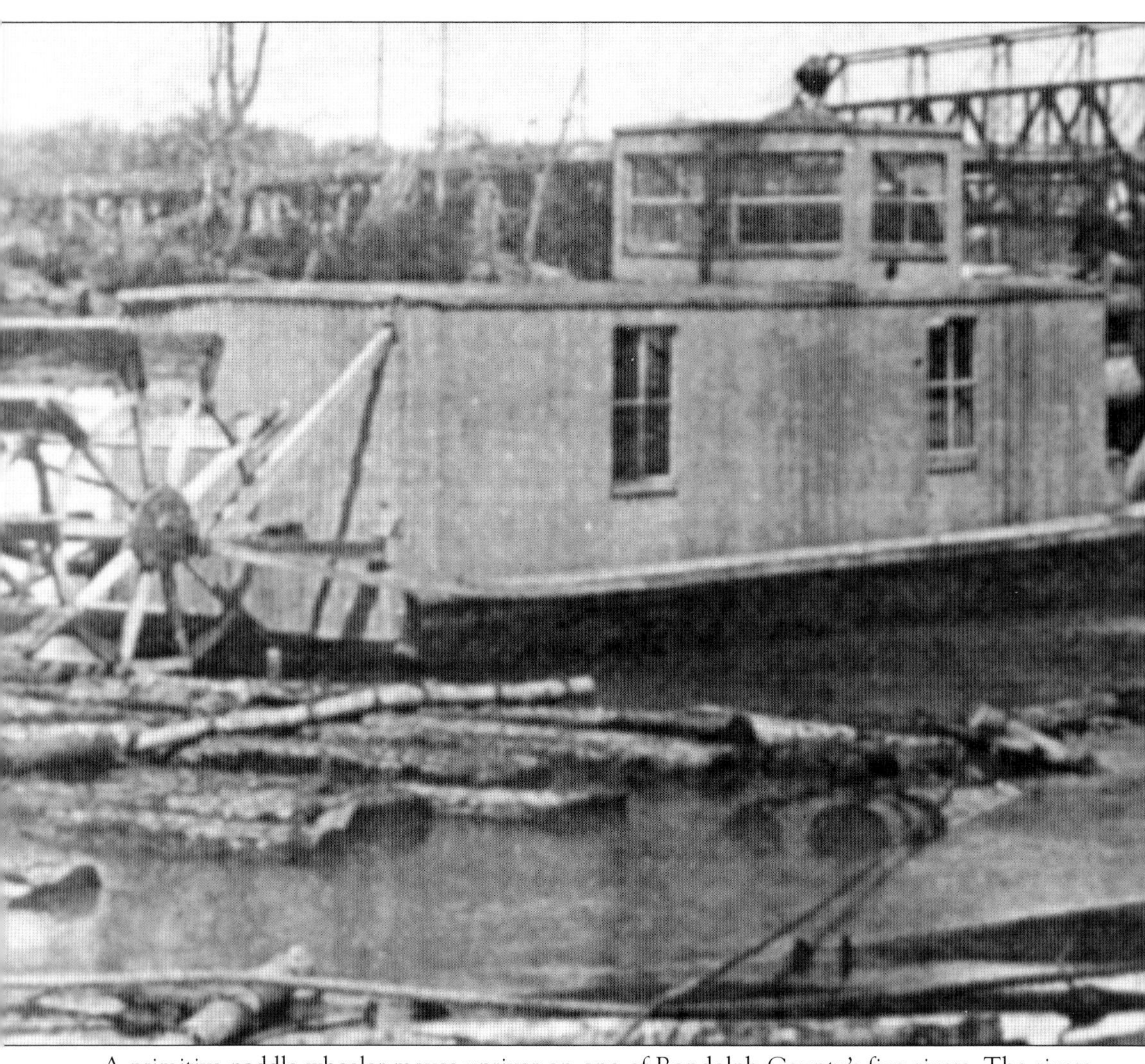

A primitive paddle wheeler moves upriver on one of Randolph County's five rivers. The rivers provided transportation, commerce, and even homes to many people. Many lived in houseboats along the waterfront in Pocahontas. Often, these "river rats" fed their families by fishing and selling fish to townspeople.

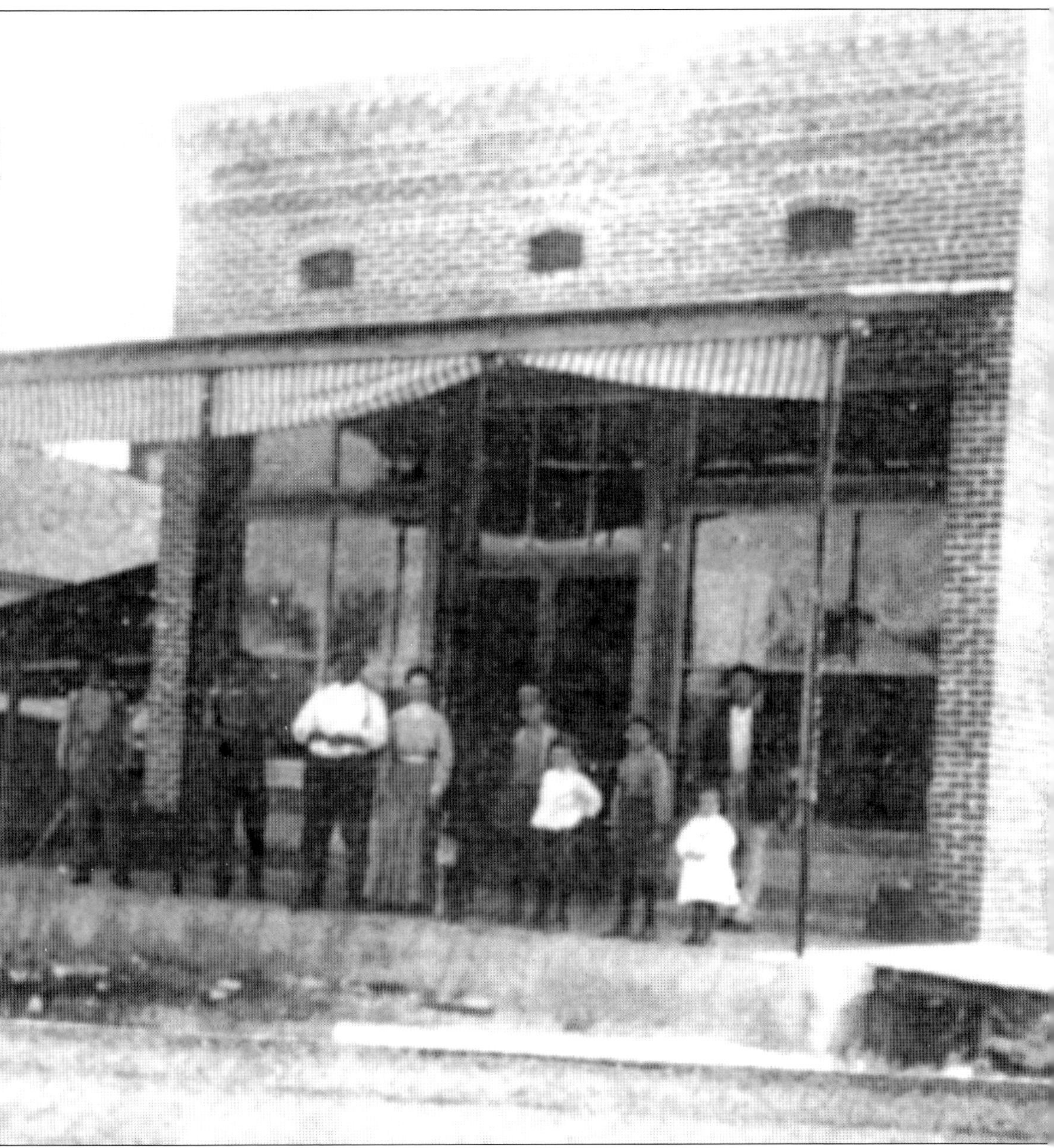

The Bode family stands in front of the Bode Store in O'Kean in eastern Randolph County in 1909. Most of the small town had been destroyed by a fire in October 1908. The Bode Store was the only store left, since the fire destroyed the two-story Sanders Store. It was noteworthy for its large front windows. The dirt streets in front of the store were a muddy mess during the wet season. The building was erected by Ferdinand Spinnenweber of Pocahontas.

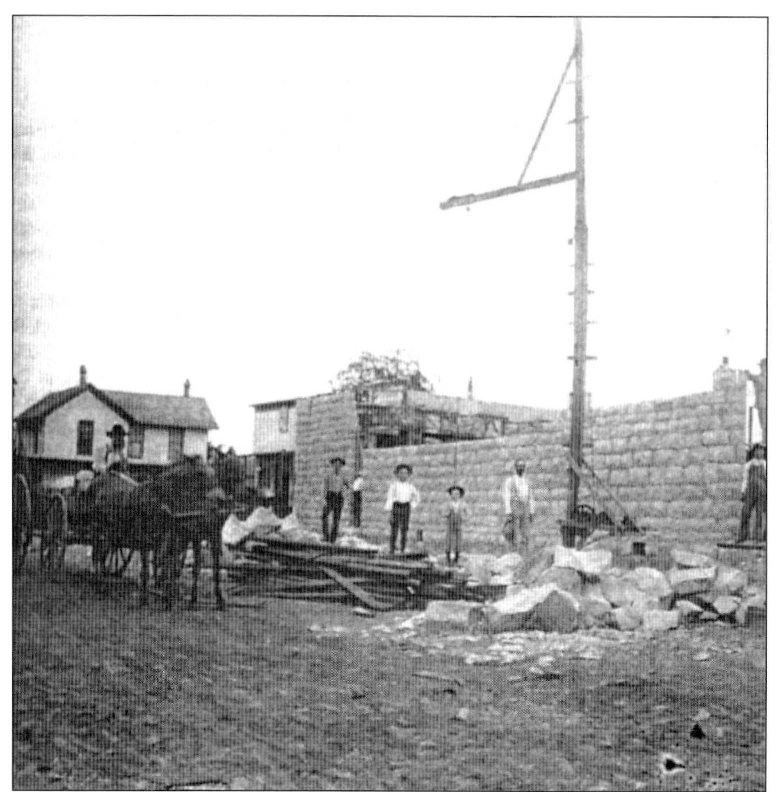

The Weaver Building is seen under construction on Main Street in Maynard. It was built to serve as a general mercantile store. Later, the store was operated by Irvin Davis and then by Ryburn Rapert for many years. The building later served as a church and was torn down in the mid-2010s.

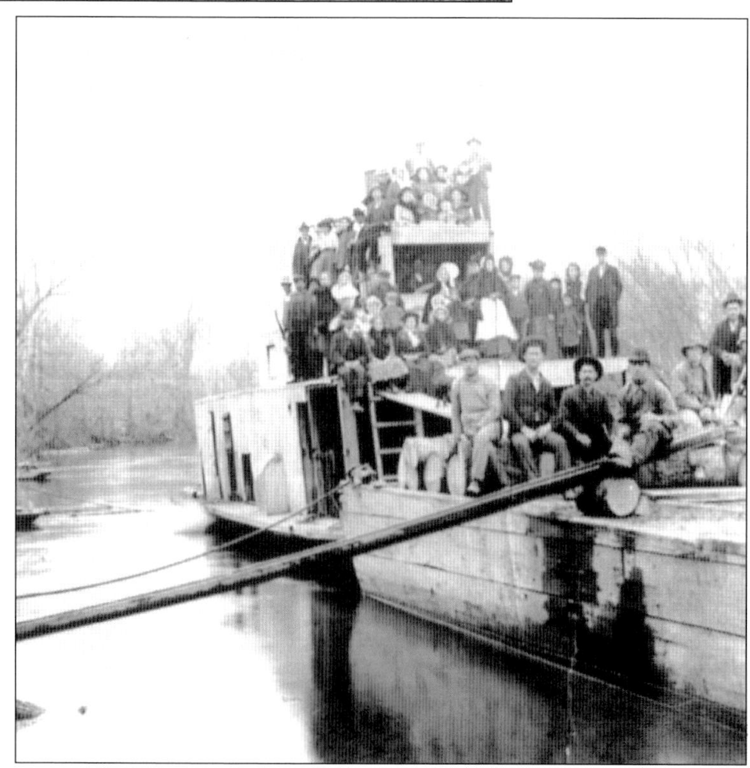

A barge load of logs is ready to be transported down the Current River to the handle mill. The boat appears to have many people on board.

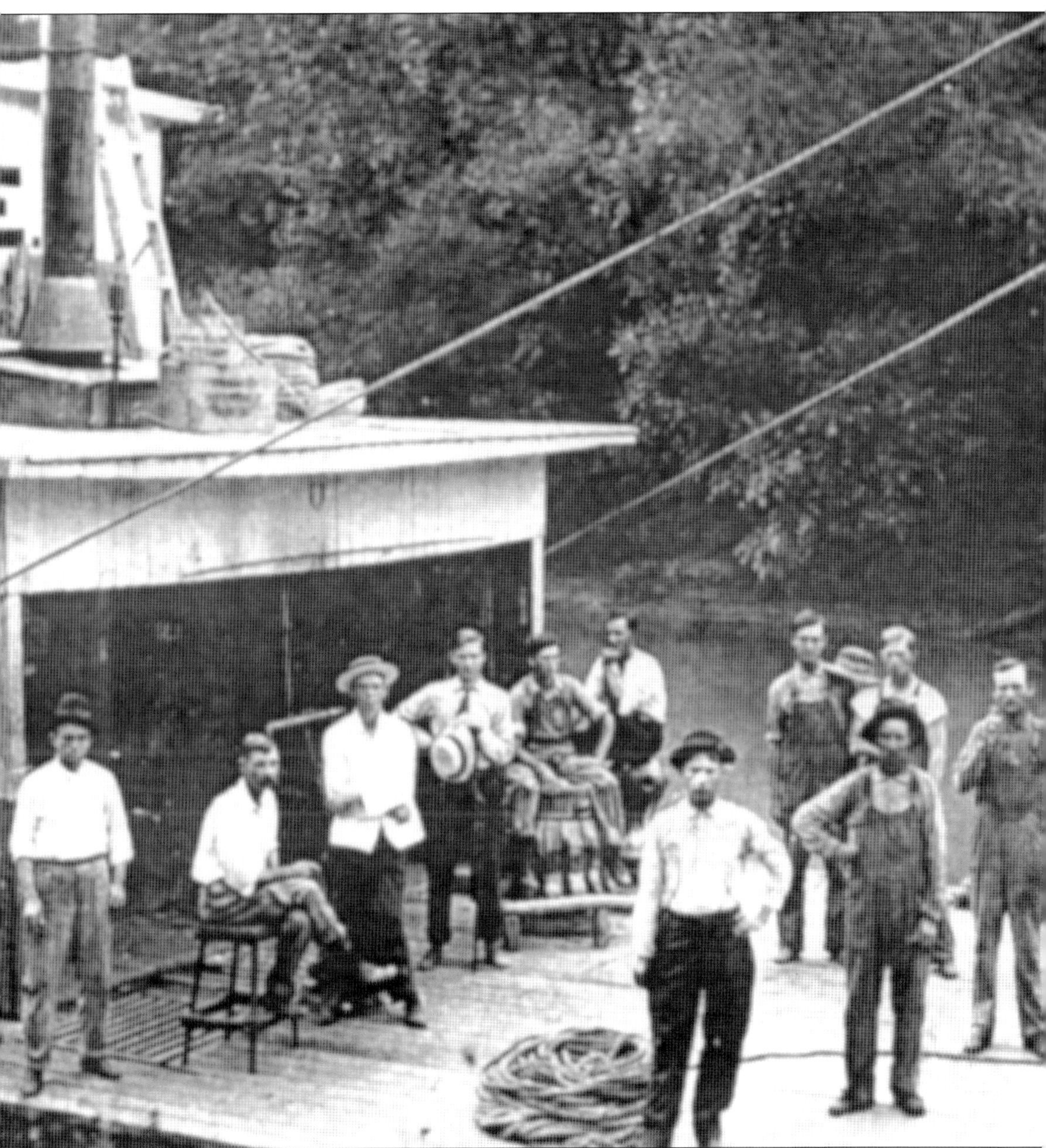

The *Riverside* was a snag boat on the Black River, which cleared the river of downed trees and other obstacles. This photograph was taken in 1913. Guy Legate is third from left in a straw hat. Legate worked on the boat as a cook; he was 21 years old. The captain of the boat was Harry L. Owens. The crew lived on the boat and worked on the Black River from the mouth of the Current River north to Poplar Bluff. It was 50 feet long and 20 feet wide.

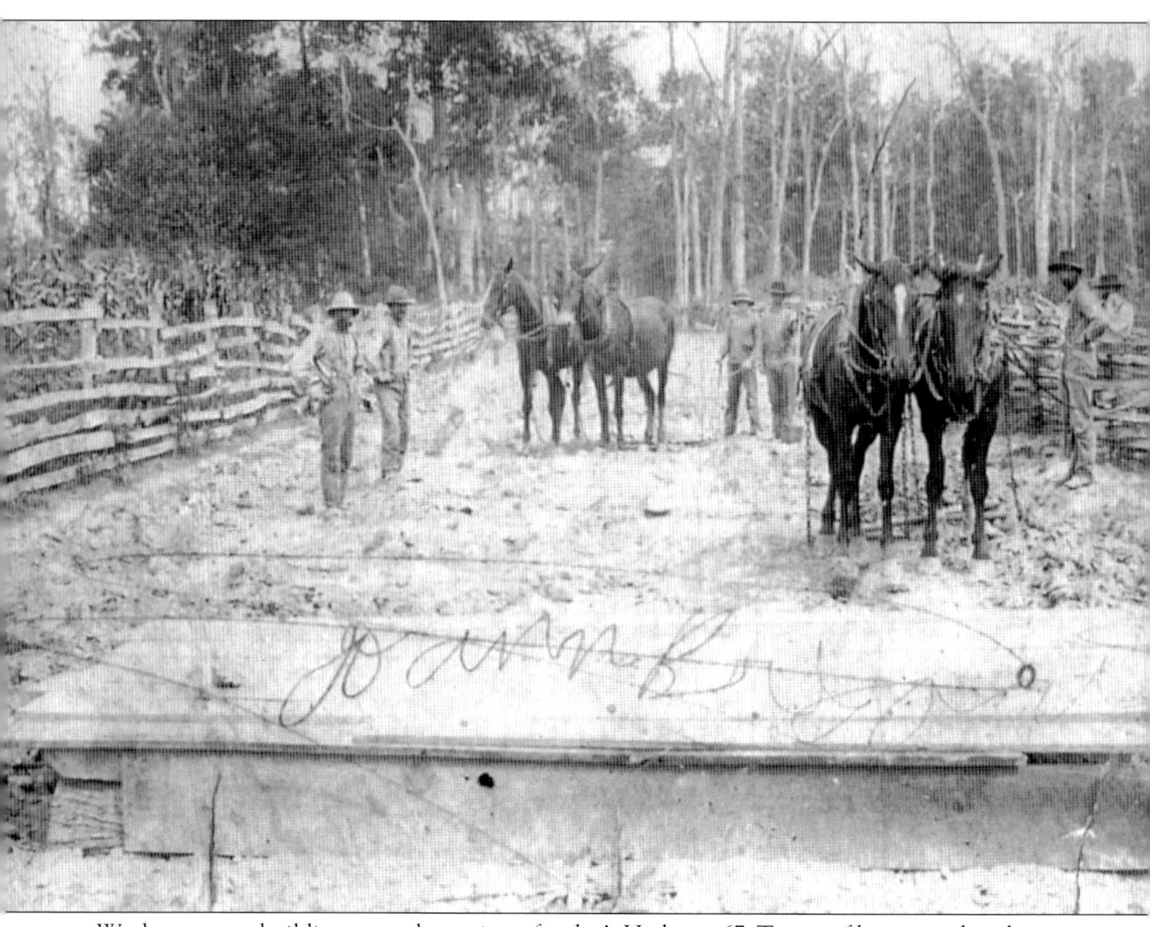

Work crews are building an early section of today's Highway 67. Teams of horses and mules were used to build the roadbed. Arkansas invested a lot of money in building roads in the early 1910s and 1920s. These road-building programs led to several political scandals, since the money was often misspent.

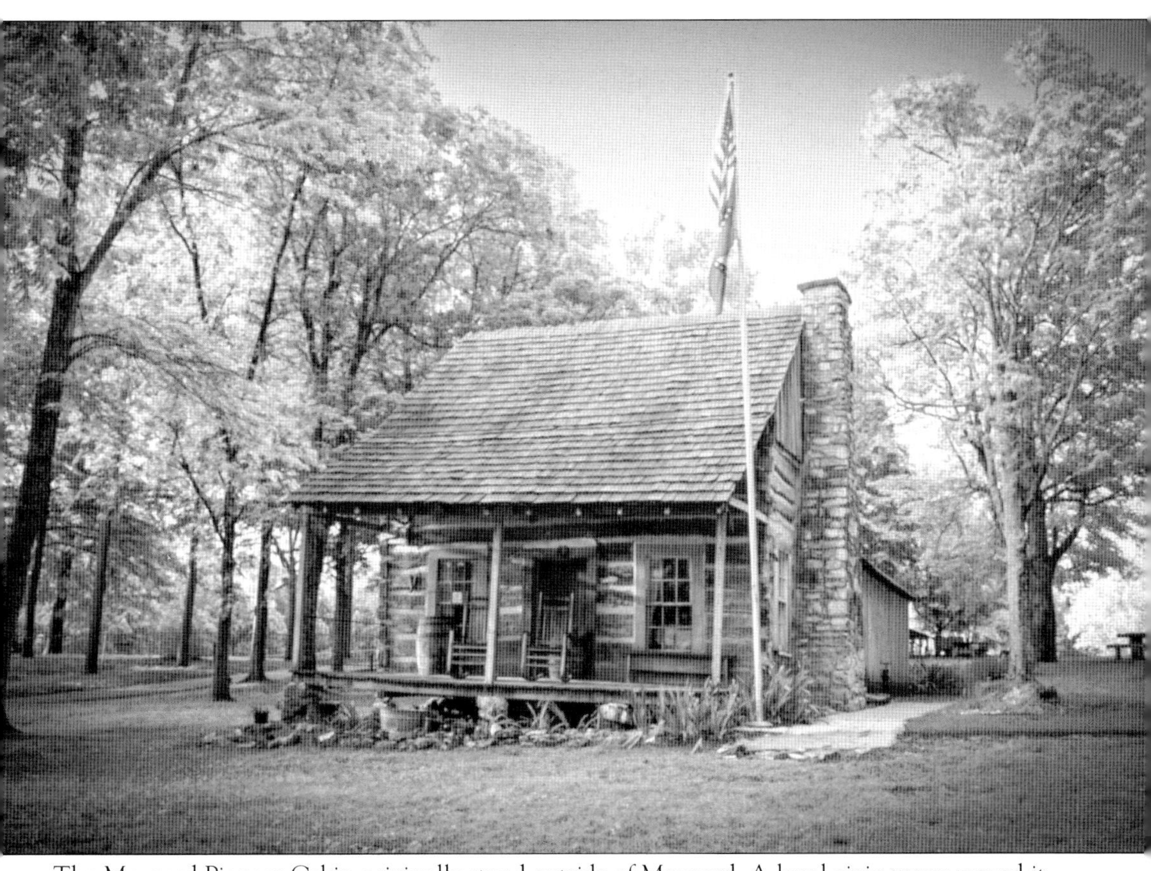

The Maynard Pioneer Cabin originally stood outside of Maynard. A local civic group moved it to a park in the late 1970s. Today, the town of Maynard hosts Pioneer Days in September, which draws thousands every year.

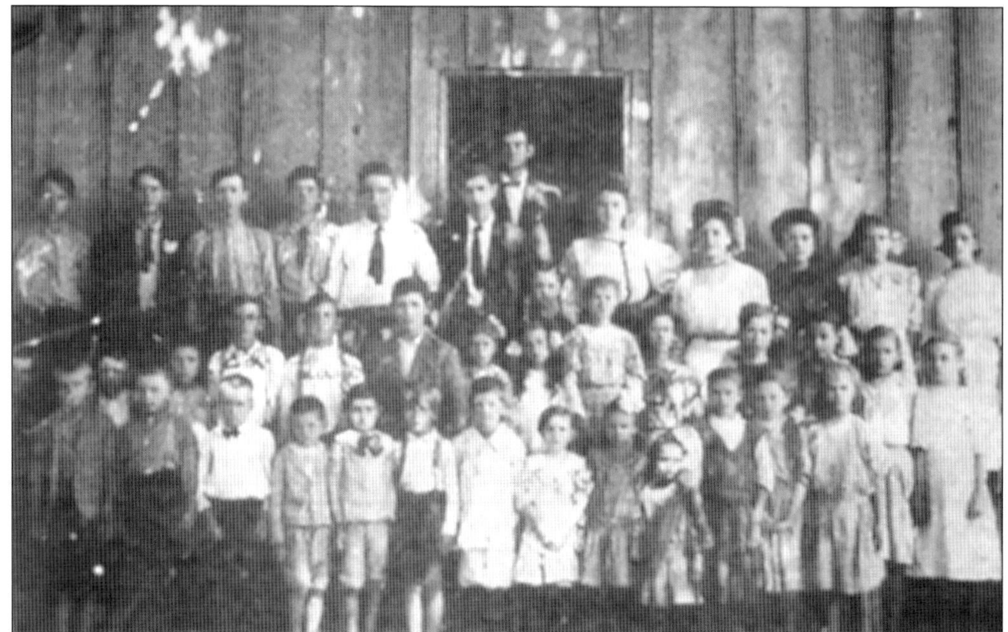

Pictured is the Shiloh School near Pocahontas. The tall man at the back is Drew Bowers, whose father was pastor of First Baptist Church in Pocahontas. Drew was an attorney, candidate for Congress and governor, and an assistant US attorney for several years.

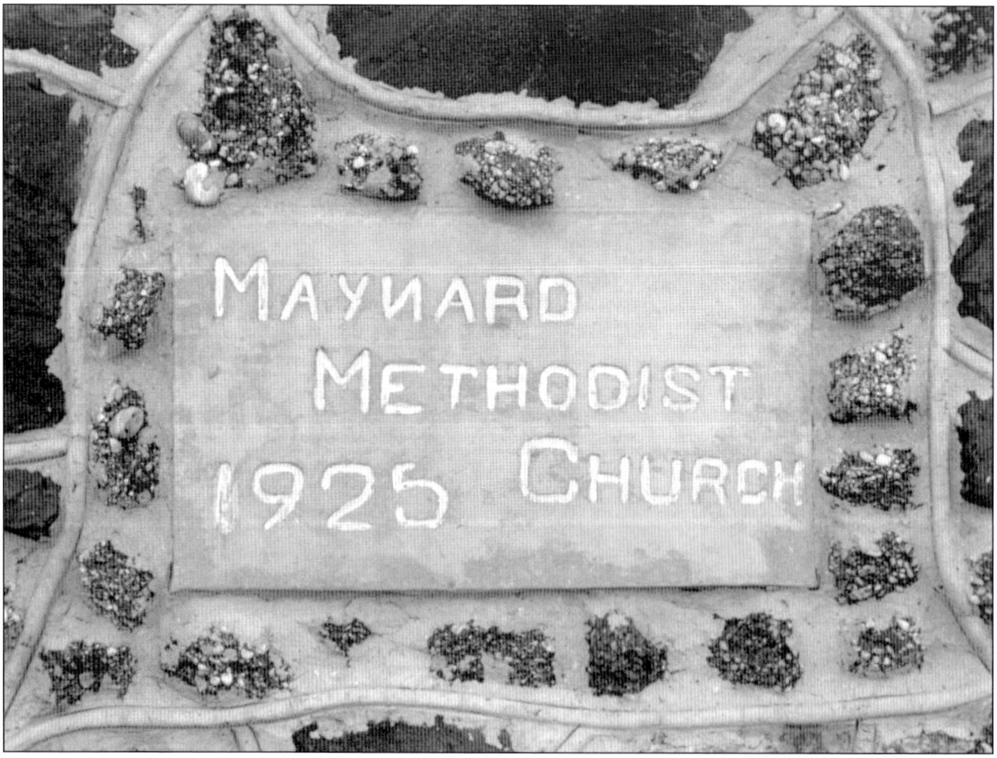

This is the cornerstone of the Maynard Methodist Church, which is near Maynard High School. The building has a unique design, with stadium seating.

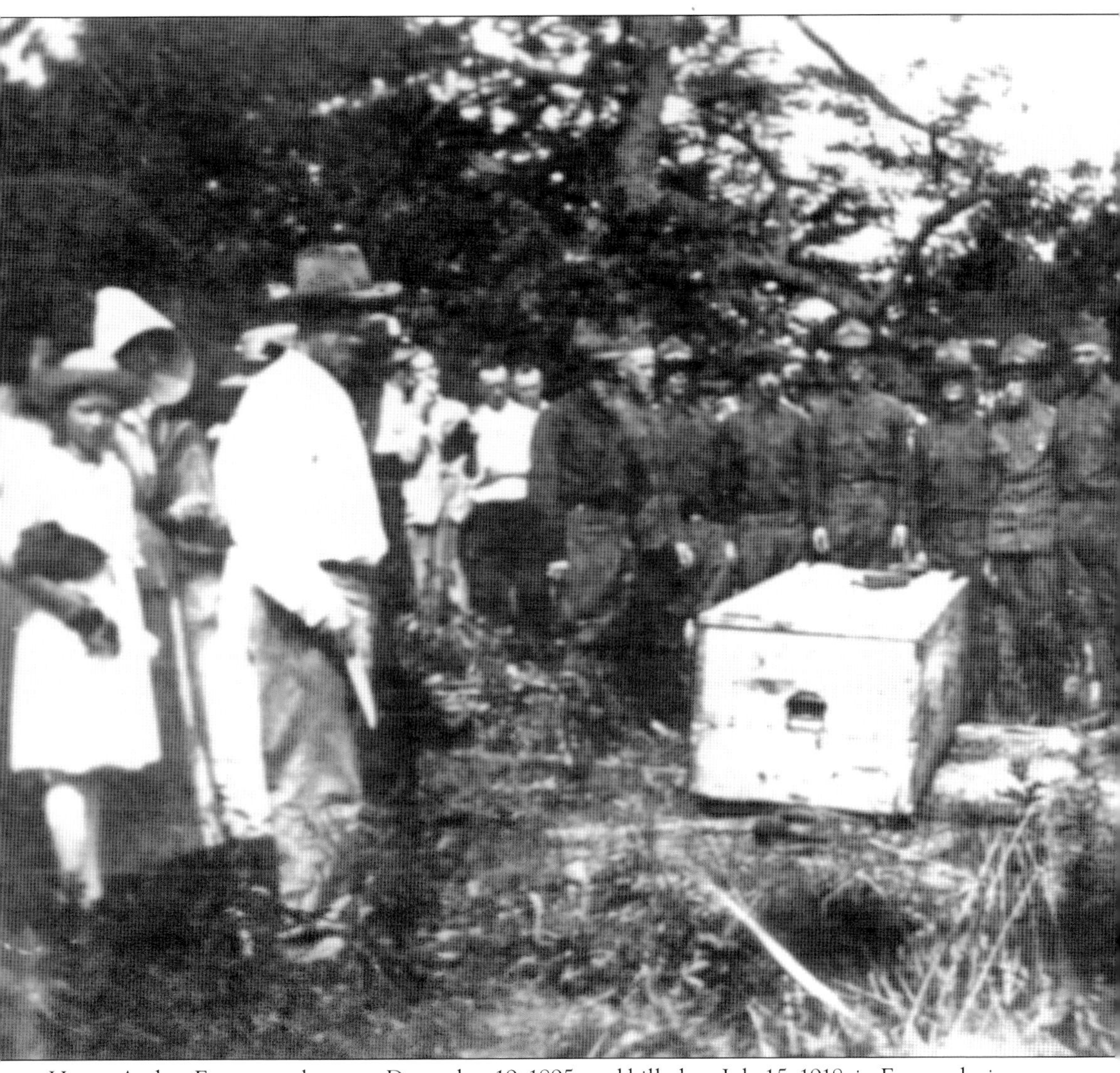

Henry Arthur Foster was born on December 19, 1895, and killed on July 15, 1918, in France during World War I. He was buried at the White Cemetery near Dalton in western Randolph County.

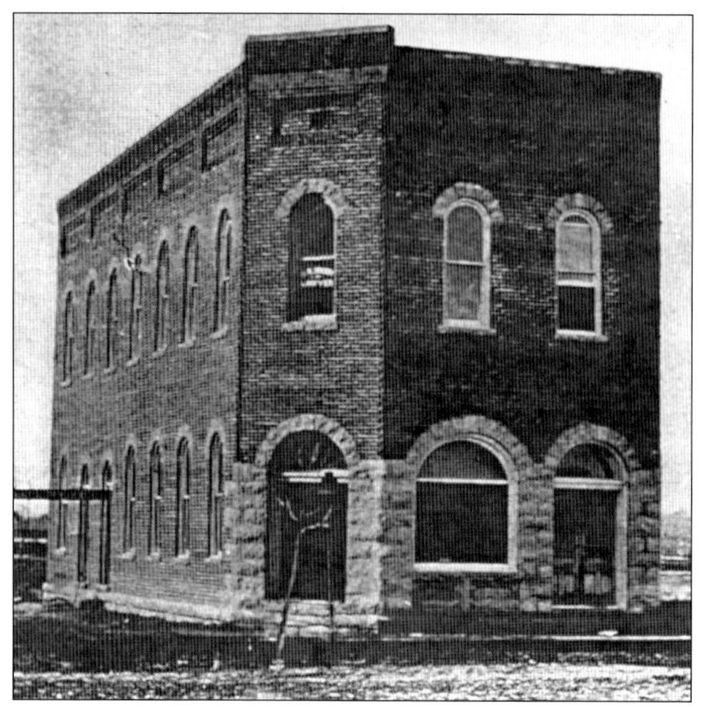

Incorporated in 1902, the Bank of Biggers had capital stock valued at $20,000. B.F. Bigger served as vice president, while S.C. Tipton was president. The town of Biggers grew rapidly after B.F. Bigger purchased land on the Current River. Not only did the town have a bank, it was also home to a hotel, a doctor, multiple saloons, and a grist mill.

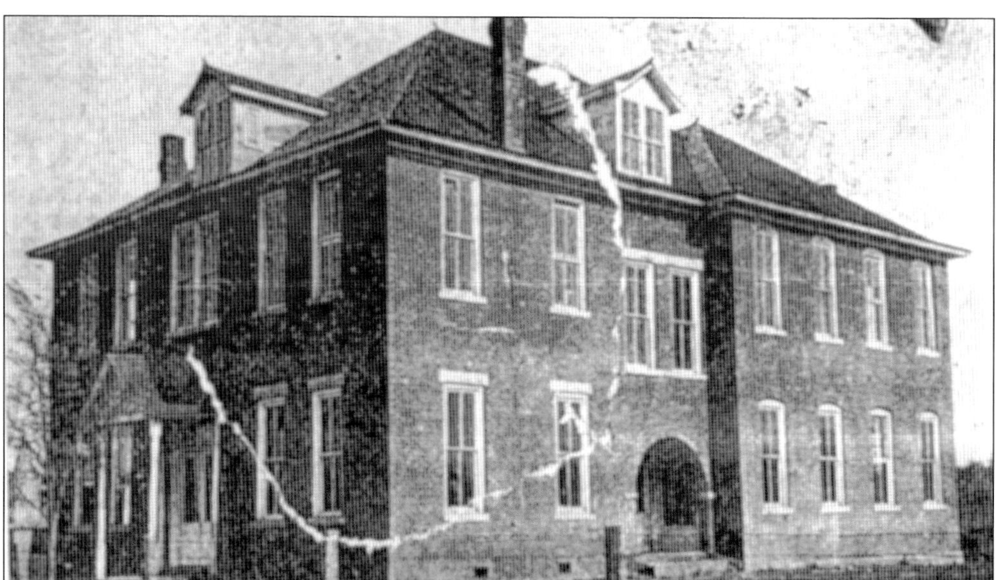

This photograph of the Maynard Academy, sometimes called the Ouachita Academy, was taken in 1903. Arkansas Baptist College established academies around the state, often called "mountain schools." The Abbot family of Maynard began this school before the college took it over. An advertisement in 1910 bragged that "Maynard Ouachita Academy is located in the foothills of the Ozarks, far away from the death-lurking swamps of the South, and the dangers associated with the metropolitan areas of the North and East." The academy operated for 28 years, from 1900 to 1928, when the Maynard School District purchased the building. Many graduates of the Ouachita Academy became teachers and had a huge impact on the region's educational system.

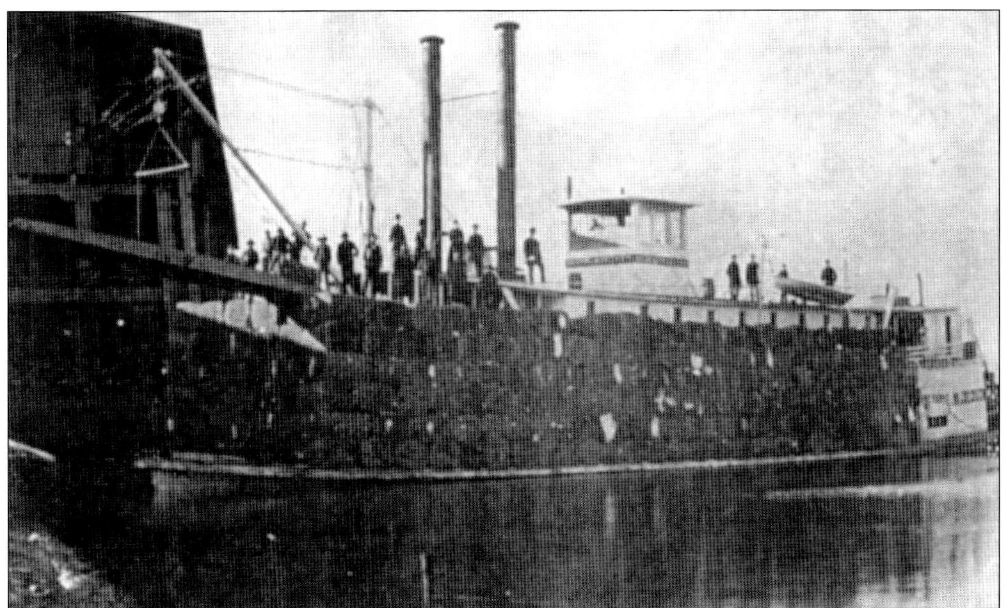

The *George W. Decker* is loaded down with 300 bales of cotton in 1894. The cotton was grown and ginned at Cherokee Bay. At the time, the Black and Current Rivers were the primary means of moving freight. The cotton was loaded at Sims Landing on the Current River. A close examination shows cotton buyers wearing dark suits and derby hats. At least three women are on board, standing near the smokestacks.

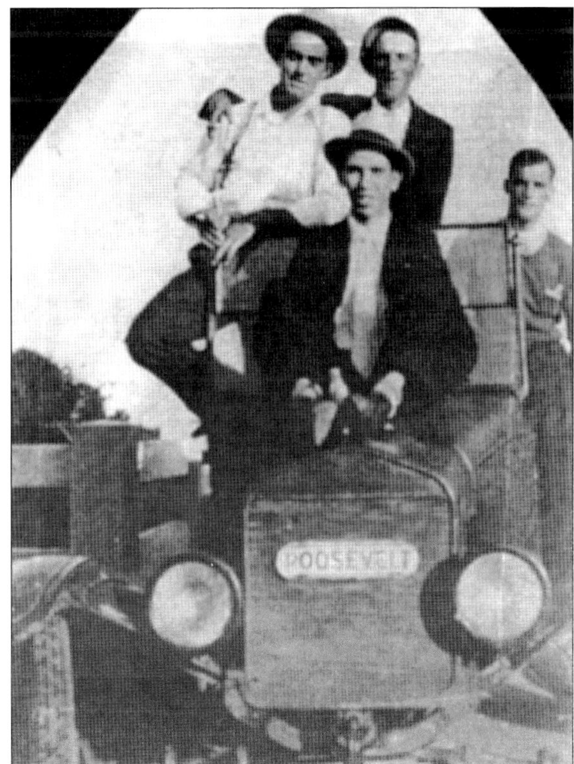

This photograph from the early 1930s shows four young men out for a drive. George Baltz, the owner of the Model T Ford, is sitting on the hood. The others are Harry Sisson, Ben Frankenberger, and Toney Schmidt. The "Roosevelt" sign on the front of the car is the equivalent of today's bumper stickers.

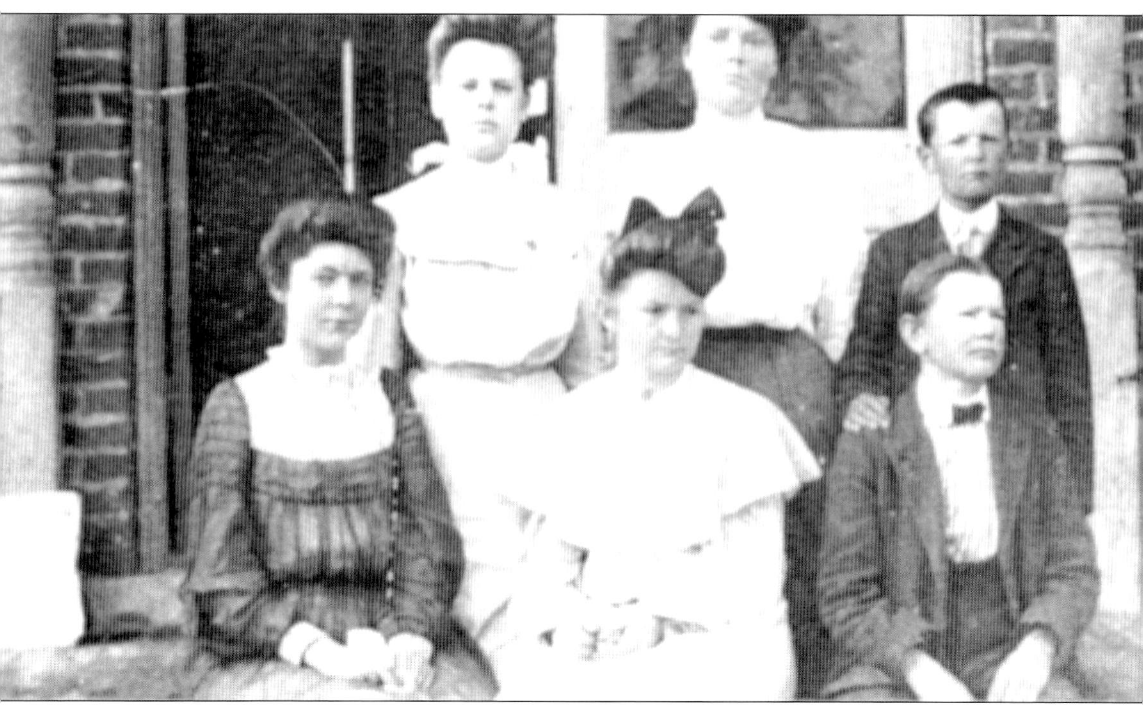

Members of the Ouachita Academy elocution class in 1906 are, from left to right, (first row) Ada Redwine, Janie Weaver, and Raymond Reynolds; (second row) Kate Hill, teacher Miss Marks, and Erick Reynolds.

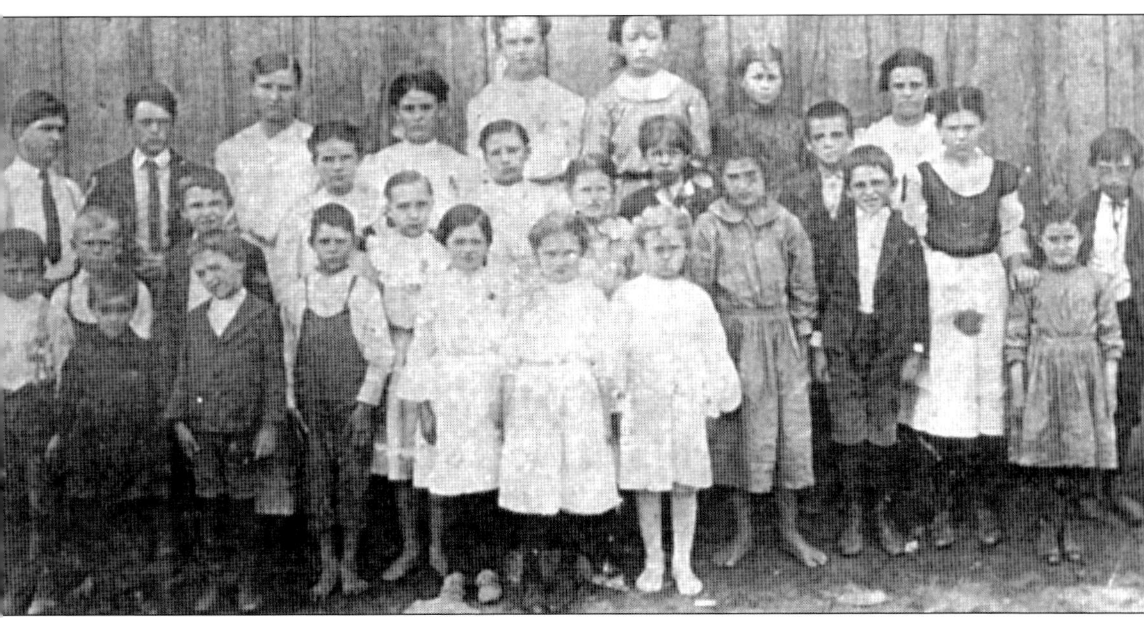

In this photograph of the O'Kean School during the 1921–1922 school year are, from left to right, (first row) Walter Ball, W.H. "Bud" Austin, two unidentified, Dave Spicer, unidentified, Ted York, Ralph Hunt, Elmo French, Ad Higgins, Eugene Storey, Dorsey Brandon, Bunt Ball, Lavelle Spicer, Nolen Brown, and unidentified; (second row) Leo Bode, Clyde Sanders, Lester Austin, Tee Dailey, Fred Haney, Henry Brandon, and Ralph Brandon; (third row) Ethel Haney, Ziphia Haney, Martha Ellen Hunt, Marguerite Sanders, Marie English, Nina Shelton, Hazel Martin, Hope Blansett, Inez York, Ethel Austin, Juanita Getson, Paul Barham, Cordelia Rowen, and Virginia Barham; (fourth row) unidentified, Herman Shelton, Eugene Byrd, Claude York, Jessie Shelton, Homer Shelton, John Getson, Clyde Witcher, Josephine Rummel, Jewel Stone, Notra Dean, Lawrence Storey, Dolaphis French, Grace Haney, Lawrence Shelton, Beulah Stone, Beatrice French, Ruby Brandon, and Ida McCarthy; (fifth row) Samantha Getson, Notra Bramlett, Mavis Byrd, teacher Vanus Higgins, Hazel Austin, Thelma Sanders, and Busche Gregory.

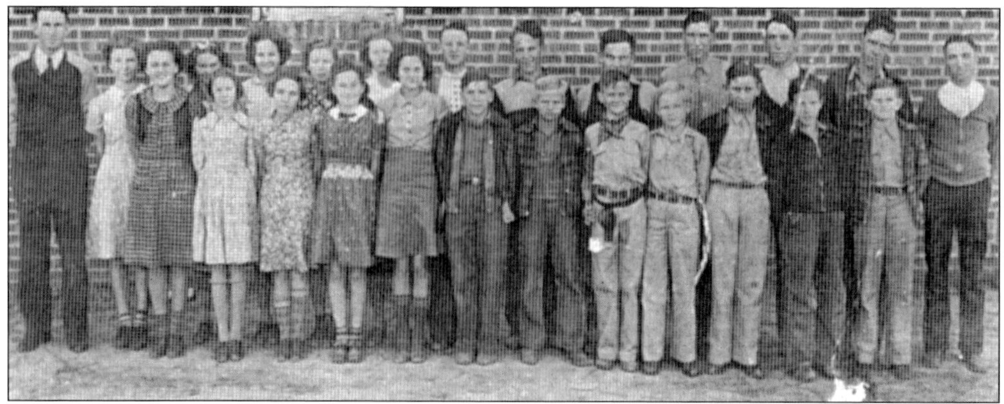

This is the Surridge School in March 1936. At far left is teacher Taid Ford. The students are, from left to right (first row) Blanch Kell, Hope James, Martha Nell Ellis, Helen Marie Brooks, Delma VanWinkle, Dub E. Jones, Darrell Armstrong, Thomas Wells, Jack Allen Starr, Billy Ellis, Billy Joe Million, and Thomas James; (second row) Essie Dowdy, Fay Head, Geneva Riggs, Eunice Yankee, Ethel Carter, Bobby Harvester, Doris Reed, Everett Lee Sutton, Gerald Caffery, Odis Nipps, Grover Brinkley, and Lehman Nipps.

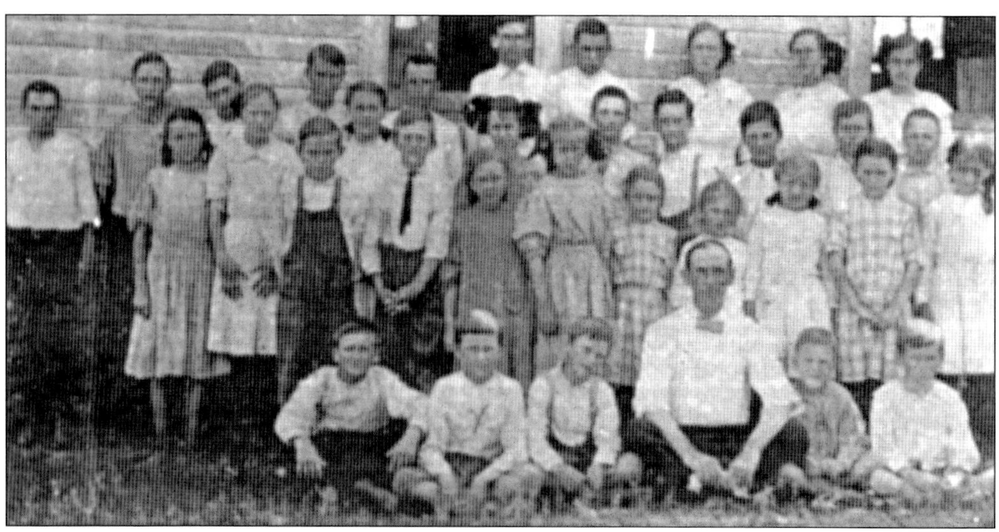

The Clearview School is pictured in 1913. From left to right are (first row) Ula Broadway, unidentified, Jake Hart, teacher Daley Mondy, Josh Stephens, Jess Hart, unidentified, Oreo Loar, Linna Stephens, unidentified, Thelma Broadway, Ouida Stephens, and Stella Broadway; (second row) Butch Warner, Tive Hurn, Irvin Thompson, Tom Warner, Martin Mondy, Marvin Thomson, Thelma Loar, Henry Witcher, unidentified, Della Hart, Edd Hart, and Delmont Loar.

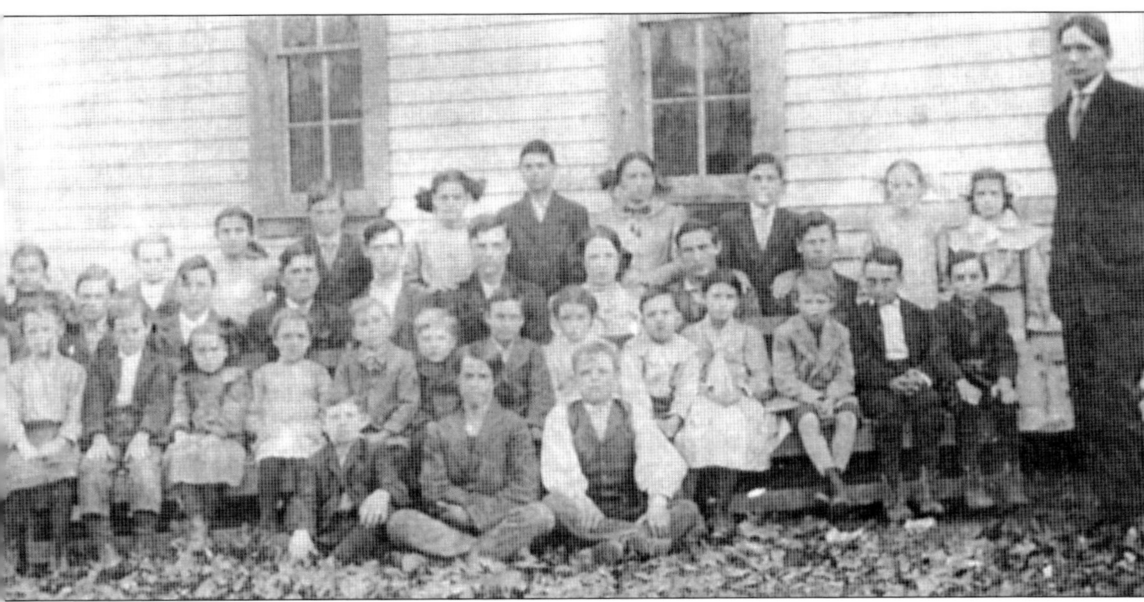

This photograph of the 1911 Brakebill School was taken on February 16, 1911. Elvis Abbot served as teacher. From left to right are (first row) Nevin Seawell, Willie Spray, and Virgil Haley; (second row) John Pence, Dovie Seawel Long, Gusszie Murdock, Etta Waldron King, Jewel Tucker Bridges, D.L. Tucker, Theodor Galemore, Gene Galemore, Irene Galemore, Clyde Mock, Goldie Harris, Ottis Kidd, Marvin Waldron, and Lecil Mock; (third row) Joe Wilson, Waldo Sewel, Martin Shaver, Jess Seawell, Roy Sewel, Lela Haley Pence, Dock Condict, and Will Russell; (fourth row) unidentified, Arnold Wison Beaver, Blanch Harris, Hite Mock, Bary Seawell Blythe, Oscar Shaver, Grace Mock Johnson, and Villdia Kid Templeton.

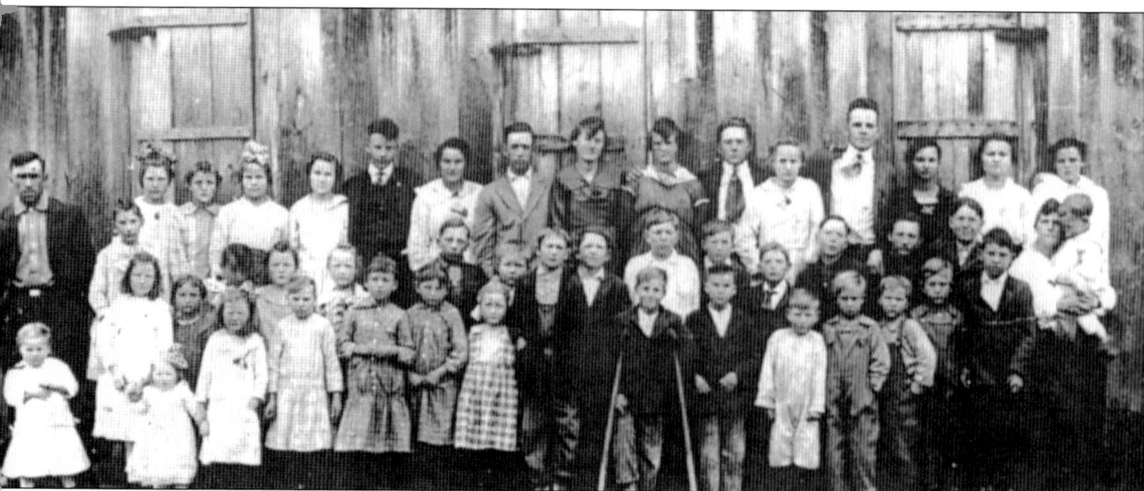

The Duff School was three miles southeast of Supply and south of the Elmont School in Clay County. Pictured are, from left to right, (first row) Opal McConniehat, Marie Creer, Laura Greer, Little Dillbeck, Vera Garrison, Lois Garrison, Cletus Johnson, Bob Morris, Tommie Pierce (on crutches), Lossie Pierce, Francis Whitworth, Monroe Legate, Buel Morris, Sterling Legate, and Loren Whitesorth; (second row) Alice Greer, Ida Mae Johnson, Girtie Frances, Vada Stackhouse, Bessie Johnson, Everett Johnson, Henry Stackhouse, Ellis Greer, Ernie Cavitt, Arvil Greer, Troy Miller, Henry McKee, Lowell Morris, Bill Ligatge, and Captolia Pierce; (third row) teacher Tom Pride, Horace Pride, Flossie Reed, Myrtle Pride, and Leona Stackhouse.

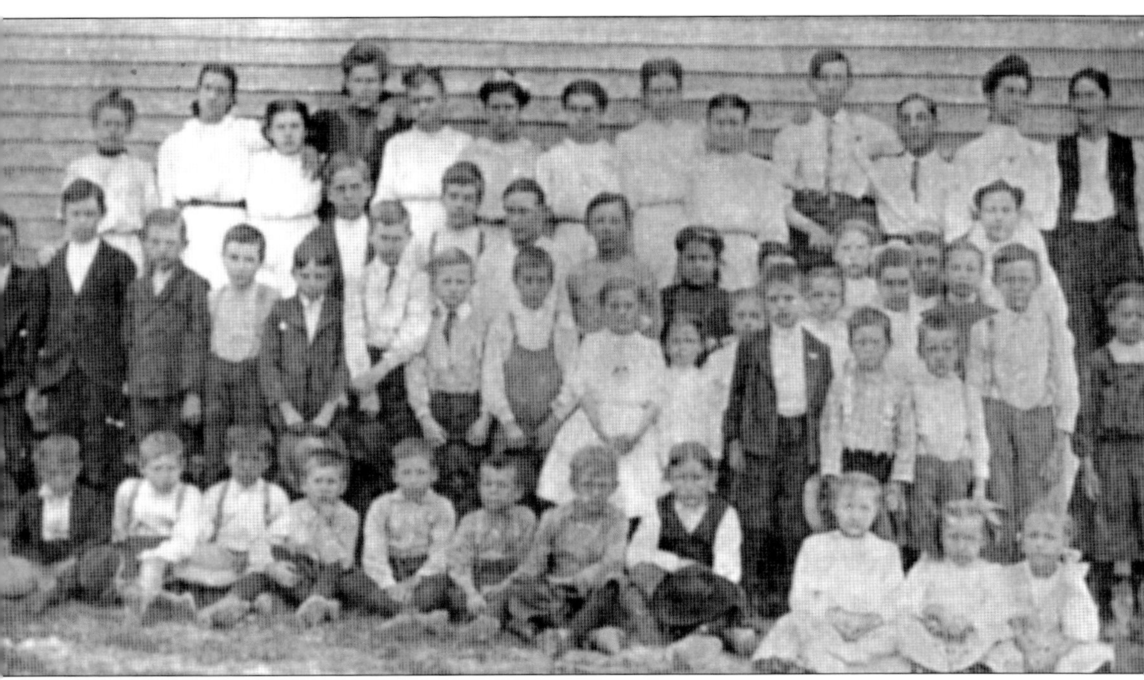

The Stokes School is pictured in 1908. The teacher at the time was Effie Parks. The students are, from left to right, (first row) Monroe Morgan, Carl Ballard, Amon Buxton, Arvel Evans, Boyd Robinson, Talmage Robinson, Joe Frazier, Ezra Pickerel, Lucy Phillips, Mary Purdy, and Ella Mack; (second row) Clyde Ulmer, Gravel Thomas, Henry Phillips, Bunk Mack, George Morgan, Clifford Sago, Morris Sago, John Mack, Ruth Ryburn, Iris Ulmer, Bill Ulmer, Sherman Davis, Frank Barker, Willis Barker, and Gracie Davis; (third row) Clifton Harris, Buster Mack, Naman Harris, Raymond Daniels, Eliza Buxton, Mary Cahoon, Darsena Morgan, Velma Cahoon, Sadie Harris, Ethel Mack, Elsie Purday, Imar Ballard, and Essie Ulmer; (fourth row) Sally Robinson, Ethel Johnson, Ada Roberts, Rodie Barker, Ecil Phillips, Annie Milam, Annie Mack, Sadie Harris, Mandy Nearns, Ed Buxton, Bill Purdy, and Luther Smith.

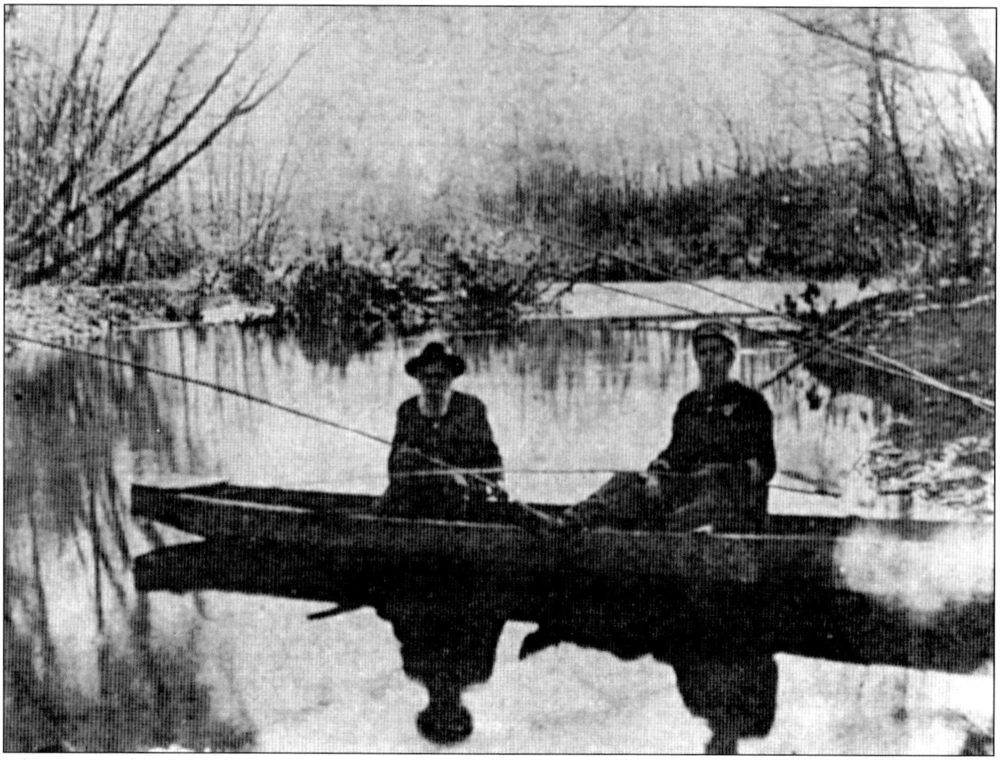

This 1912 photograph shows Sam Harmon and Henry Seawell fishing on the Fourche River. Both men were Civil War veterans but fought on opposing sides. Seawell, who fought for the Confederacy, was wounded during the war, and Harmon always jokingly claimed he was the Union soldier who shot him.

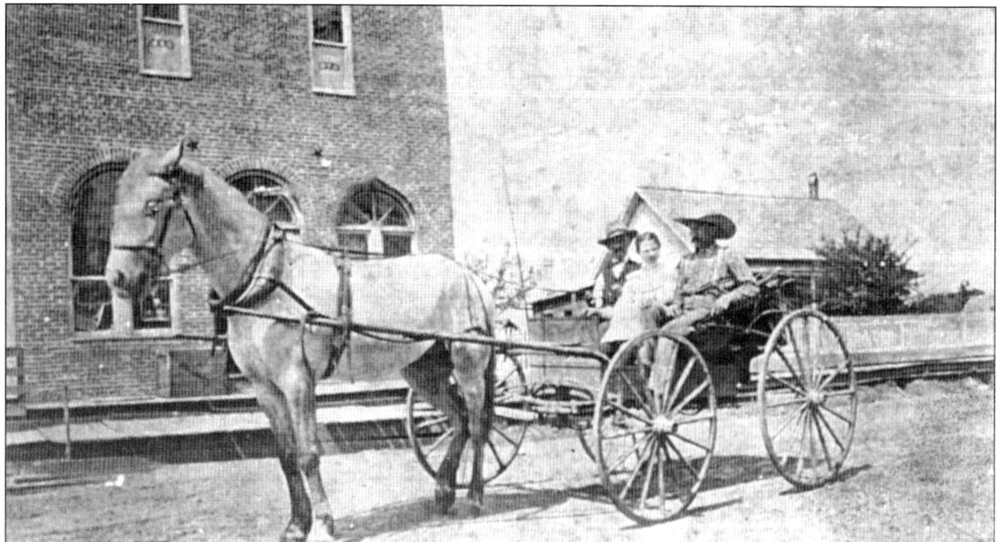

This 1905 photograph of Lee Poyner, Tommie Lewis, and Bill Lewis was taken on Main Street in Maynard. The building in the background housed the *Maynard Enterprise* newspaper. The upper floor was the Maynard Odd Fellows hall for many years.

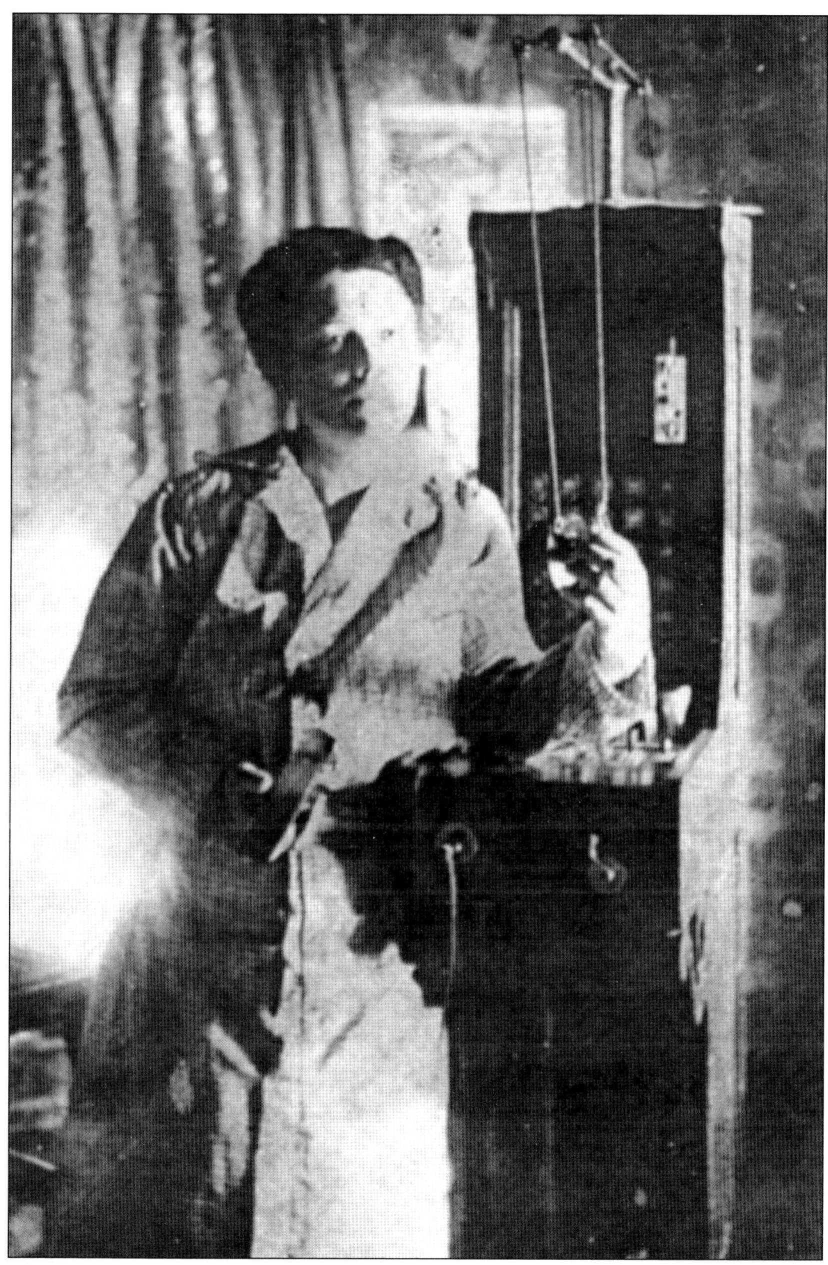

Addie Parker was the switchboard operator at Maynard in 1918. The switchboard had 25 drops, so there could have been as many as 25 phones at Maynard, but the exact number is unknown. Mose Wilson, an uncle to Addie Parker, owned the phone system. Parker had previously been the switchboard operator at Pocahontas and worked out of an office on Marr Street for some time. The Pocahontas phone system went bankrupt, and Parker and her husband moved to Maynard. At that time, phone service cost 25¢ per month, and payment often came in hams, sorghum, and other items. The phone itself cost between $9 and $12 to purchase. Later, Addie Parker returned to Pocahontas, where she served as the night operator for a new phone company. It is worth noting that there was no long-distance phone service at this time. To talk to someone on the phone, they had to be part of the same phone company as the person making the call.

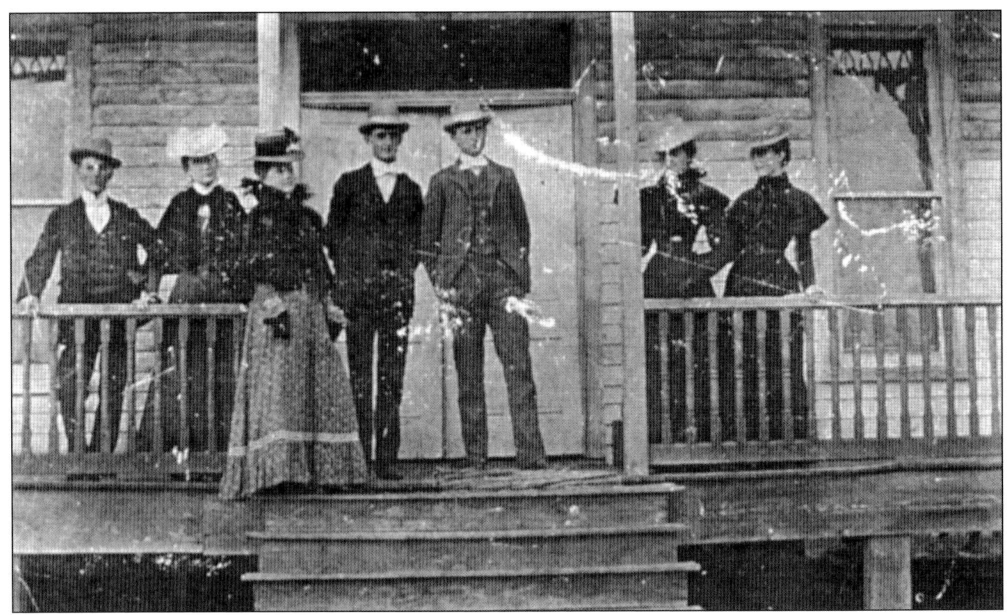

Friends pose for a photograph around 1900 on the porch of the Dr. H.A. Slaughter home at Maynard. From left to right are Henry Abbot, Lena Redwine Abbot, Kate Moore, John Downing, Baird Weaver, Nell Gamble, and Emma Purdy.

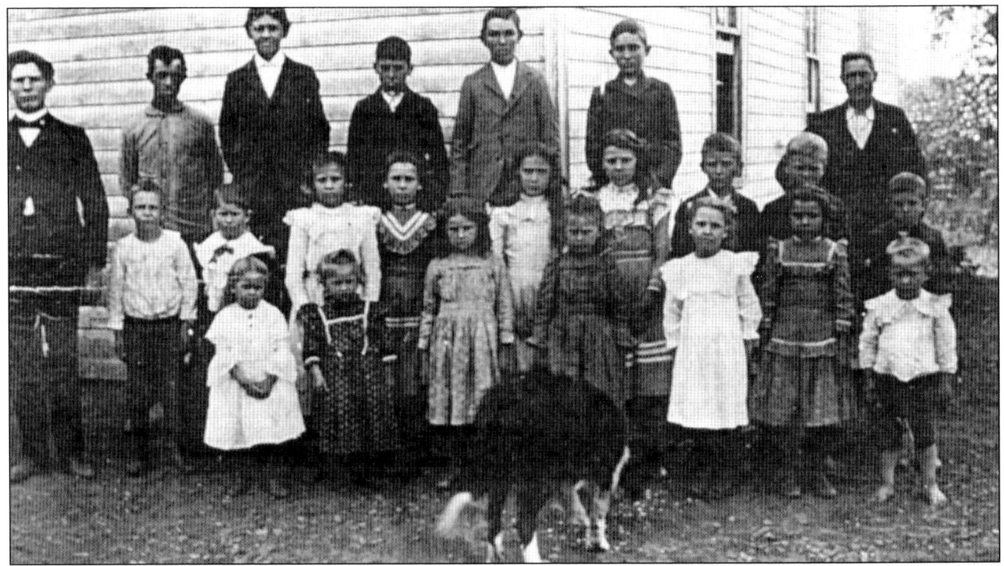

This New Home School photograph is from 1900 and features, from left to right, (first row) Mayme Bly Haynes, Mazie Camp, Myrtle Coleman, Ella Camp, Elsie Dunn, Pearl Dunn, and Kennan Dunn; (second row) Raleigh Dunn, Elbert Bly, Maud Camp Poe, Ethel Dunn, Minnie Dunn, Bonnie Dunn, Thurman Bly, Sugar Camp, and Allie Coleman; (third row) teacher Charley Dixon, Gid Thompson, DeWitt Moore, Eelam Coleman, John Dunn, Daly Thompson, and George Dunn.

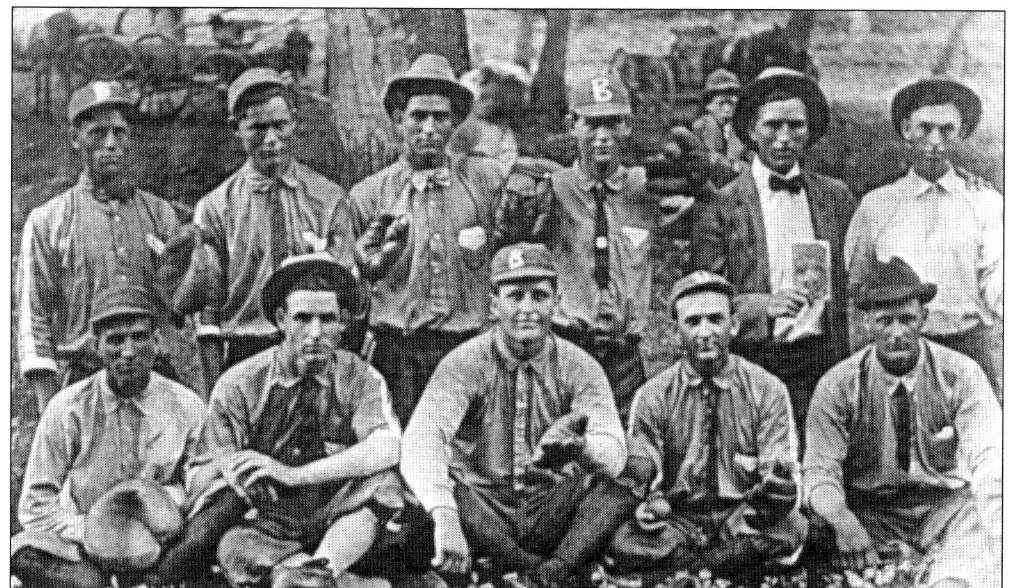

Members of the Burr baseball team around 1908 are, from left to right, (first row) Bill Palmer, Claude Wright, Henry Hold, Ad Pond, and Tom Holt; (second row) Herman Robinson, Perry Murphy, Fred Wright, Tom Murphy, Will Phillips, and Ed Grissom.

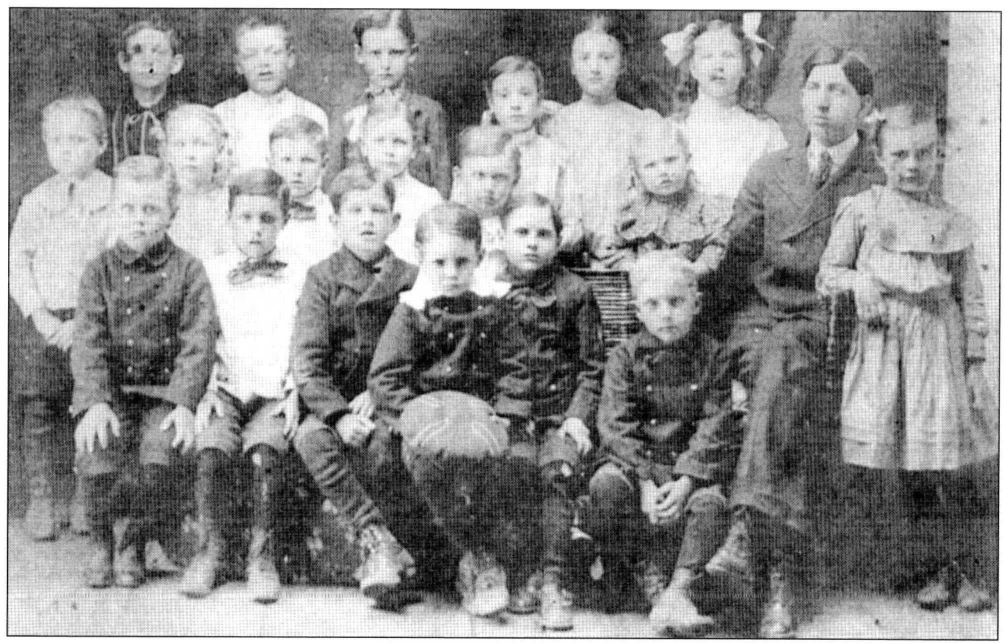

This 1907 photograph shows a Baptist Sunday school class at Maynard. Members of the class are, from left to right, (first row) Paul Maynard, unidentified, Henry Richardson, Pug Douglas, Roy Hawkins, and Les Fowler; (second row) Spurgeon Richardson, Jessie Poyner, Earl Richardson, Novella Cate, Dan Wyatt, Vera Wyatt, teacher Horace Hawkins, and Lucille Douglas; (third row) Joe Abbott, Speed Bemis, Schley Anderson, Estelle Abbott, Mollie McNabb, and Dewees Cate.

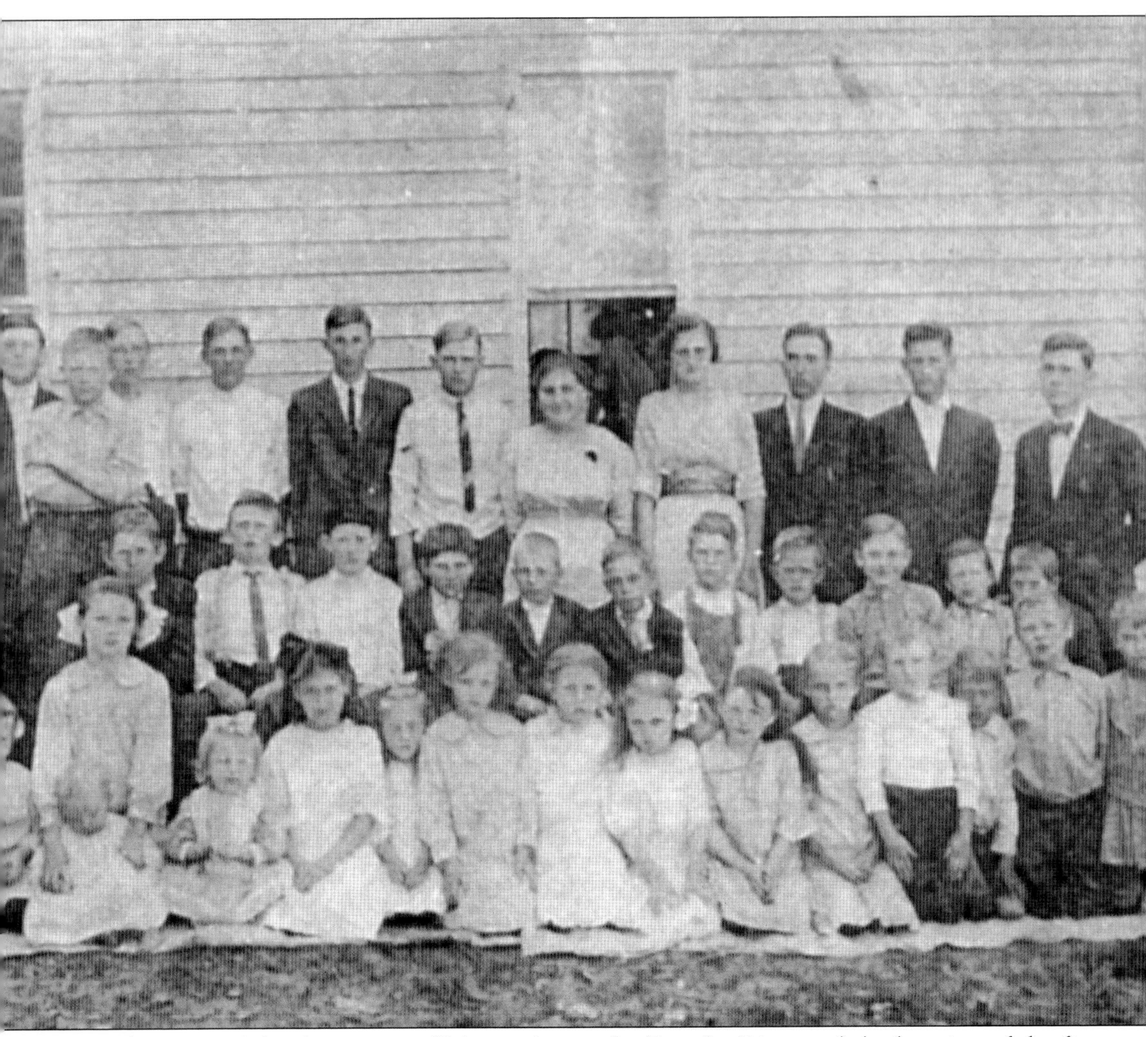

The Jarrett School was west of Maynard near the Fourche River and the location of the first Baptist Church in Arkansas. From left to right in this 1910 photograph are (first row) Grace Brooks, Mildred Carroll, Alene Carroll, Glen Brooks, Bessie Foster, Arvil Foster, Hassel Carroll, Susie Foster, Iva Jarrett, unidentified, Elmer Carroll, Uland Foster, Daly Brooks, and Eral Roberts; (second row) Clyde Foster, George Rufe Foster, Dock Brooks, and Richard Foster; (third row) John Osborn, Hosford Brooks, Charlie Thoma, Joe Fraizer, Oscar Jarrett, Claud Foster, Myrtle Williams, Idell Bridges, Irvin Jarrett, Roy Foster, and teacher Herbert H. Price.

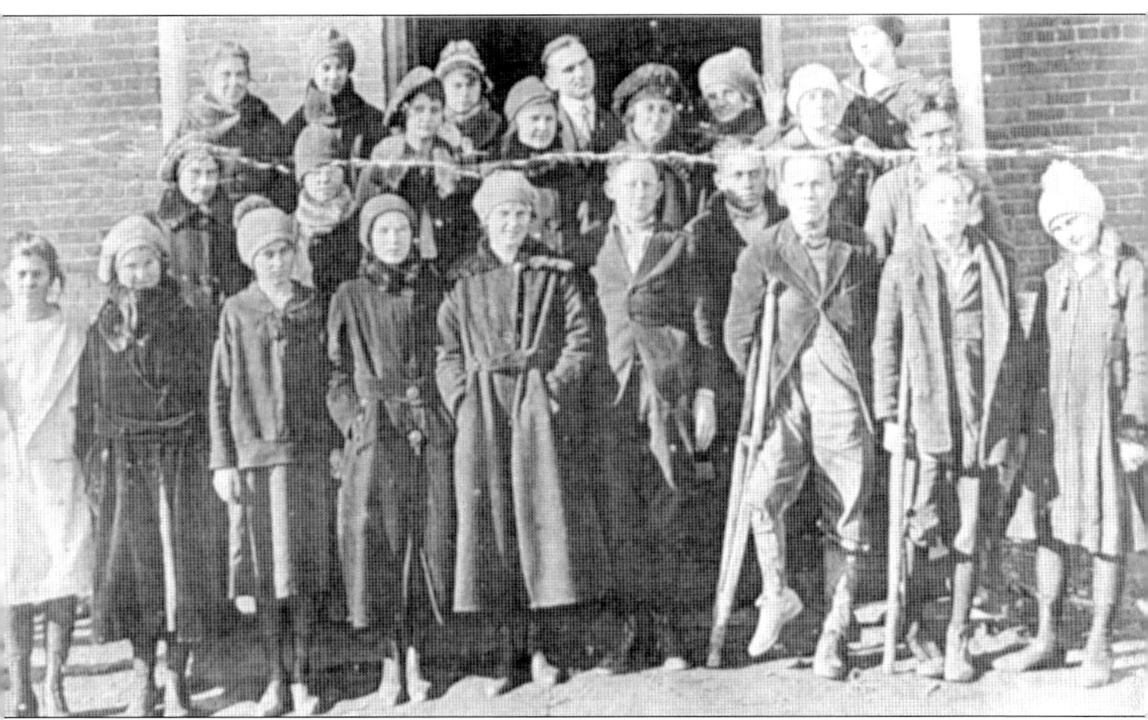

The eighth-grade class at Biggers is seen here in 1920. From left to right are (first row) Ruth Whittington, Tressie Seagraves Gazaway, Sylvia Johnson, Gramblett, Crystal Hatley Brooks, Etalka Hite Tyler, unidentified, Jim Autry, Lovell Dunn, Durell Hufstedler, Wendell Luter, and Lorine Reynolds Ulmer; (second row) Myrtle Donahue Pulliam, Addie Finney, Matilda Parrish, and Loree Johnson; (third row) teacher Mrs. Purdy, Vivian Johnson Lloyd, Gussie Hambrick Evans, Rufus A. Mock, Marie McCauley, Pearl McIllroy Mariott, Velma Cox, and unidentified.

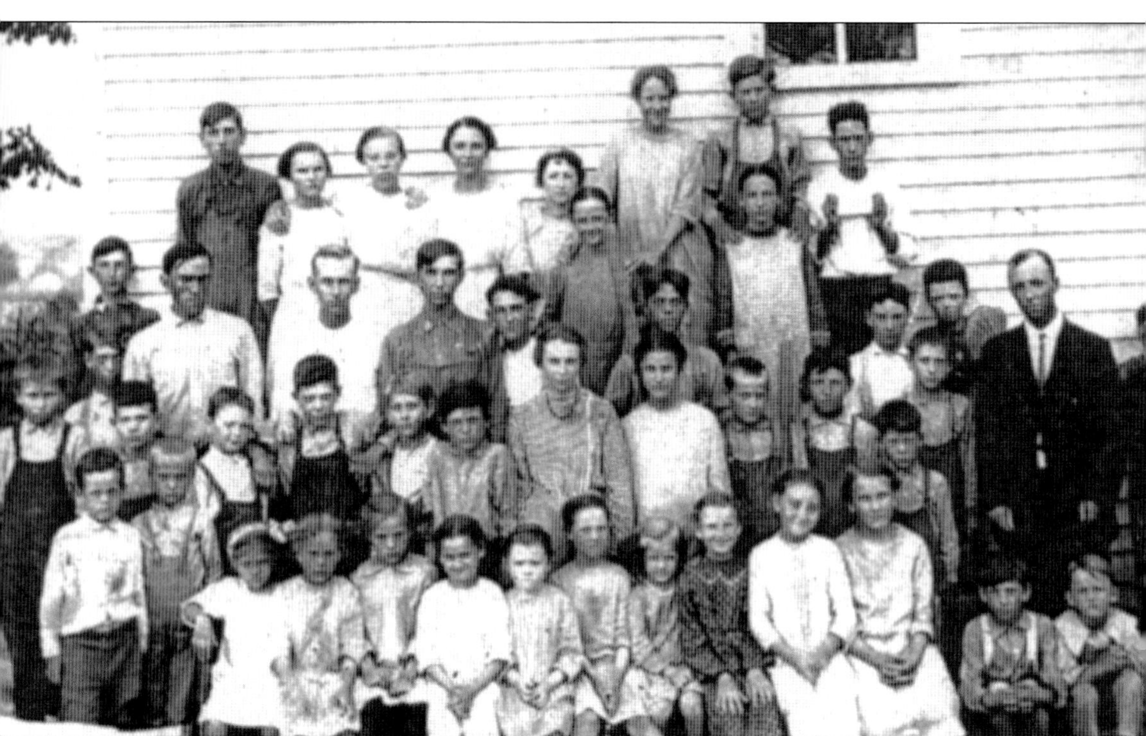

Grandview School students around 1915 are, from left to right, (first row) Donald Smith, Henry Perrin, Edna Redwine, Bonnie Duff, Elmira Dunnavin, Mary Folwer, Eula Ingram, Sadie and Lena Dudley, Eva Wallace, Letha Duff, Doris Redwine, and Cleo and Ed Knowlton; (second row) Arvil Pride, Lloyd Ennis, Niles Ingram, Halley Ennis, Everett Duff, Herman Knowlton, Della Wallace, Eva Benton, Johnnie Fowler, Leonard Brown, Homer Wallace, Green Boyd, and Sherman Fowler; (third row) Adam Perrin, Tom Pride, Elmer Duff, Earnest Shepherd, Hulen Knowlton, Oma Knowlton, Ida Mae Dudley, Oren Perrin, Charlie Cox, and Chester Ingram; (fourth row) Arsh Parish, Roy Jolly, Mayme Fowler, Ella Redwine, Estil Parish, Amy Knowlton, Nora Elsie Dudley, and Douglas and Charlie Fowler.

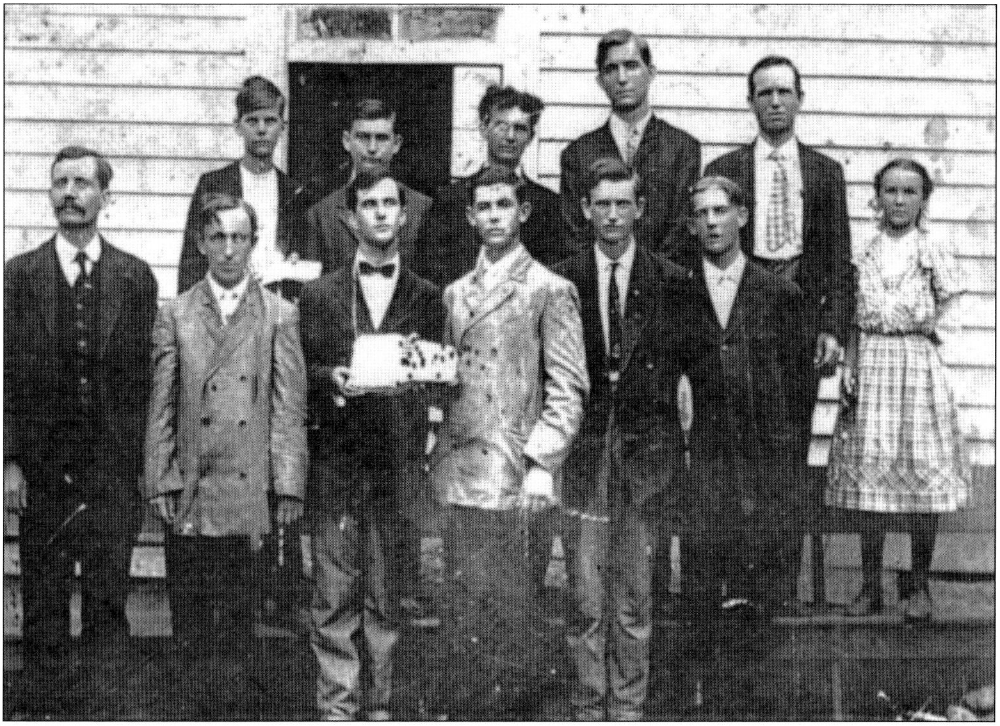

The new converts class at Oak Grove Methodist Church in Attica in 1908 are, from left to right, (first row) Reverend Baty, Dee Knots, Arthur Tyler, Daly Lacy, Rob Hart, and Marvin Simonton; (second row) Arthur Weatherford, George Browdy, John Newton, Joe Snodgrass, and Jack Cole.

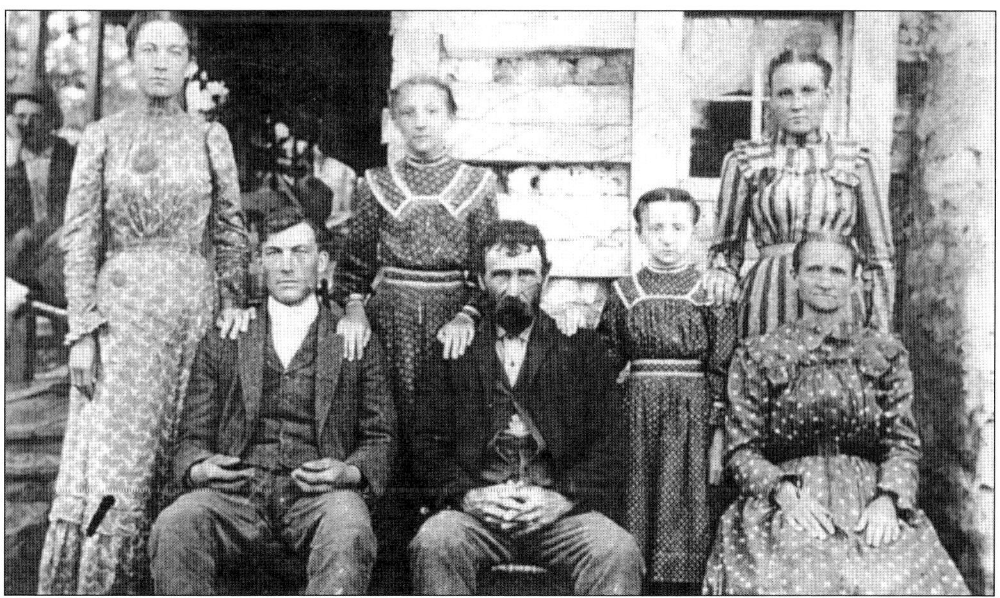

The Jim McDaniel family lived near Attica around the turn of the 20th century. From left to right are Mrs. Sular McDaniel, Sular McDaniel, Willie McDaniel, "Uncle Jim" McDaniel, Lucy McDaniel, "Aunt" Emma McDaniel, and George McDaniel.

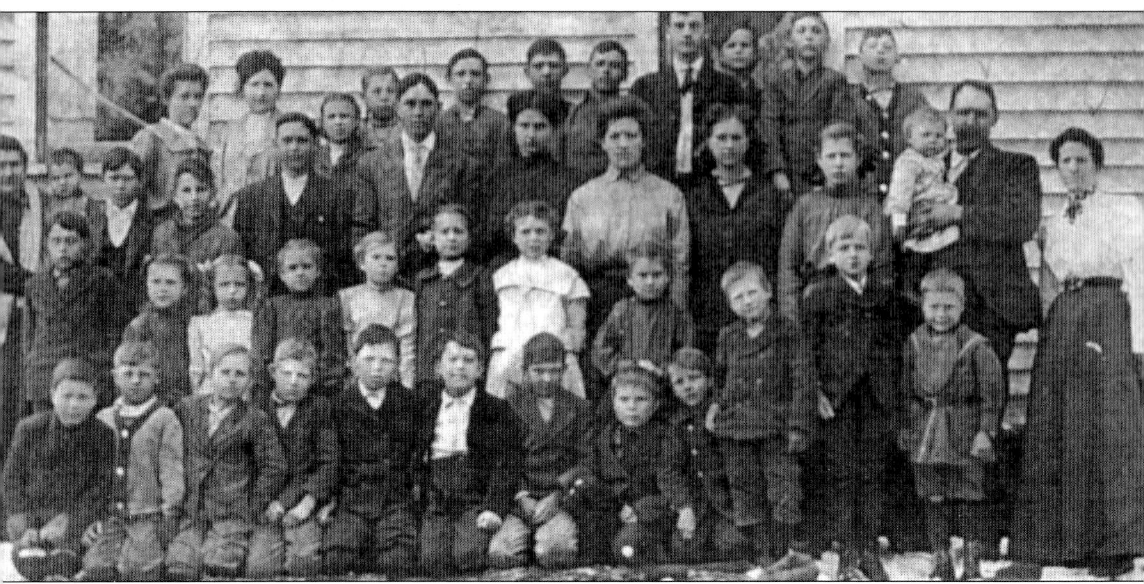

The McIlroy School was near Dalton in northwest Randolph County. This undated class photograph shows, from left to right, (first row) Luther Harnden, Bunk Horsman, Clifford Romine, Gary Fry, Cleo Nuckles, unidentified, Dan Wren, George Harnden, two unidentified, John Houston, three unidentified, Detta Romine Rickman, unidentified, Elsie Hincha, and unidentified; (third row) Mrs. Cordle holding baby, Jesse Haas, James Houston, Burl Rickman, Earl Pickman, Ethal Wren, Myrtle Cochran, Lela Riley, Grace Fry, Avery Nuckles and Mrs. Nuckles; (fourth row) Ethel Horsman, Annie Rickman, Letha Nuckles, Lora Horsman, Verrnie Wren, Lester Wren, Daley Rickman, teacher S.D. Bennett, Lee Riley, Tom Rickman, and Eric Horsman.

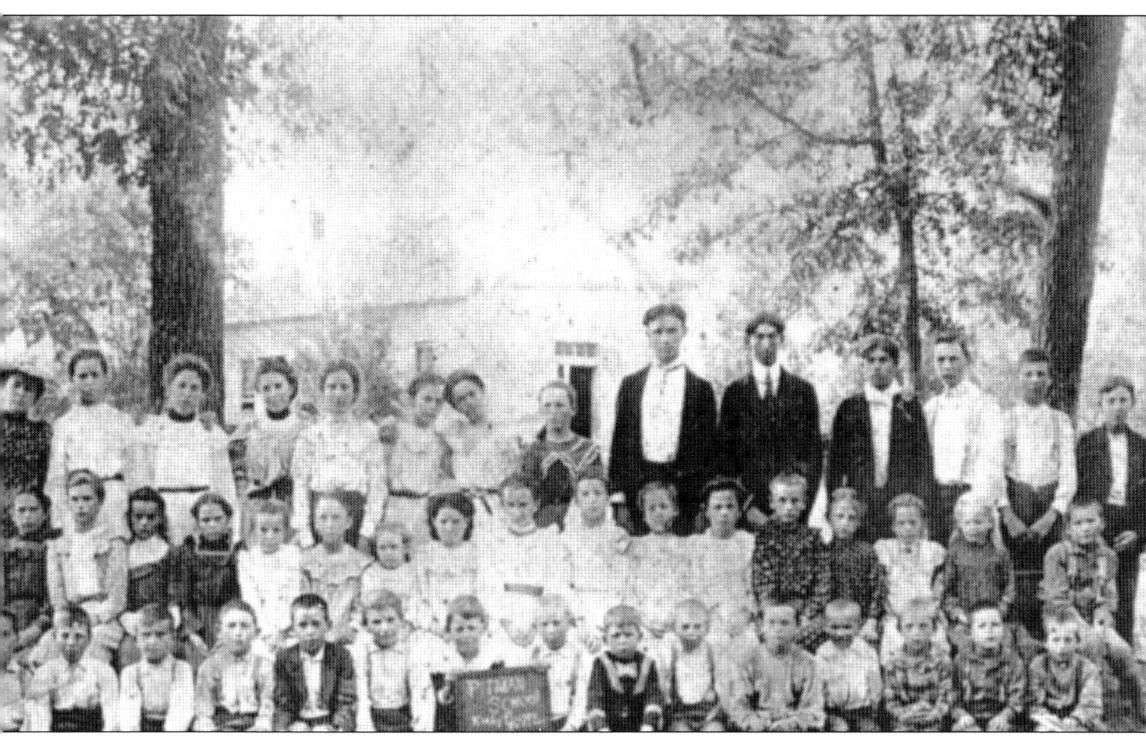

Students of the Pittman School summer term pose in 1903 with the school building in the background. The teacher at this time was Kirby Foster. From left to right are (first row) Lloyd Shemwell, Clarence Cockrum, Bud Sanders, Harry Rhodes, Carlos Moore, Red Ruff, Malin McNabb, Tom Belk, Marvin McNabb, Willie Belk, Roy Sharp, Earl Lewis, Herbert Inness, Addie Sharp, and ? Nelson; (second row) Dessie Scates, Jessie Ruff, May Louis, Geneva Scates, Rita Louis, Leona Inness, Mary Belk, Lena Nelson, Ona Sanders, Amy Louis, Louise McNabb, Lona Cockrum, Nora Berry, Clara Cockrum, Grace Equal, and unidentified; (third row) Jane Brown, Fanny Moore, Della Robb, Rosa Robb, Hattie McNabb, Tommie Shemwell, Eva Skates, Alberta Belk, Kirby Foster, Frank Horton, George Robb, Katy Skates, Tom Cockrum, and Andrew McNabb.

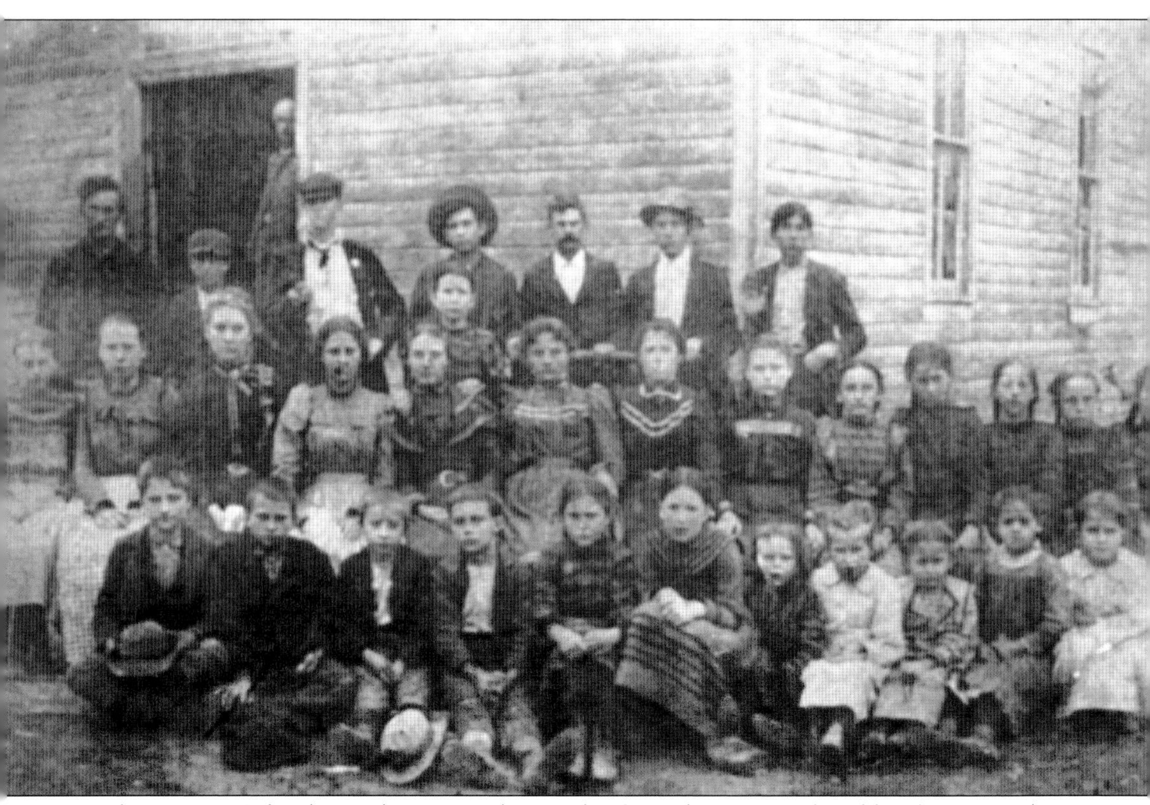

The Vernon School was about 12 miles north of Pocahontas on the old Belview Road near the Fourche River. This photograph was taken in 1901. From left to right are (first row) G.G. Shocklee, a member of the school board, and students John Shocklee, Frank Reed, Esker Shocklee, Doc Condict, Lillian Roberts, Nettie Reed, Mable Roberts, Sada Caveat, Vivian Throgmarton, Mamie Early, and Ethal Caveat; (second row) Mag Barnett, Kate Roberts, Edna Throgmorton, Estele Early, Elsie Early, Peral Condict, and Martha Early; (third row) Cyrus Barnett, the teacher, Garfield Throgmorton, David Spikes, Hyman Tyer, Wesley Barnett, Sank Spikes, and Fayette Tyer.

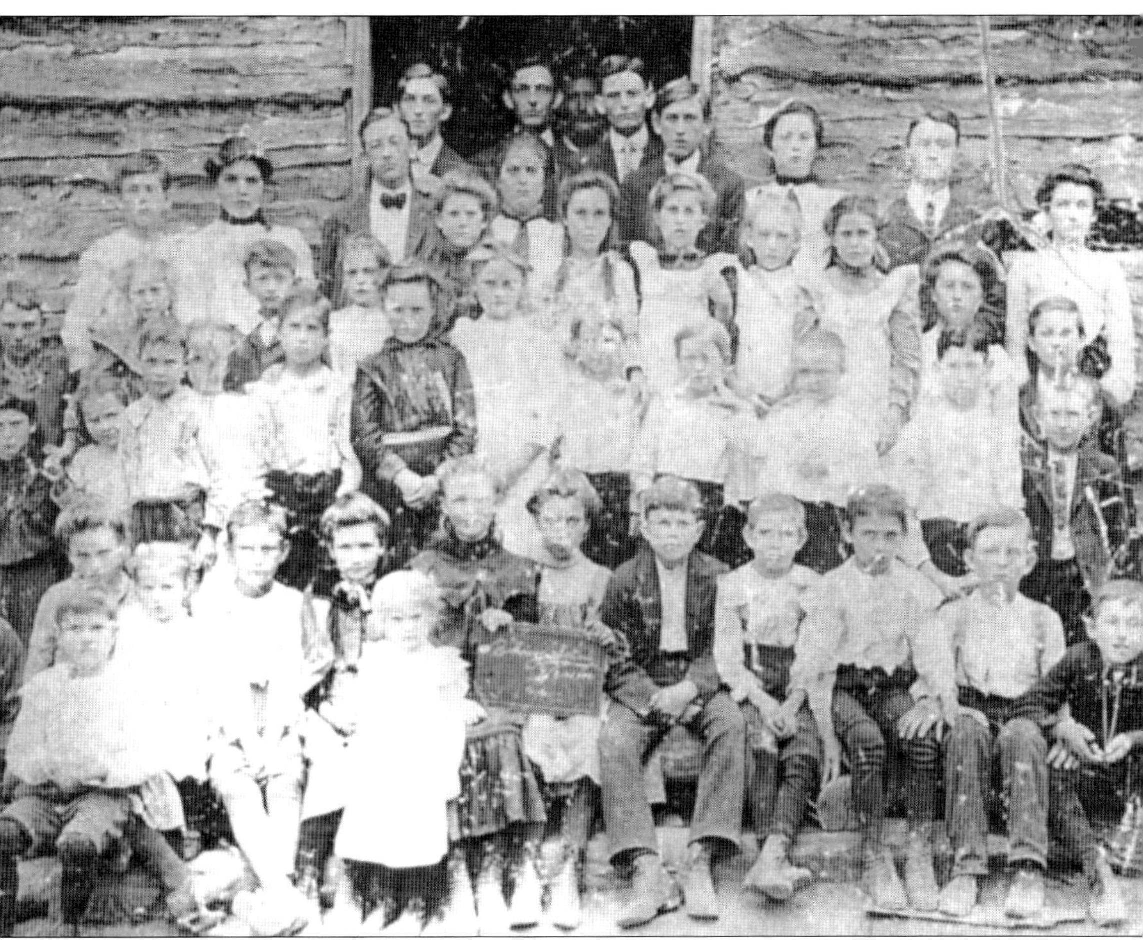

This September 2, 1904, photograph shows the Bethany School, where Lee Higginbotham taught. From left to right are (first row) Grover Poteet, Cara Rogers, Jerry Magruder, Frankie Bailey, Alf Prince, Kois Marguder, Irene Bailey, Willie Poteet, Fay English, John Looney, Albert Bailey, Omer Rogers, Oscar Prince, and Roy Kellett; (second row) Nettie Bailey, Gussie Davis, Burnett Davis, Ina Bailey, Sam English, Edna James, Jim Davis, Clark Davis, Virgil Bailey, Lee Davis, and Virgil Looney; (third row) Joe Poteet, Ella Bailey, Everett Looney, Elva Black, Ruthie Bailey, Pearl Bailey, Mollie Looney, Lora Rogers, and Albert Bailey; (fourth row) Ed Price, Beulah Magruder, Jasper Kellett, Lula Bailey, Earl English, Zula Bailey, and George Looney; (fifth row) Tom Slayton, Lee Higginbotham, and Henry Higginbotham.

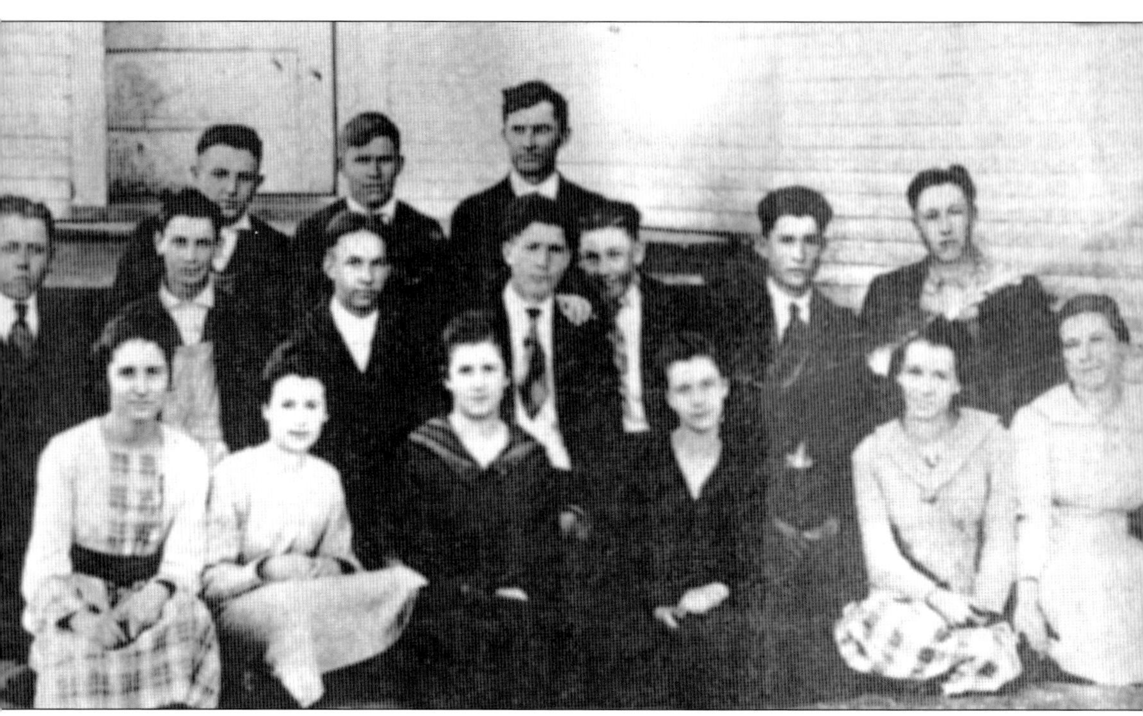

The Holmes School class of 1919 included, from left to right, (first row) Gladys Fender, Edna Ivy, Uva James, Alice James, Jessie Fender, and Grace Mays; (second row) Vernon Lemmons, Fred James, Dr. Harry Johnson, Elmer James, Burley Rogers, Arvil James, and Louie Lemmons; (third row) Wallace Mays, Harry Fairchilds, and teacher Wesley Brown.

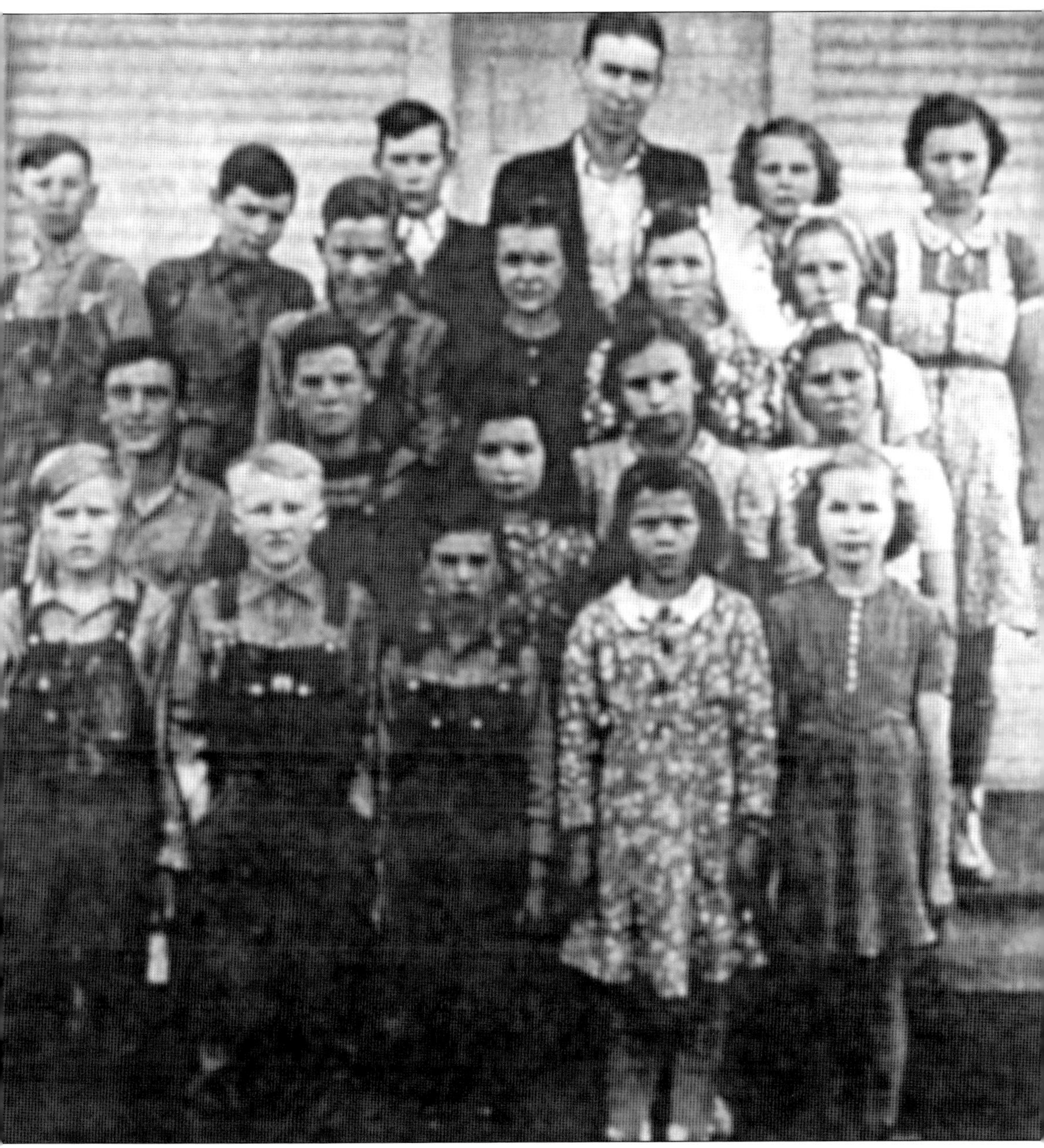

This photograph is of the Shannon School south of Pocahontas in 1941. From left to right are (first row) Sidney Burgess, W.T. Tarlton, Tommie Joe Reed, Freda Rogers, and Dephene Oldham; (second row) Junior Rose, Carlie Brown, Zella Rose, Helen Ruth Brown, and Frances Lee Brown; (third row) Weldon Leach, Jewell Dean Clark, Odesa Rogers, and Bernice Rogers; (fourth row) Kenneth Dame, unidentified, Orville Capps, teacher John Tiner, Inez Robinson, and Helen Dame.

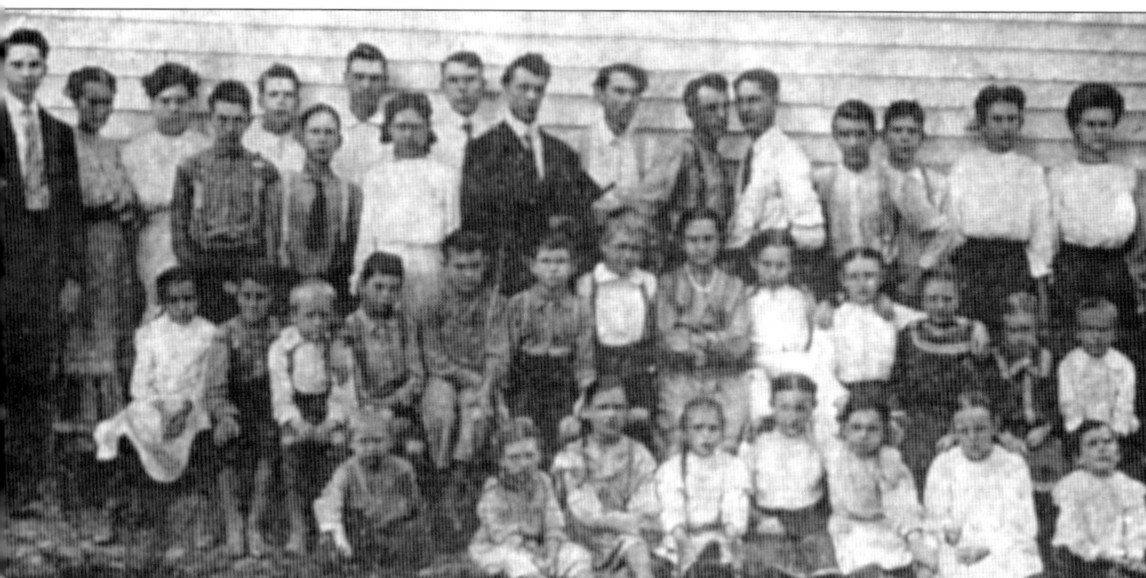

This is a class photograph of the Harmony School in 1909. From left to right are (first row) Arthur Law, Mazie Chesser, Grace Slayton, Flora Chesser, Edna Ehrhardt, Ethel Penn, Ollie Penn, and Guy Lemmons; (second row) Joseph Schaechtel, Grace Price, Nema Chesser, Lora Chesser, Mazie Chesser, Gertrude Schaechtel, Louis Lemmons, Jess Mulvaney, Bert Beegle, Glen Mulvaney, Vernon Lemmons, Leo Frankenberger, and Mary Frankenberger; (third row) Clyde Chesser, Almaus Penn, Clem Stoley, unidentified, Elmer Mulvaney, Marion Cox, Walter Cox, Anne Cox, unidentified, Bert Stoley, Neal Persful, Drew Beegle, Sarah Tish Chesser, and teacher A.P. Weatherly.

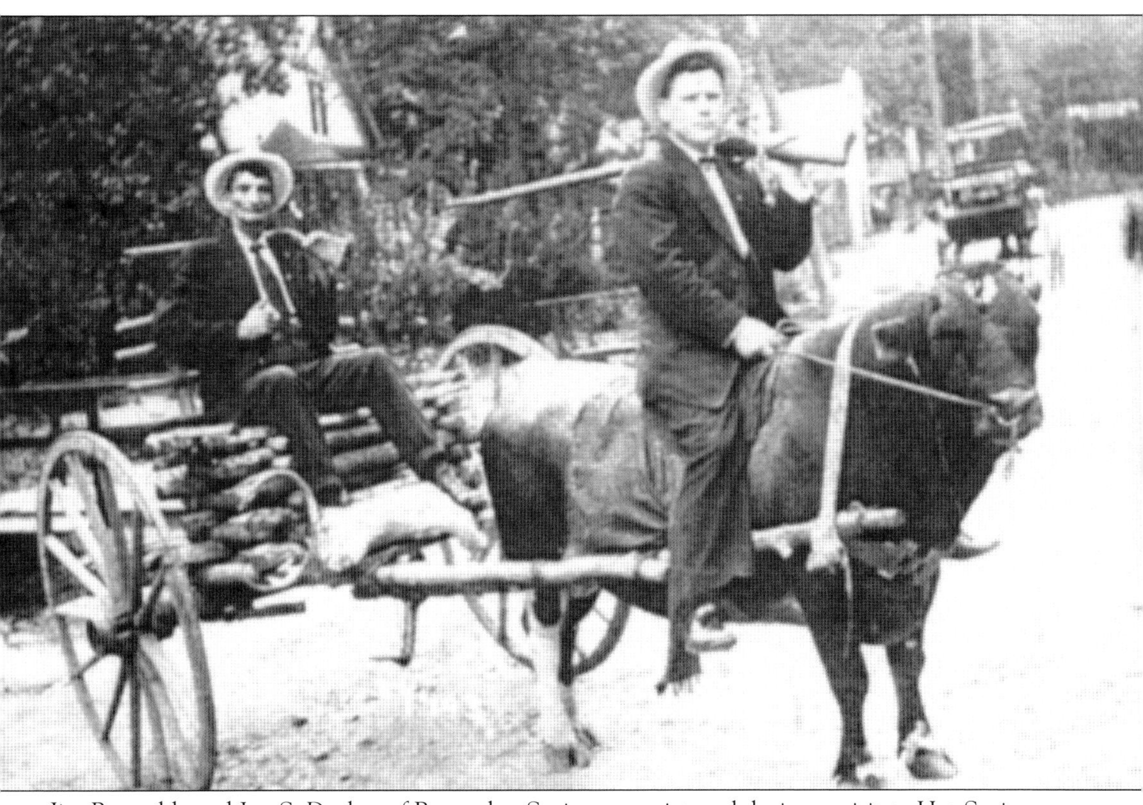

Jim Reynolds and Joe S. Decker of Ravenden Springs are pictured during a visit to Hot Springs in 1908. Decker is astride an ox and carrying a gun over his shoulder.

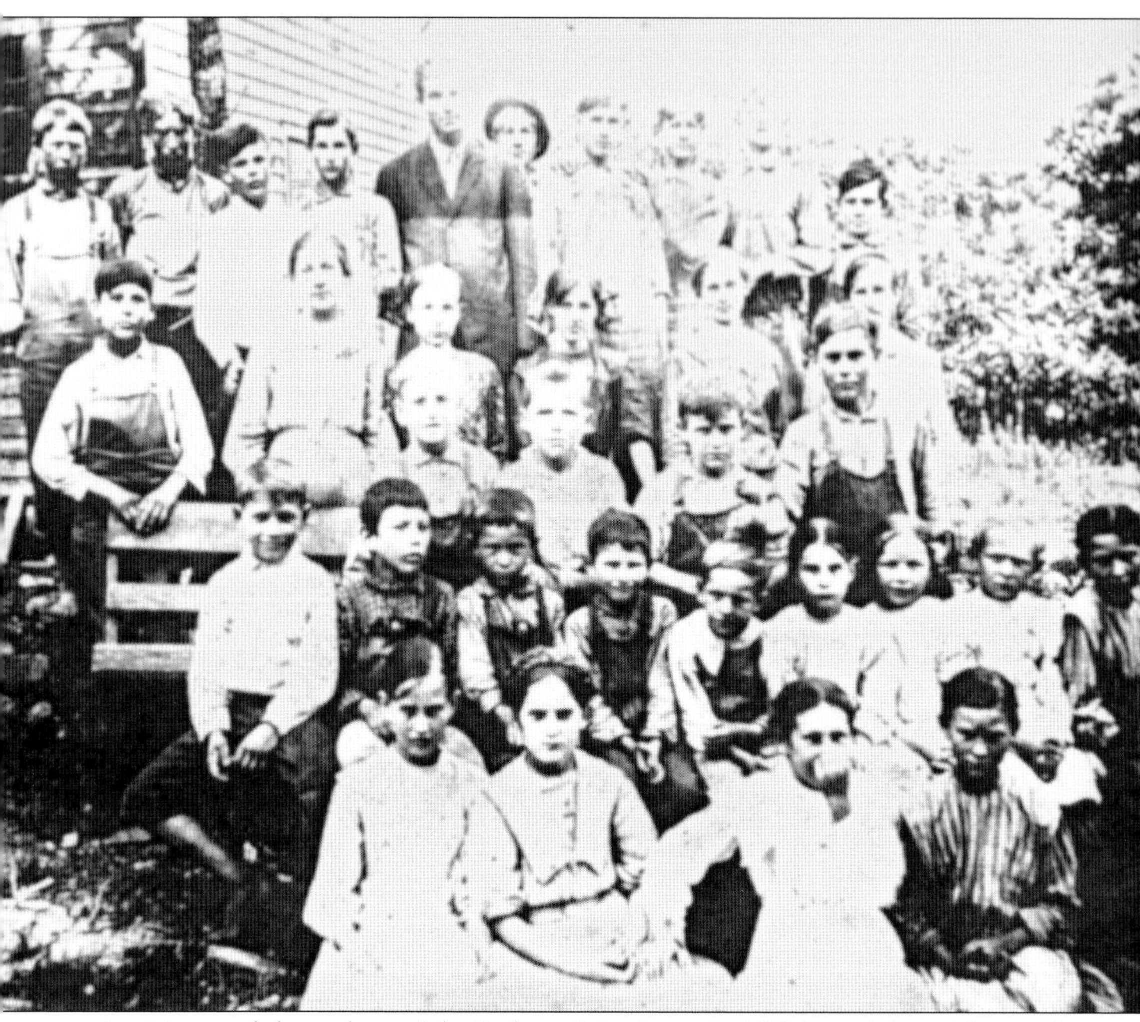

Joe Privett and the students of the Bethany School pose in 1912. From left to right are (first row) Julia Sullenger Clements, Irene Bailey Crawford, Jessie Mariott James, Edith Allison, and unidentified; (second row) Philip Shultz, Cleo Allision, Manuel Allison, Harvey Sullenger, Jed Rickman, Media Belle Sullenger, Gladys Bailey Brown, Lessie Mariott McElroy, and Maggie Allison; (third row) Noel Rickman, Bryan Shultz, Dolph Kellett, and Virgil Bailey; (fourth row) Garland Shultz, Hazel Shultz Kellett, Frankie Bailey Cooper, Hester Shultz, Bailey Crawford, and Ina Bailey Marriott; (fifth row) Clark Davis, Tommie Gaines, Henry English, Cad Sullenger, teacher Joe Privett, Virgil Higginbotham, Albert Bailey, Jim Davis, Buster Rogers, and Edward Allison.

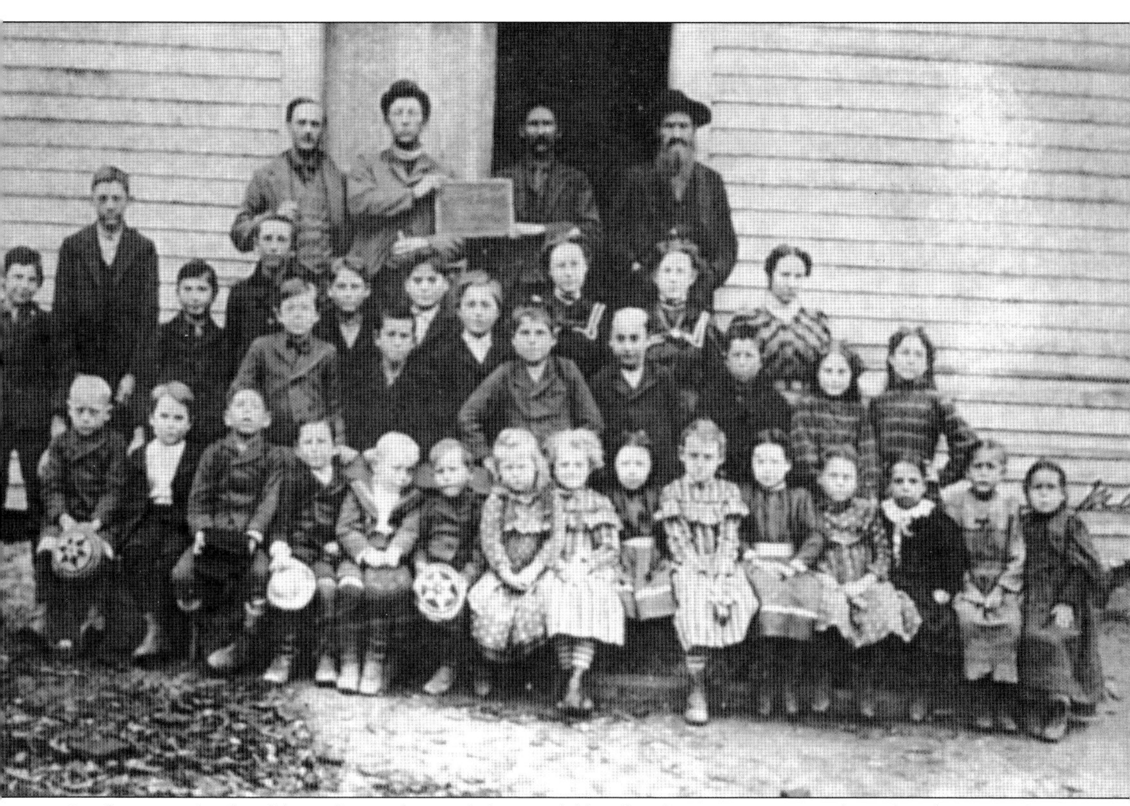

Students and school board members of the Birdell School pose in 1901. The school was eight miles west of Pocahontas on the Eleven Point River. The teacher was Hutchie Phipps. From left to right are (first row) Claud Barden, Edward Story, Almus Gazaway, Jessie Mondy, Joe Barden, Lewis Gazaway, Stella Glover, Myrle Hufstedler, Sylvia Lomax, Mell Huffstedler, Jodie Lomax, Janie Glover, Matilda Gazaway, Abby Stringer, and Mary Stringer; (second row) Clarence Mondy, Wesley Baldridge, John Mondy, Harley Stringer, Curtis Lomax, Elisha Story, Ben Stringer, Walter Lemmons, Frank Lemmons, Albert Gazaway, Dell Hufstedler, Joe Mondy, Kate Hufstedler, Roger Stringer, Francis Story, Bertha Story, and Willie Langley; (third row) board member James Lomax, teacher Hutchie Phipps, and board members Mace Mondy and Joseph Huffstetler.

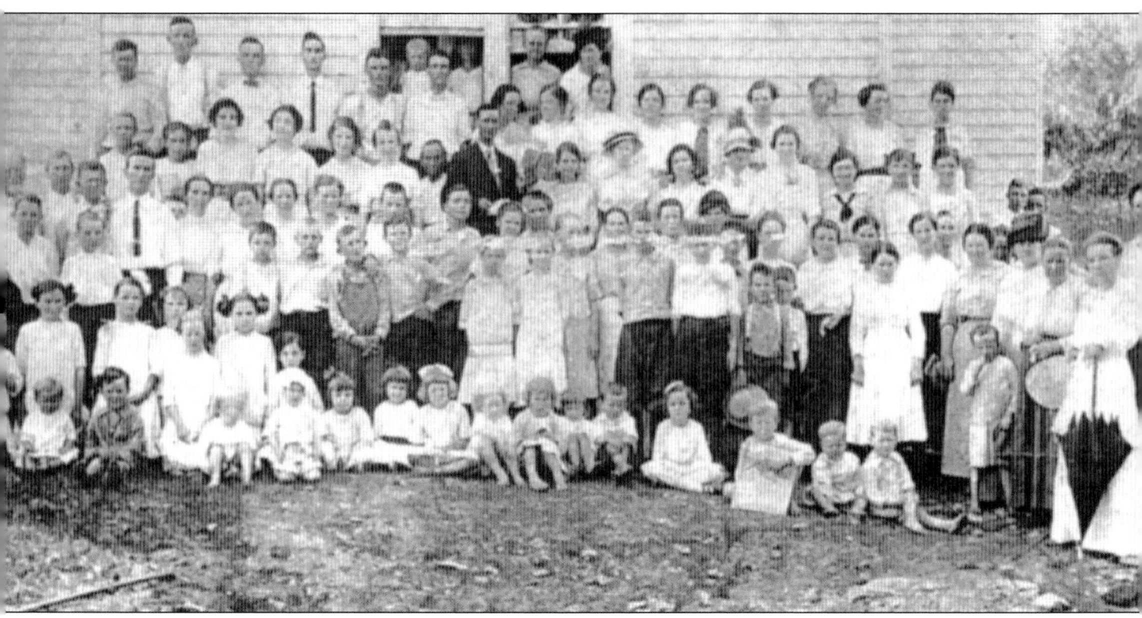

Singing schools, such as this one at the Church of Christ at Maynard in 1914, were popular entertainments. The schools offered training classes, which were considered social events and were usually highly attended.

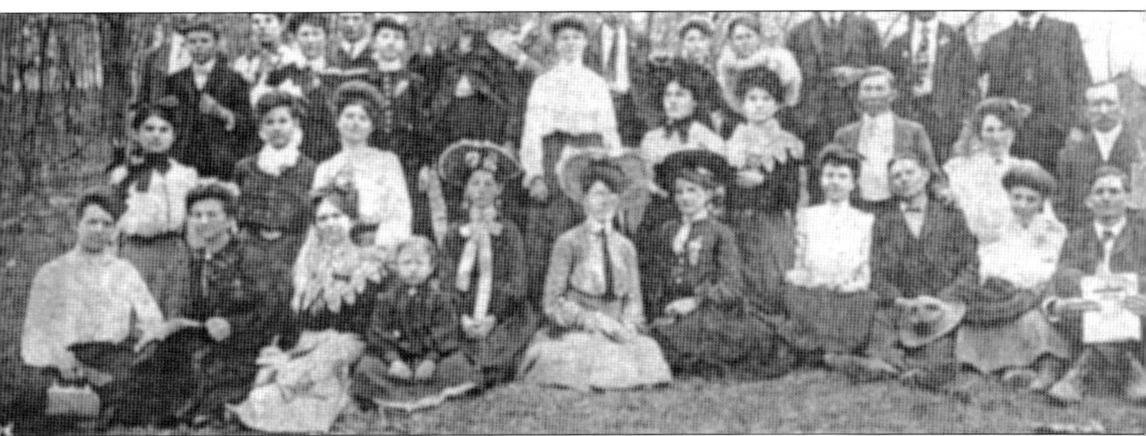

This photograph is of a singing school in 1903 at the Free Will Baptist Church of Warm Springs. The participants are wearing their best clothing.

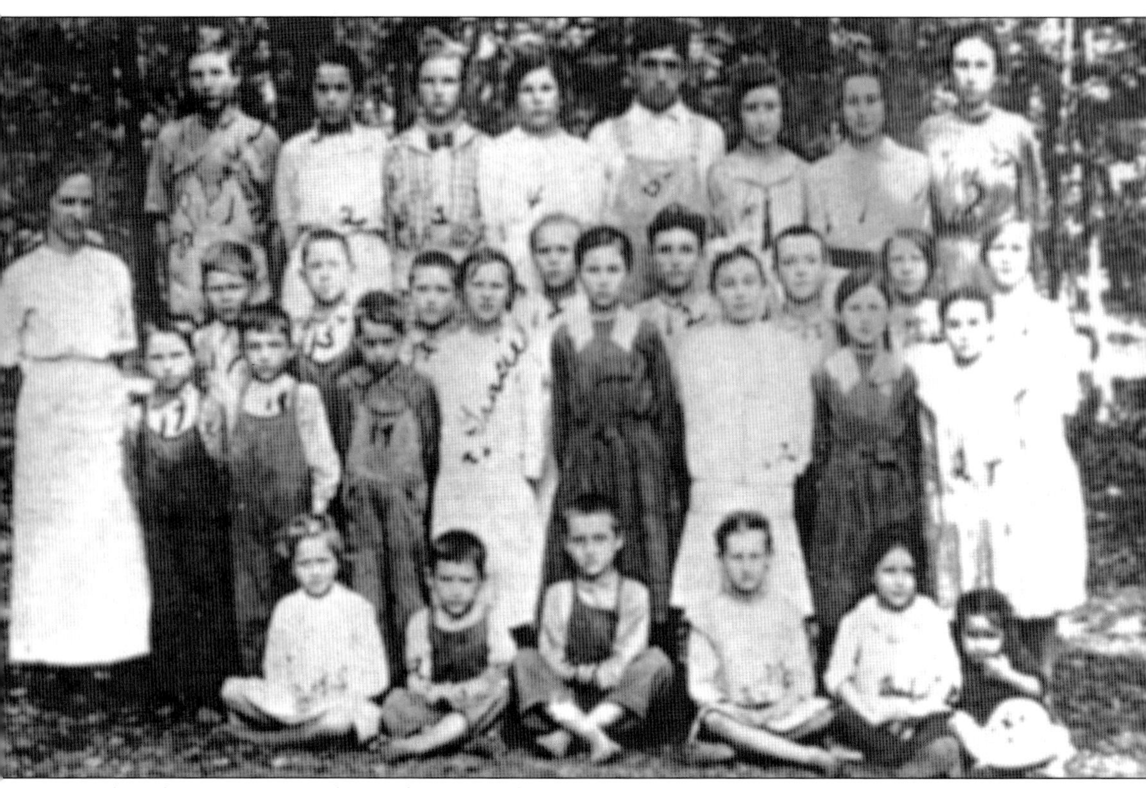

This photograph is of the High Point School in 1914. This was a one-room school serving first through eighth grades.

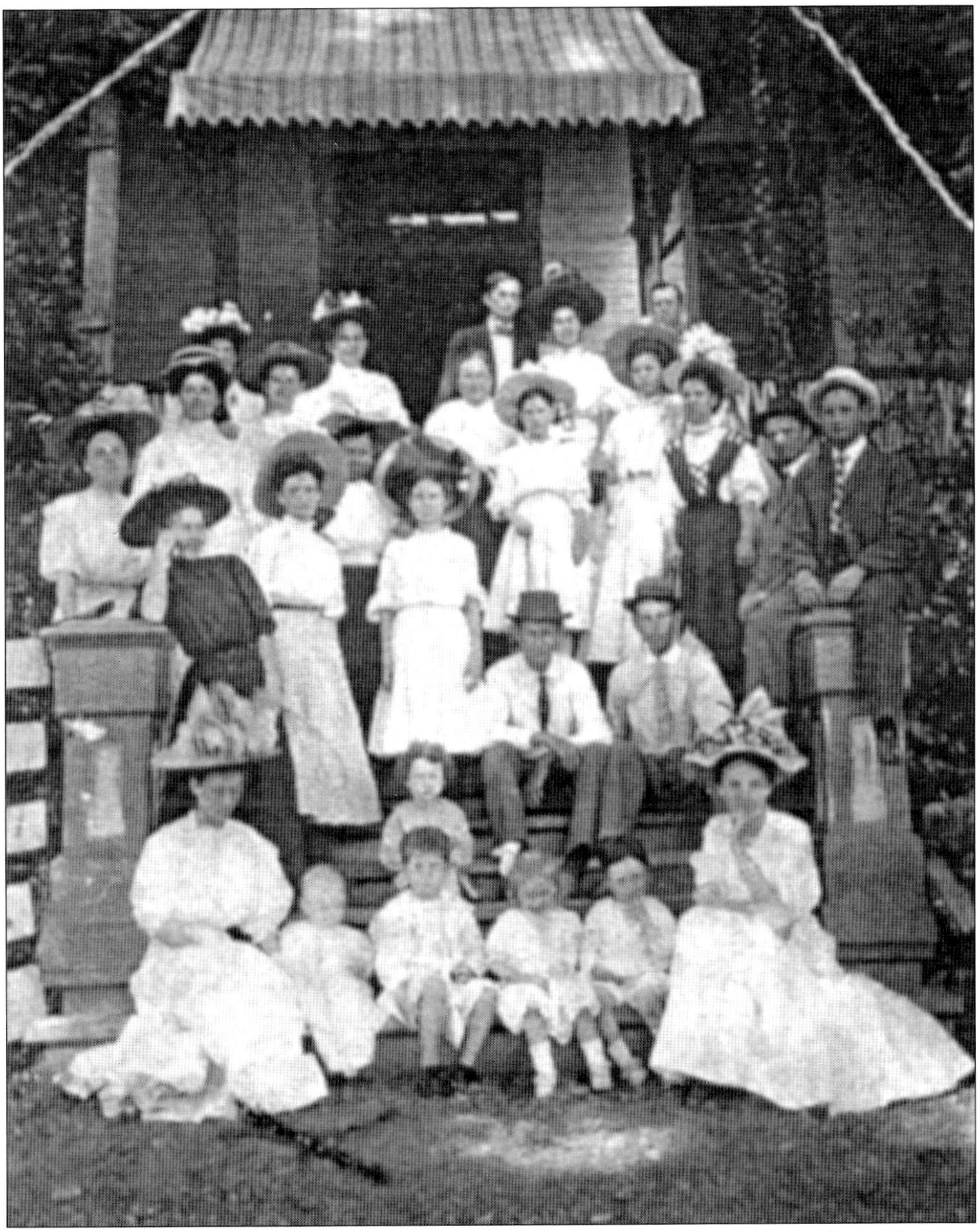

This image captured in Ravenden Springs in 1900 shows citizens dressed up in front of a local hotel. There are at least five men in the photograph as well as a few young boys.

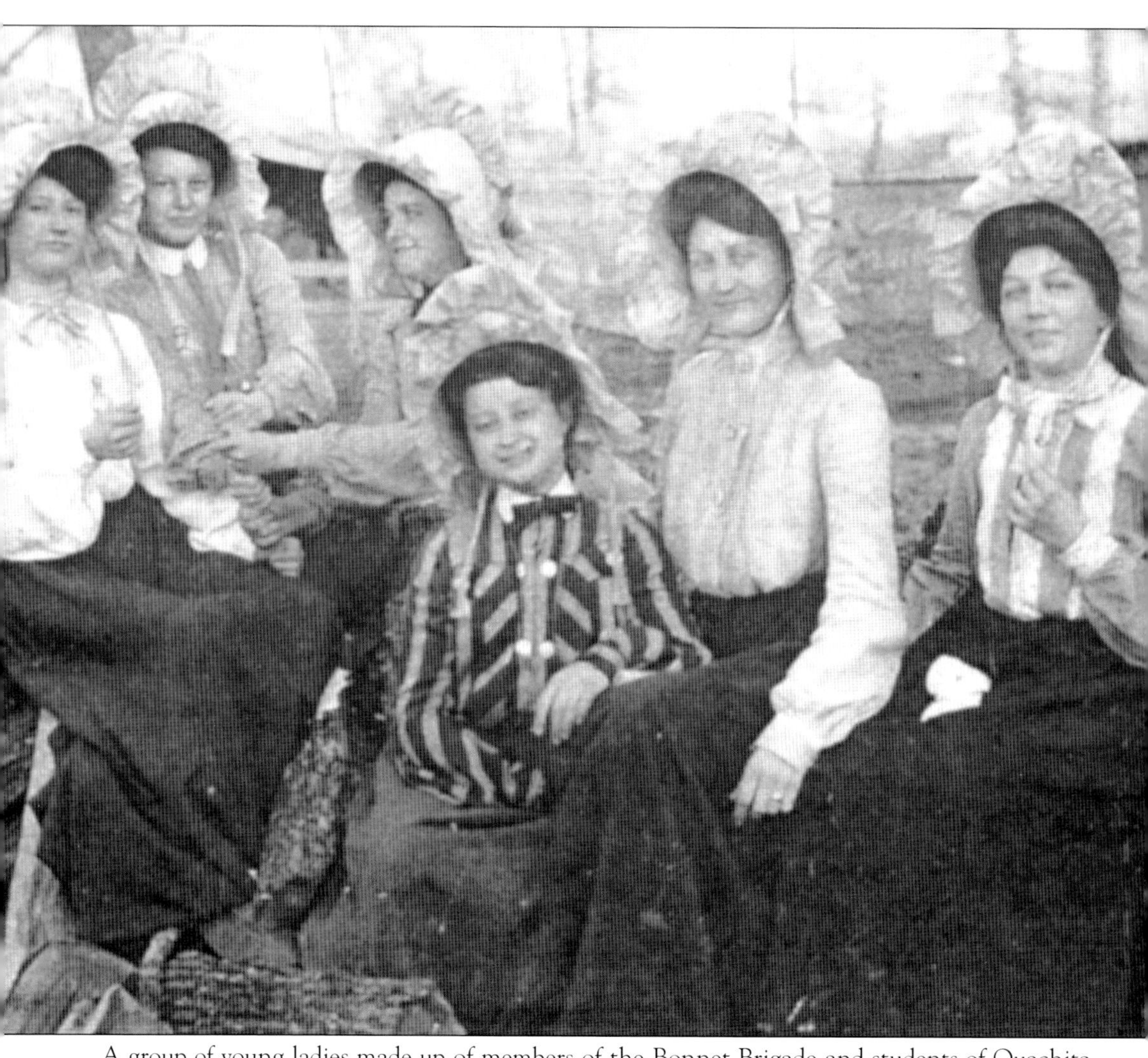

A group of young ladies made up of members of the Bonnet Brigade and students of Ouachita Academy pose in Maynard in 1905.

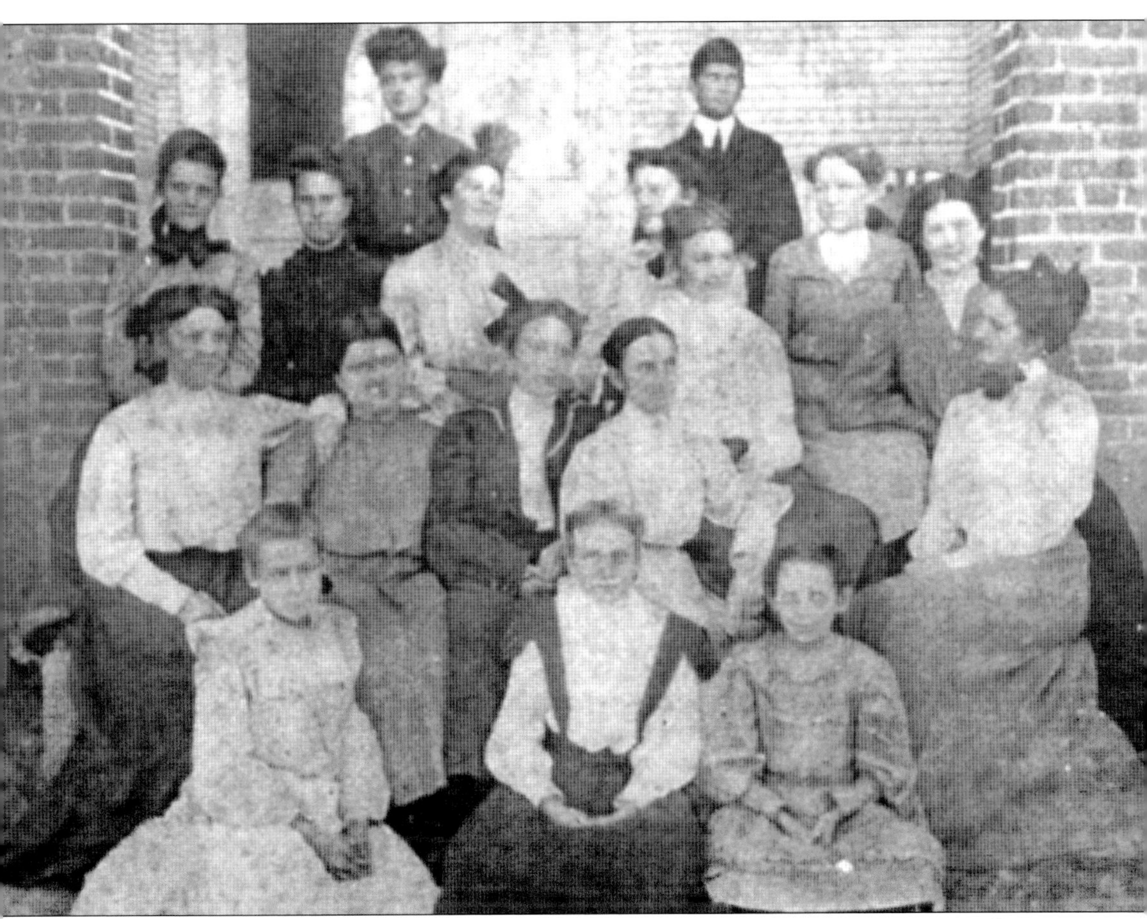

Students of the music class at Ouachita Academy pose in 1904. The teacher was Miss Dudley.

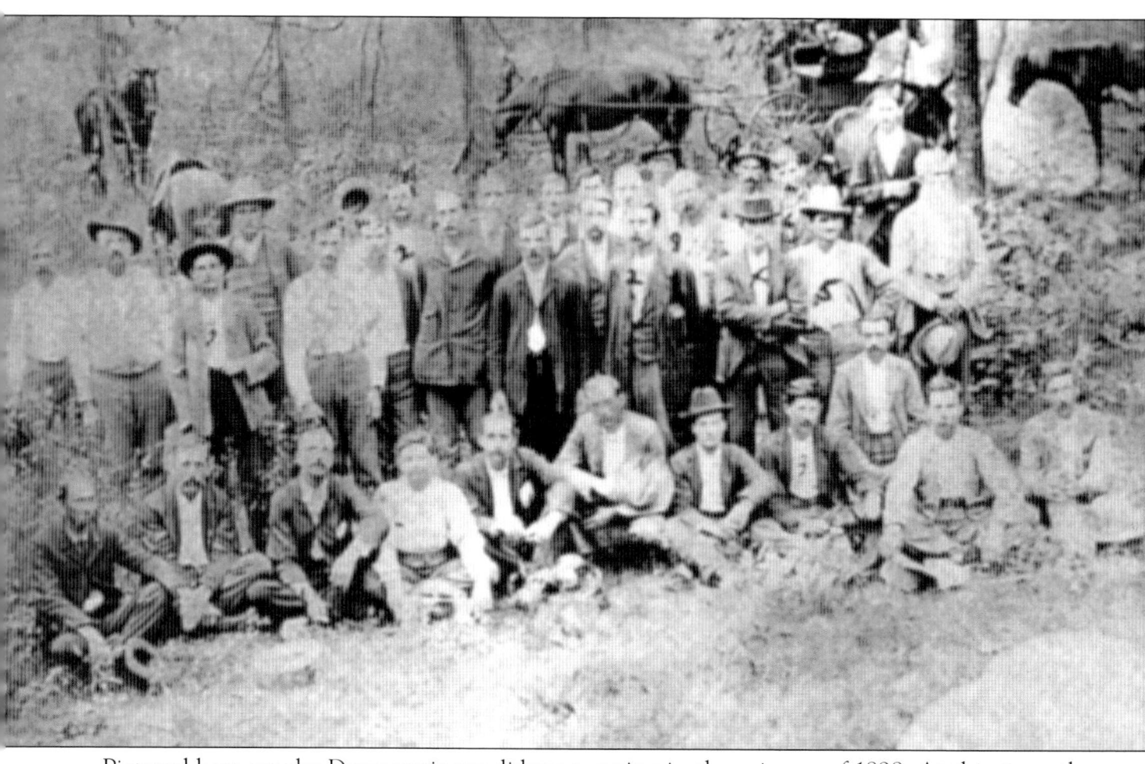

Pictured here are the Democratic candidates running in the primary of 1898. At this time, the Democratic primary would have been the major election of the year, since the Republican Party was almost nonexistent in Randolph County, as in much of the South. Winning the primary meant winning the election.

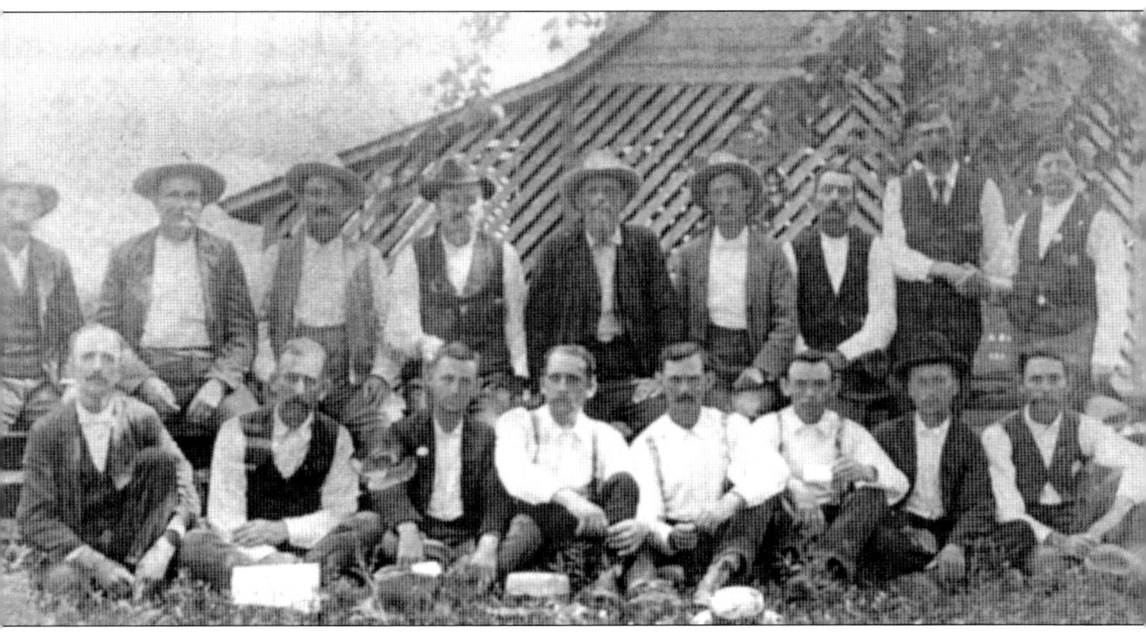

In the election year of 1900, candidates for office posed for this photograph. From left to right are (first row) Ben F. Spikes, Solomon M. White, Tom Campbell, Rufe Shaver, William Johnson, Cad Bishop, Herbert Rice, and Bud Abbot; (second row) Wiley Russell, William Hogan, Ben Bowden, H.R. King, Mr. Poteet, Mont R. Armstrong, J.C. Duvall, Don M. Robinson, and Gus Reynolds.

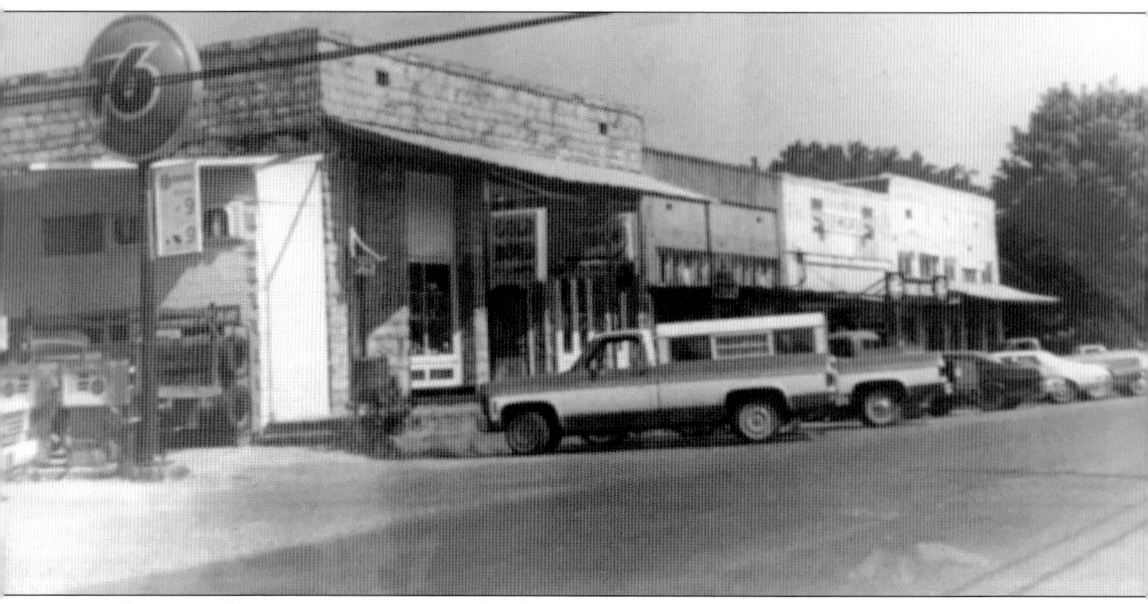

This view of Main Street in Maynard is from the 1970s. The building at left with the large Gold Bond sign is the Weaver Building.

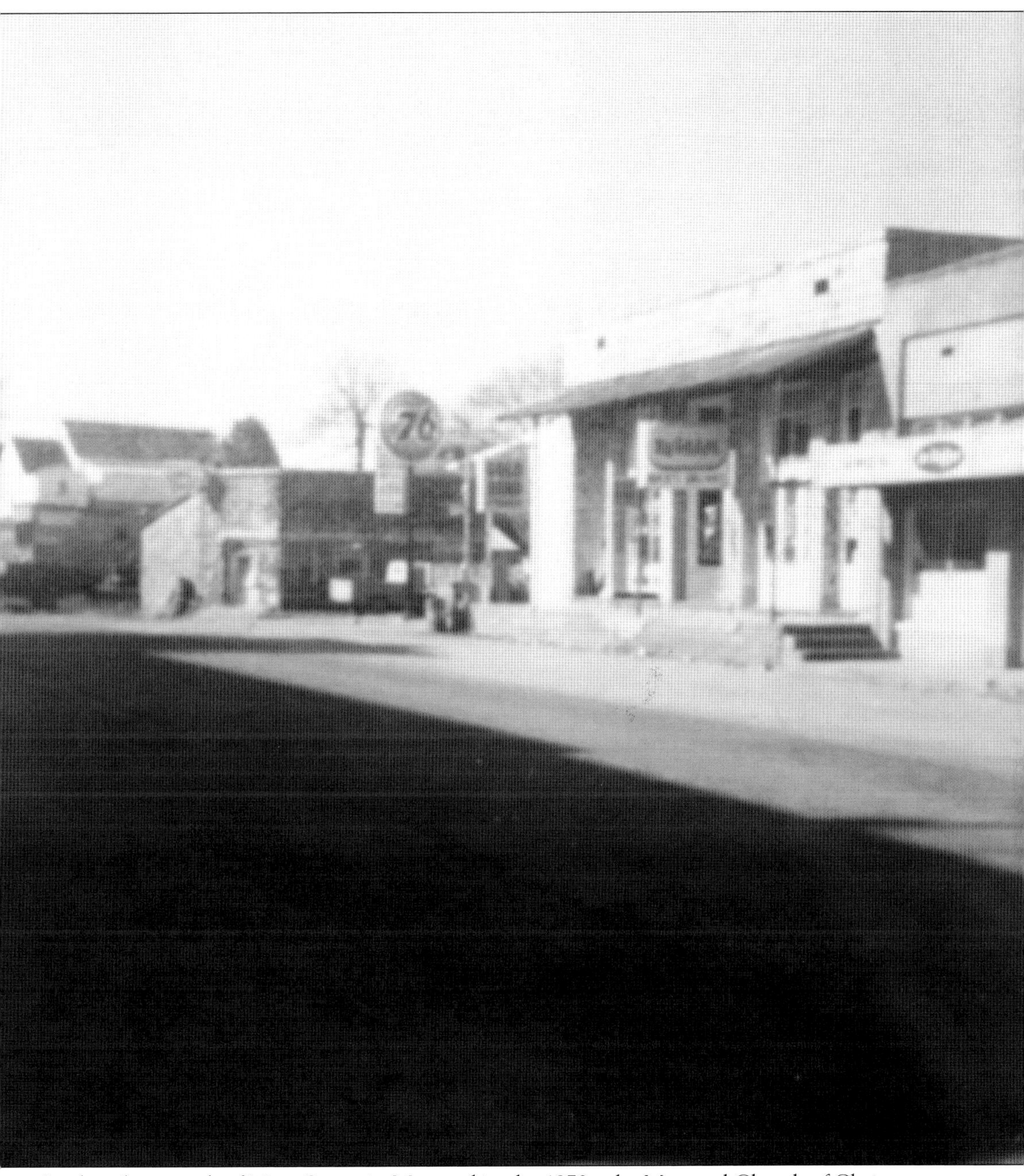

In this photograph of Main Street in Maynard in the 1970s, the Maynard Church of Christ can be seen in the background. At the time, Maynard still had a vibrant business district.

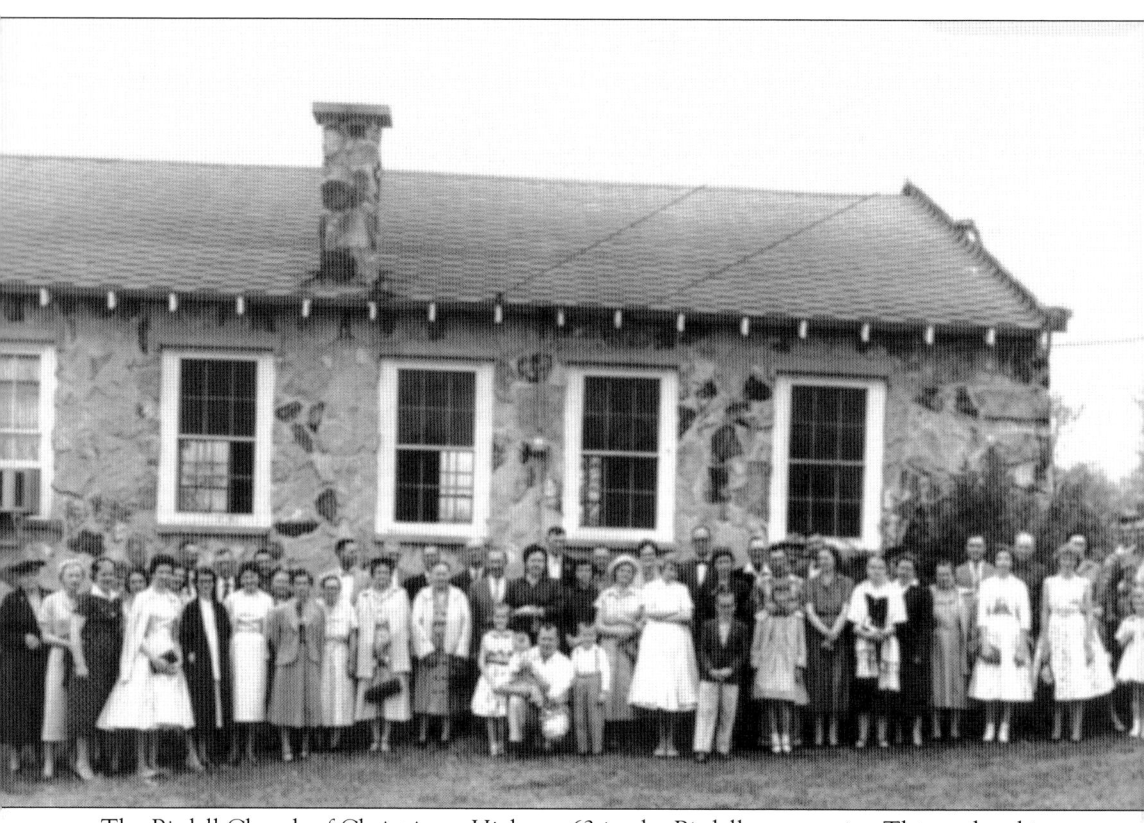

The Birdell Church of Christ is on Highway 63 in the Birdell community. This undated image shows a crowd gathered outside the building.

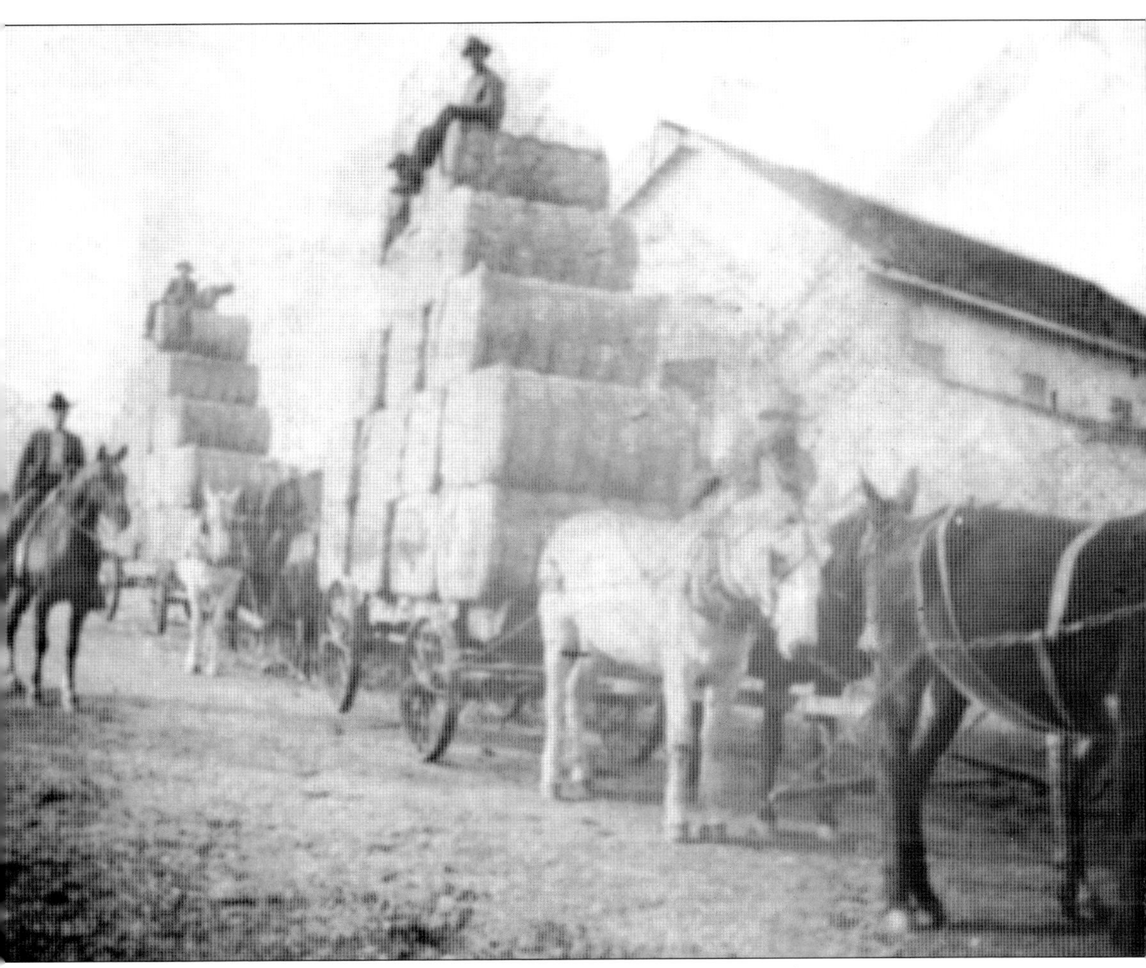

Cotton bails are stacked high on a wagon at Ravenden Springs in 1915.

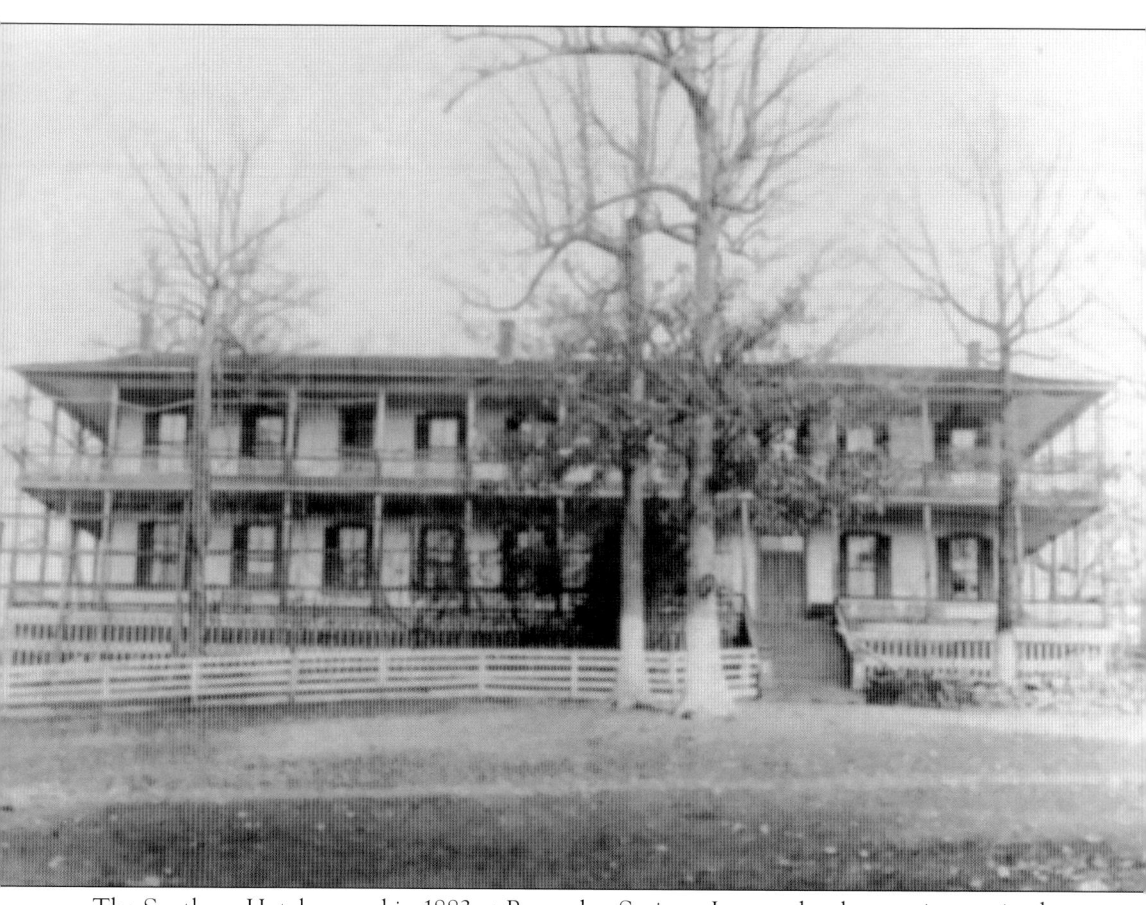

The Southern Hotel opened in 1883 at Ravenden Springs. It proved to be a major tourist draw as people vacationed in Ravenden Springs. During the heyday of the town, there were multiple hotels and businesses.

About the Randolph County Heritage Museum

The Randolph County Heritage Museum was created by Five Rivers Historic Preservation Inc. as part of the Pocahontas sesquicentennial celebration in 2006. The museum building was given to Five Rivers by Joe Martin, a local banker and community leader. Martin descended from some of Randolph County's leading families. The museum houses permanent displays that tell the story of Pocahontas and Randolph County. It also houses an archival collection open to researchers, and preserves documents, photographs, and a significant newspaper collection for generations to come. A dedicated staff of volunteers is committed to making the collection available to the public.